Improvisational Poetry

from the Basque Country

The Basque Series

Other books by Gorka Aulestia

Basque-English Dictionary

English-Basque Dictionary
with Linda White

Basque-English English-Basque Dictionary
with Linda White

GORKA AULESTIA

Improvisational Poetry

from the Basque Country

Foreword by
William A. Douglass

Translated by
Lisa Corcostegui and
Linda White

University of Nevada Press ▲▲ *Reno Las Vegas London*

Basque Series Editor: William A. Douglass
A list of books in the series follows the index.

This edition has been translated with financial assistance from Spain's
Dirección General del Libro y Bibliotecas of the Ministerio de Cultura.

The original work, *Bertsolarismo*, by Gorka Aulestia, was published in Spain
in 1990 by Bizkaiko Foru Aldundia (Bilbao).

The paper used in this book meets the requirements of American National
Standard for Information Sciences—Permanence of Paper for Printed Library
Materials, ANSI Z39.48-1984. Binding materials were selected for strength
and durability.

Library of Congress Cataloging-in-Publication Data

Aulestia, Gorka, 1932-
   [Bertsolarismo. English]
   Improvisational poetry from the Basque Country / Gorka Aulestia;
      translated by Lisa Corcostegui and Linda White ; foreword by
      William A. Douglass.
      p.   cm. — (The Basque series)
   Originally presented as the author's thesis (doctoral)—University of
      Nevada, Reno, 1987.
   Includes bibliographical references and index.
   ISBN 0-87417-201-2 ; (alk. paper)
   1. Basque poetry—History and criticism.
2. Music (Improvisation) I. Title. II. Series.
PH5290.A93 1993
899'.92109-dc20   93-22447
                                            CIP

University of Nevada Press, Reno, Nevada 89557 USA
Copyright © 1995 by Gorka Aulestia
All rights reserved
Book design by Kaelin Chappell
Printed in the United States of America

9 8 7 6 5 4 3 2 1

to Mertxe and Iker

CONTENTS

FOREWORD

When speaking of the origins of any people's popular or folk art forms, the phrase "lost in the mists of time" comes readily to mind. And so it is with Basque improvisational poetry, or *bertsolaritza*. However impossible it may be to establish a historical baseline, we may at least underscore with confidence its uniqueness. Many cultures have rich and extensive oral literatures, often combining some form of poetic composition, either spoken or sung, which is then transmitted down through the generations with little recourse to the written record. To my knowledge, however, it is only in Basque culture that we find elaborated the spontaneous composition of verses that are simultaneously set to music and "performed" as song.

It might be argued that in Basque, as an agglutinative language (one whose grammar makes extensive use of a small universe of infixes and suffixes), it is easy to create rhymes, which in turn facilitates versification. However, such a predisposition scarcely preordains the *bertsolari*, or versifier. Rather, he (since nearly all are males) is more the expression of a deep-seated cultural pattern and the product of a historical necessity. For if the language, in all of its distinctiveness, is the metonym of Basque ethnic uniqueness, the bertsolari may be regarded as its highest practitioner and protector. This is especially true because, until the present century, Basque all but lacked a written literature and a common literary form.

Thus, the performance of what, until recently, was regarded by the Basque intelligentsia as the rude output of crude men, nevertheless provided a people with a voice and an appreciation of a language that seemed destined for extinction. Indeed, it is one of the many ironies of Basque history that bertsolaritza has never been more popular nor more varied in its form and content than at present, despite the emergence of a vigorous written literature in unified Basque and competing forms of expression such as Basque-language television, radio, magazines, and newspapers.

Bertsolaritza, then, has managed to make the transition from the nineteenth-century rural tavern to the late-twentieth-century television set. While it is true that no village festival is complete without its bertsolari performance, there are also regional and national competitions in which the Basque Country honors its best versifiers. No longer the exclusive provenance of gifted, if illiterate, men who were "born with the talent," bertsolaritza is now described in manuals and learned in classrooms by young men and women. Bertsolaritza, like so much else in Basque culture, now reflects more its late-twentieth-century, urban-industrial setting than the lifestyle of the peasants and fishermen of former times. In short, today's bertsolari, if still a cultural icon, is as much a reflection of profound change as of continuity within Basque society. It is this very fact that augurs well for the future of bertsolaritza.

The author of this present work, Gorka Aulestia, is a master at creating bridges between his native Basque culture and the English-speaking world. During his more than a decade with the Basque Studies Program of the University of Nevada, Reno, he published dozens of reviews of Basque literary works in journals such as *World Literature Today*. Indeed, he was practically the only reviewer in English of Basque-language works, and he embraced his role with near missionary zeal. His *opus magnum*, a Basque-English, English-Basque dictionary, opened a whole new range of possibilities for two-directional cultural interaction. Its production and publication constitute one of the most important and enduring legacies of the Basque Studies Program. Now, with publication of *Improvisational Poetry from the Basque Country*, Gorka Aulestia provides the English-language audience with its first in-depth treatment of the literary form, including an account of the historical and cultural breadth of bertsolaritza. Once again both the Basque- and English-speaking worlds are profoundly in his debt.

WILLIAM A. DOUGLASS
Reno, Nevada

ACKNOWLEDGMENTS

I wish to gratefully acknowledge the kind assistance of William A. Douglass, Juan Mari Lekuona, Nelson Rojas, William Jacobsen, Jr., and Carmelo Urza in the preparation of this book.

I extend my sincere appreciation to the people who provided me with the necessary information—both archival and oral—to complete this work: Juan Mari Lekuona, José Antonio Arana, Antonio Zavala, Samuel Armistead, José María Aranalde, the family of the bertsolari "Xalbador," and the *bertsolariak* Xabier Amuriza, Jon Azpillaga, and Jon Lopategi.

Last, but not least, I express my gratitude to my wife, Mertxe de Renobales, for her patience, support, and the typing of the manuscript.

INTRODUCTION

Basque literature is divided into two separate but complementary parts, written and oral. Basque written literature has characteristics that make it difficult to compare with the literatures of neighboring peoples. The literary schools and movements such as classicism and romanticism that formed and were formed by the great western literatures are not completely applicable to Basque literature.

The salient feature of Basque literature is the Basque language, Euskara. Euskara is a minority language even within its own geographical territory and has only recently been used openly in public life. Historically, the use of Euskara has been controlled and speakers have been persecuted on many occasions, especially during the Franco regime.

It is also important to point out that written Basque literature was very late in developing. The first Basque book, *Linguae Vasconum Primitiae*, by Bernard Detxepare, was published in 1545.[1] According to general opinion, even though the book was written in the midst of the Renaissance, the meters used, such as *cuaderna via*, are reminiscent of those employed in the Middle Ages. Moreover, Basque literature is divided along geographical lines, just as the Basque Country itself is divided between Spain and France. In the north, in the area of France where Euskara is also spoken, Basque literature appeared more than two centuries before it did in the south. This division has created noticeable differences that must be taken into account in any examination of the literature.

Early Basque literature is also largely religious. From the sixteenth century to the middle of the nineteenth, there were very few secular Basque writers. The great majority were clerics who wrote about religious themes. Their point of view involved more didactics and apologetics than literature. Religious literature of the sixteenth century was also for the most part a product of the religious struggle launched by the Council of Trent (1545) against dawning Protestantism. The majority of classical Basque writers in the seventeenth and eighteenth centuries were also clerics who wrote primarily to preach the word of God and to defend the beauty of the Basque language. This ascetic prose gave rise to the narrative and the novel, which, however, did not appear until the beginning of the twentieth century.

In the opinion of several Basque scholars, Basque oral literature is of a quality equal to the oral literatures of neighboring populations. The word *literature* derives from the Latin word *litterae*, and upon hearing it the tendency is to think of the written form. This reflects the conditioning that the classical world has imposed on us and may be one reason why oral literature has been overlooked and neglected for centuries. Oral literature does not conform to the rules imposed by the classics. As J. Walter Ong wrote: "A basic difficulty in thinking about words today is our tendency to regard them largely or chiefly or ideally as records. We are inclined to think of them as, at their optimum, written out or printed." [2] For a long time the majority of people interested in this subject matter regarded the concept of oral literature as a *contradictio in terminis*. They did not accept the possibility that there might have been a true literature in preliterate societies, such as existed among Europe's primitive peoples prior to the arrival of the Indo-Europeans. Today, this view is rejected and even seems quaint. Thanks to the research of specialists in oral traditions, the very concept of literature is evolving. Over the last few decades appreciation for oral literature has grown in part because of the research conducted by Milman Parry (1902-1935) and Albert B. Lord. Thanks to them, today it is generally accepted that the majority of early books such as the Bible, the *Iliad*, and the *Odyssey* have their roots in oral traditions. According to John Miles Foley, a specialist in oral literature:

> Oral cultures are by no means primitive; we cannot anymore smile benignly and admire the simplicity of the noble savage . . . no matter where we look in the world, we find either traces of an oral tradition that preceded (and in some cases still subsists alongside) written traditions or an ongoing oral tradition still very much alive.[3]

Parry became interested in the subject of oral traditions in the 1920s. The year 1928 marked a milestone in literature with his creation of a new method of literary analysis. Using Homer's *Iliad* and *Odyssey*, Parry contrasted oral and written forms of thought and expression and thus contributed to the growing interest in the oral aspects of literature. He employed extremely stringent standards, creating a very personal synthesis between the ancient texts and modern thought. His method was not without foundation. On the contrary, it was grounded in a carefully defined theory drawn from an arduous analysis of Homer's verses.

It had been generally accepted that Homer's style was based on preestablished formulas. However, there had been no in-depth studies of Homer's personal and creative role in the conception of the *Iliad* and the *Odyssey*, the importance of tradition, or how these *formulas* technically functioned in the composition of poetry. Parry challenged the traditional studies of the Homeric epic poem. He asked himself whether Homer had really existed at all and, if so, whether the *Iliad* and *Odyssey* were personal works originating exclusively with him, or merely the fruits of an inherited tradition. To answer these questions, Parry offered a point of view that was radically opposed to what had been traditionally upheld. In two theses, *L'Epithète traditionnelle dans Homère: Essai sur un problème de style homérique* and *Les formules et la métrique d'Homère*, presented in 1928 at the Sorbonne in Paris, Parry proved that Homer had worked in a traditional and epic style that was created over many generations and had relied on many formulaic phrases and expressions. In his analysis of Homer's two famous works, Parry observed that the renowned Greek poet constantly utilized formulas, which Parry defined as "a group of words which is regularly employed under the same metrical conditions, to express an essential idea."[4]

Parry's painstaking scientific research demonstrated that Homer employed an oral tradition passed on from previous generations of singing poets who had continually reshaped songs to reflect the time in which they lived. Homer frequently used formulas or short phrases (noun or name plus epithet) as idioms and prefabricated phrases to tie his great poetic works together. It became evident to Parry that a much greater part of Homer's work may be attributed to this system of formulas than was believed. Only a part of what had been considered to be Homer's work was original. According to Parry, it would not be possible for one poet to create so many of these formulas.

Parry went beyond his assertions concerning the important role of tradition in Homeric poetry and examined oral tradition in depth. He compared the results of his Homeric studies with the experiences of other cultures rich in oral tradition. He studied the oral epic poetry tradition of the Slavic Balkans in the Serbo-Croatian area of the Montenegrin Republic of Yugoslavia.

Accompanied by Albert B. Lord, his colleague and assistant, Parry made two journeys to Yugoslavia between 1933 and 1935. During the second expedition, which lasted from June of 1934 to September of 1935, he compiled a great deal of valuable material regarding the oral and epic Serbo-Croatian poetry of Bijelo Polje, Kolašin, Gacko, Stolac, and Bihac as well as that of some villages of Macedonia.

These trips proved very beneficial not only because of the great number of verses and songs that were collected, but also because of the scientific rigor in the methods employed in the research. When Parry applied his hypothesis about Homeric poetry to the epics of Slavic communities, he concluded that it was not possible to understand the former fully without delving deeply into the nature of oral poetry. In his encounters with the *guslars*, illiterate Slavic bards of the Moslem religion, he determined that they composed oral and epic poetry without the aid of written text. Although the guslars' decasyllabic rhythm differed from the hexametrical verse of the ancient Greeks, their poetry, like Homer's, employed formulas and had meter.

Unfortunately, Parry did not live to carry out his plan of publishing the hundreds of epic texts collected from Yugoslavia nor did he finish the comparative analysis of the material. He died in an automobile accident in 1935.

Lord, however, continued Parry's work, analyzing the data on Homeric poetry with a meticulous and creative methodology. He also advanced their common work on the Serbo-Croatian guslar during subsequent travels by adding material to their previous research. Today all of this work is preserved at Harvard as the Milman Parry Collection of Oral Literature.[5]

Parry's work revolutionized the field of Homeric studies. Lord's research has also been very significant in helping us understand the concept of oral tradition. Lord's first analysis, entitled "Homer and Huso I" (1936), dealt with problems in epic Homeric poetry. In 1938 he published another work, "Homer and Huso II," where he first defined the concept of theme as "a subject unit, a group of ideas regularly employed by a singer, not merely in any given poem, but in the poetry as a whole."[6] Between 1949 and 1959 he published important works dealing with oral literature and heroic and folk songs of the Serbo-Croatian people.

Lord's famous *The Singer of Tales*, was published in 1960. This work, already a classic on oral tradition, is based on the body of knowledge of traditional epic and oral poetry. Lord formulated a critical methodology from the analogy derived in the study of Homeric poetry and the guslar. His work provided a new way of looking at Homer and the Serbo-Croatian bards. In this manner, Parry's work lived on by providing data from interviews from his field trips as well as many recordings of oral performances of Serbo-Croatian epic singers. In his book, Lord also highlighted the elements of oral tradition present in ancient and medieval poetry. He demonstrated that similar modulations are present in Homeric poetry, the French chanson de geste, and Old English. He also studied in detail the process whereby the guslar acquires the essential technique for singing the epic songs of his land. In Lord's opinion, the Serbo-Croatian bard is not simply a mechanical robot, but rather, an artist whose special ability lies in the mastery of technique, themes, and formulas.

Since the publication of his book, Lord's theories of oral tradition have been applied to other literatures, and research on classical Greek and Old English has greatly increased. More than a thousand books and articles have been published that are in some way related to Parry's and Lord's research.

Although most critics who have analyzed Parry's and Lord's studies have found them to be valid, there are a few scholars who have not looked favorably on them. Ruth Finnegan, a specialist in oral literature, is an example. She is the author of several books and has studied oral literature extensively, especially in Africa.[7] Finnegan's dissension stems from the restrictions that Parry and Lord attached to the concept of oral literature. She suggests that the experiences taken from the Serbo-Croatian communities should be complemented with other, similar ones such as those that she encountered in Sierra Leone and other African countries. Finnegan proposes a multifaceted approach to the concept of oral and popular literature that views oral composition as a universal process.

Finnegan also disagrees with Lord's statement concerning the quality of improvisation of the Yugoslavian guslar and contends: "Contrary to the impression in *The Singer of Tales* and elsewhere that oral poetry is always composed in-performance, this is not true empirically. . . . Memorization rather than improvisation is in fact involved."[8]

My work, although directly related to Parry's, Lord's, and Finnegan's studies, focuses on another expression of oral literature: bertsolaritza, or Basque troubadourism. This popular poetic form has ancient origins and is a living heritage of a region whose indigenous language is non-Indo-European.

Basque oral literature has some very interesting and unique characteristics. Luis Michelena (1915-1987) stated that "Basque popular literature, which is essentially oral, is probably as rich and varied as the literature of any other society."[9] Outstanding examples of this oral tradition are the *pastorales*, a form of popular theater from the province of Zuberoa, and bertsolaritza, the art of improvising sung verse. Both of these genres have tenaciously survived and remain active although others have disappeared.

In the Basque province of Zuberoa, the word *phastuala*, or pastorale, has a broad meaning. It embraces various types of theater, drama, tragedy, and comedy. The pastorale may have originated from poems composed by shepherds to express their bucolic sentiments. However, it is difficult to trace its remote origins and establish definite dates. The earliest information we have on the pastorale is provided by Arnaud Oyhenart (1592-1667) in a letter to a priest in Lapurdi. Beyond that, images discovered on the walls of churches such as the one in Santa Garazi (Zuberoa) allow us to trace this form back to the eleventh century.[10] It is probable that the pastorale is more than a thousand years old. There is no consensus about its origin. According to Georges Hérelle, one of the most respected specialists of this genre of music and drama, the pastorale bears a resemblance to the medieval mystery plays. However, the form employed in the mystery plays fell into disuse toward the end of the sixteenth century. Others, such as Manuel Lekuona (1894-1987), believe that the pastorale dates as far back as ancient Greek theater and do not see it as simply a vestige of medieval theater.

Basque pastorales do, in fact, contain elements of ancient Greek theater such as poetic verse, music, song, dance, and an open area serving as a stage. In the eighty-six pastorales that have been preserved, religious mysteries and the feats of medieval knights are the predominant themes. While pastorales from the eighteenth century to the present have maintained traditional elements, their themes have grown to reflect a character that is more Basque. The music of the pastorale is of a religious nature and traditionally archaic, featuring sung rhymed quatrains. Sometimes Gregorian melodies were utilized. Traditionally there were two performers: a *xirulari* (a person who played a type of Basque flute, the *xirula*) and a drummer. Today the pastorales are being modernized for sociocultural reasons. Secular and popular melodies are used and are performed with new instruments such as the cornet, bass drum, and clarinet. Themes vary according to the modern concerns of the Basque Country and include emigration, sociopolitical problems, and standardization of the Basque language. The actors are not professionals, but rather, interested townspeople. The pastorale is essentially popular theater because it is created, written, and performed by and for the people.

Traditionally only men were allowed to perform; if a particular scene called for a female character, a man disguised as a woman played the part. Today the cast is mixed. The length of the play has also been modified. In the past, pastorales began in the morning with a kind of procession to attract attention and ended in the evening. Today there are evening events that last approximately four hours with no interruptions. This adaptation to modern life has made it possible for the pastorale to endure and to attract the attention of thousands of spectators throughout the Basque Country.

Pastorales are performed almost exclusively in Zuberoa, and the residents of small towns participate. This tradition has been maintained without interruption since at least the sixteenth century. Not even the anticlericalism of the French Revolution altered this custom.

In recent years this time-honored form of theater has been revived with great success. Two particularly outstanding modern pastorale authors are Etxahun de Iruri (1908-1979) and Junes Casenave (1924-   ). Unlike similar genres such as rural French and Italian theater, which disappeared in the middle of the nineteenth century, pastorales are enjoying a popularity they never had in the past. From a phenomenon limited exclusively to the smallest Basque province, they have grown in importance until now there are numerous performances that attract people from all corners of the Basque Country.

The second phenomenon of Basque oral literature that attracts the attention of natives as well as foreigners is bertsolaritza. Bertsolaritza has some elements in common with the pastorale: the style of popular verse (rhythm and rhyme) and song. Additionally, in spite of the fact that they are different artistic expressions, both have endured until the present and have adapted to the modern world.

Just as Parry was the great pioneer student of oral literature in the United States, Manuel Lekuona similarly established the scientific basis for research of literature in the Basque Country. Since he focused heavily on bertsolaritza, it is with good reason that he is considered responsible for giving Basque troubadourism the prestige that it enjoys in the Basque Country today. During the nineteenth century and at the beginning of the twentieth, bertsolaritza was scorned. The bertsolariak (versemakers) were regarded merely as clowns who enlivened popular festivals. Many Basques saw nothing more than vulgar nonsense in this popular poetry and considered it, at times, offensive. The fact that most of the bertsolariak were illiterate and given to late nights and hard-cider drinking contributed to the lack of respect for this art form. No one wanted a bertsolari in the family, and performances were prohibited in some towns.

During his years as a professor of Basque, Latin, Greek, and Hebrew at the seminary in Gasteiz, Manuel Lekuona came to the conclusion that the norms established for the study of bertsolaritza were of little use. He felt that comparing this oral poetic expression to norms established for written literature could only lead to a lack of appreciation of the art form. Convinced that troubadourism was a manifestation of a very ancient oral culture, he began by placing it within the framework of oral literature. Unlike the educated poet who expresses himself through writing, the Basque artist creates his popular poetry through improvised song. According to Juan Mari Lekuona (1927-   ), this form of literature was born in the mouth, was enjoyed through the ears, and endured not because of the written word, but because of the collective memory of an active people. Writing has been a great medium for the cultural progress of humanity, but it is not the only medium. The illiterate can also possess great culture.

José Miguel de Barandiarán (1889-1991), Lekuona's colleague and a prestigious ethnologist, published his anthropological studies in the academic journal *Anuario de Eusko Folklore*. Those studies helped Lekuona to understand more fully that the Basques had a purely oral culture for many centuries. He had long suspected this, and history supported his belief. The Basque speaker has always used the words *ohitura* and *usadioa* (both words mean "custom") in social interactions. Basque law has long been based on oral tradition. Custom prevailed over written law. A code of written laws appeared long after custom became established and has been applied somewhat superficially to the multisecular Basque race in recent times. According to Basque jurist Adrián Celaya: "Until 1452 there were no written laws. Even the venerable *fuero viejo* [collection of old laws] was nothing more than the regulation of customs, brought about by repetition of behavior since remote times."[11]

In his most important works Manuel Lekuona revealed his thoughts concerning the new method for studying bertsolaritza. In 1918 he published "Métrica vasca." In 1930 he presented several papers at the conferences of Eusko Ikaskuntza (the Basque studies society) in Bergara that were later published in *Poesía popular vasca*. The publication of *Literatura oral euskérica* in 1935 (reprinted in 1965 as *Literatura oral vasca*) coincided with the "Day of the Bertsolari" (the name of a championship competition for Basque troubadours). This is considered to be Lekuona's classic and became a cultural milestone.

Manuel Lekuona assigned a prehistoric date to the origin of Basque troubadourism. In his opinion, Basque oral literature is rooted in the pastoral period, a time earlier than and distinct from the agricultural one. The pastoral era is chronologically situated in the Neolithic period and reaches back to approximately 5000 B.C. Lekuona felt that troubadourism must have arisen in the pastoral culture and was characteristic of the contemplative shepherd whose leisure time contributed to the creation of this popular poetry. Consequently, bertsolaritza is a form of artistic expression among primitive pastoral societies. The shepherd is also a folk poet who improvises verses around bucolic themes.

Such theories, while defended by Manuel Lekuona as axioms, are debatable. However, it is undeniable that in the Basque Country this artistic phenomenon has endured throughout the centuries with great vitality and highly defined characteristics. The themes of Basque oral poetry have evolved but essentially have not changed with respect to technique, form, and improvisation. In many ways, bertsolaritza is reaching the apogee of an ascent begun two centuries ago because of its ability to adapt to present-day sociopolitical changes in the Basque Country.

The purpose of this study is to present a clear and complete overview of the nature and history of Basque troubadourism. I have collected and utilized existing bibliographic data as well as direct testimony from important bertsolariak and representatives of the Basque people's oral tradition. The general public is my intended audience, as are academicians interested in oral literature and improvised and sung popular poetry. This work deals with oral literature in Euskara, one of western Europe's few surviving non-Indo-European languages. It is my hope that it makes a valuable contribution to a better understanding of similar ancient artistic phenomena.

PART I

The Nature of Bertsolaritza

CHAPTER ONE

The Concept of Oral Tradition

and Basque Oral Literature

In order to understand Basque troubadourism, we first must examine the relationship between Basque oral literature and the oral dimension of other literatures.

In the opinion of most writers, Basque written literature was limited and slow in developing. While other nations have had many writers, representing many different literary movements, there have been relatively few Basque writers, and there are huge gaps if we look at past centuries. Modern living has made us dependent on writing as a convenient method for preserving literary works. Consequently, the Basque Country is at present experiencing an increase in both the quality and the quantity of its written texts. Nevertheless, the written word has yet to supplant oral literature in the soul of the Basque people. This is probably due in large measure to the absence of schools and universities throughout Basque history. Until recently Basque written literature has had little impact and few direct social repercussions.

Unlike other great nations that recorded their history in written form and then disappeared, the Basque people, with prehistoric origins, did not write about their lives. Instead, they left a rich legacy of another type. This heritage consists of Euskara, their living and ancient language, and a series of oral and popular artistic expressions such as pastorales, romances, and ballads. The

Basques tried to preserve their perception of life, their sentiments, and their beliefs through oral expression. This practice in part made up for the lack of a written culture that might normally have interpreted the Basque social and artistic environments over the centuries.

If we accept the definition of oral literature as "everything that has been said and then retained by the collective memory of the people,"[1] we can say that literary and folk creativity in the Basque Country has been present in all literary expressions: poetry, theater, storytelling, and couplets. Bertsolaritza, or Basque troubadourism, and theatrical performances are equally valid forms of oral literature.

In addition to bertsolaritza and popular theater, we must also cite romances, ballads, ancient war songs, *eresiak* (hymns), and the *kopla zaharrak* (old verses) as traces of Basque folk poetry from the Middle Ages. The eresiak were often dirges sung in verse form and improvised at funerals by hired mourners, creating a kind of elegiac bertsolaritza. The kopla zaharrak have a great deal in common with bertsolaritza, as we will see.

These manifestations of oral literature are expressions of a people's lifestyle. The genres reveal that lifestyle's spiritual and artistic character. Even though they represent folk culture, the genres are very useful for understanding the spirit of the people. In the opinion of writer and Bascophile Rodney Gallop:

> Although all poems and stories taken down from peasant lips
> are not necessarily of intrinsic literary beauty, there is a great
> fascination as well as sound scientific value in their collection
> and study, for there are few things in which a nation reveals its
> character so fully as in its folk-literature.[2]

Basque troubadourism is a form of oral literary expression. The bertsolariak are folk poets and improvisers. In most cases, they are versifiers rather than poets. However, among these artists there are often sparks of great poetry. If the verses do not always reach the artistic levels of written poetry, it is because the bertsolari must improvise spontaneously on any given subject. This phenomenon is deeply rooted in folk culture by means of the people's collective memory. This technique of improvised creation and oral transmission is characteristic of socially and linguistically closed communities. The Basque Country still preserves many remnants of a rich prehistoric culture transmitted through oral tradition.

Oral literature is born and endures independently of written literature. Its production is linked to sociocultural circumstances that existed in the time before Basque written literature became a reality, or at least a common occurrence. The bertsolari himself served as the "book" of that time, and the people's collective memory of his creation ensured that few new "editions" would appear.

Although language is essentially oral, studies conducted on language and literature in the past few centuries have greatly neglected oral aspects while concentrating mostly on the written text. The oral factors have been regarded as simple deviations from the written form. The much-used expression "oral literature" itself lacks logic and seems contradictory. The very word *literature* implies writing, and the use of the term "oral" cannot counterbalance the weight of that implication.

It is clear, however, that the origins of language and literature are essentially oral in nature. It is difficult to calculate exactly how many languages have been used on this planet throughout human history, but it is quite evident that the majority of them never attained written form. According to the linguist Ong, of the approximately three thousand languages spoken in the world today only seventy-eight have a recognized written literature.[3]

Oral literature's most distinguishing features include the following: it is created in the mind and not recorded on paper; it is retained in memory and not preserved in books; and it is recited before an audience and not read in private.

Societies that possess a predominantly or exclusively oral culture have their own special characteristics. Their world is interpreted through the spoken word alone. Their literature endures orally, and the continuation of the culture depends on those individuals who verbally impart their cultural heritage from one generation to the next. Verbal transmission and retentiveness are of utmost importance in these cultural activities.

The differences between the bard working in an oral medium and the poet-writer are clear: The former is never free of tradition. The sources of his art are not his readings, but rather the years of listening to older bards who never sang an oral composition twice in exactly the same way. The bards did not possess pen or ink. Most of them did not even know how to read or write. Their working environment was very different from that of the educated poet. The bard's source of creativity to generate his next phrase rested on an ability for rapid thought without the benefit of being able to rework his prior utterance.

Oral texts are not concrete and therefore permit the existence of more than one version. Indeed, each performance is a re-creation. Instead of reciting an oral composition from memory, the bard recomposes it. In a sense, each performance is a debut. The oral poet does not merely replicate a mechanical process of metrical and stereotypical formulas that limit his creativity. Instead, the troubadour's song may take various forms. Written text, in contrast, generally exists in a single version that becomes fixed and is the exclusive property of one person. Although written text is generally richer in detail and logic, it lacks spontaneity.

As we probe more deeply into the characteristics of oral literature we find that the actual author is a collective and anonymous entity: the community. Consequently, we can say that this art form is created by and for the people. The artist is born into the community and interprets its sentiments. Greater sensitivity is required to express artistically the community's feelings. The artist as an oral poet becomes a pioneer, an intermediary, and a witness for the people. He must be in tune with the people and be able to laugh and cry with them. In this way the artist becomes the greatest exponent of the oral tradition.

When applying these concepts to the Basque Country, we must note that in general the Basques were illiterate until the nineteenth century. Their only school was nature and the church, where they heard priests preach Sunday sermons. They relied on their memories to preserve and reshape their common literary heritage.

The church used verses for instructional purposes. During the sixteenth and seventeenth centuries no literary works at all were published in the southern part of the Basque Country. A few catechisms constituted the entire written wealth of the Basque Country. However, even these must be placed within an oral literary context. Since the people did not know how to read, the priest read aloud to them and the congregation memorized the oral pastoral message. Moreover, the catechistic and pedagogical objectives of these pious texts were influenced by the fact that they were destined for an illiterate public. In this fashion the books of catechism, written from the perspective of popular oral literature, passed into the collective memory of the people.

The farmhouse kitchen was another focal point for the promulgation of Basque oral literature. After dining moderately and praying the rosary with grandmother, there were informal lessons. On some occasions grandmother retold ancient stories and tales while the family husked corn. At other times grandfather sang the old *bertsoak* (improvised oral poetry sung before an audience) that he remembered or the new ones he had heard in the marketplace after Sunday mass. Basque culture was transmitted to younger generations in this way through the centuries. In his renowned book *Euskaldunak* (1950), Nicolás Ormaetxea, alias "Orixe" (1888–1961), describes these family gatherings: "In the Basque Country the task of husking corn signified a 'literary evening' in which our oral literature was transmitted."[4]

The general public was the ultimate creator of oral literature and as a consequence imposed its own rules. Oral texts were not the exclusive property of one person as is the case with written literature. The public was the trustee of this oral tradition and had the right to change, reshape, and at times even adulterate some passages. A simple poem and a humble melody by an anonymous author gradually acquired life like an embryo growing inside the community's womb. The people nourished it orally until it became a collective work that increased the wealth of the oral tradition. In this way these texts were exposed to constant evolution and did not retain the hermeticism of a written passage. Ultimate authorship, then, belonged to the community. Consequently, it was the community that gave these works their final form through modification and adaptation. Thanks to this collaboration, the content and style of these texts gradually changed, and what once may have been unique and personal to one author became communal property.

This active community participation is also present today in Basque troubadourism. The public imposes its tastes, and the artist does not lose sight of the community's involvement. The public demonstrates its approval or displeasure by applauding and whistling. It sings in chorus with the bertsolari and sometimes finishes the last stanza by singing the last line with him. The community also participates indirectly in the selection of subjects by indicating their preferences. The majority of sociopolitical themes employed in competitions of the 1980s reflect community concerns. Finally, the bertsolari must improvise without repetition and ad-lib without using preestablished formulas. The audience demands it. This is the way the public actively participates in the creative process of this artistic phenomenon.

The mutability of ideas, the fleeting images, and the abundance of elisions in oral literature contrast sharply with the slow and studied production of written literature. Swift spontaneity is especially demanded in bertsolaritza, where the artist is given no more than a few seconds to improvise and to answer an opponent. The folk poet's imagination leaps from one idea to another, from one image to the next, with little apparent logic or cohesion. At the same time, fluidity and natural ease with images are characteristics of this folk literature.

CHAPTER TWO

Definition and

Qualities of a Bertsolari

DEFINITION

I have studied the subject of bertsolaritza for several years. However, when I attempt to translate the concept into another language, I am unable to find an adequate equivalent. I have often used the word *troubadour* to describe the bertsolari because it is similar in meaning. However, the bertsolari is more than a troubadour. Although the Basque artist exhibits elements in common with the minstrel, educated poet, songster, and actor, he is none of these.

Bertsolaritza is now treated in the same way that the Basque language was in earlier times. The Basques' ancient language, Euskara, was surrounded by such ancient and mythic mystery that many people thought it was impossible to learn. Likewise, bertsolaritza has been portrayed as a mysterious art form that may be mastered only by a privileged few, born with special talent. The Basque people, especially those from Gipuzkoa, have been great enthusiasts of this artistic phenomenon. In spite of this, when asked to define the nature of bertsolaritza, most people offer very vague replies. Even Manuel Lekuona hesitated in giving a definition and simply offered this comparison: "A bird knows how to sing without understanding how he does it. You know how to create verses. . . . But do you understand their essence? You ask me if I understand? I wish I did."[1]

At times similar answers are obtained from the best bertsolariak. Even artists who are able to improvise verses of great quality in a few seconds have a difficult time defining their art. Consider, for example, the experience of American anthropologist William A. Douglass, coordinator of the Basque Studies Program at the University of Nevada, Reno, who spent several years in the Basque Country. During one of his trips he interviewed the bertsolariak Ignacio Eizmendi, alias "Basarri" (1913-   ), and Manuel Olaizola, alias "Uztapide" (1909-1983). He recorded their conversations on tape.[2] Douglass asked them: "What is bertsolaritza?" Several minutes passed in silence; they did not know how to respond. Later they replied with rather vague answers.

Basque oral literature is a phenomenon that has survived through the centuries and has a great following in the Basque Country. This genre is not a fossil or an ancient monument preserved in a museum. Indeed, bertsolaritza is on its way to becoming an institution. By way of definition I begin by demonstrating that bertsolari is not synonymous with troubadour, poet, songster, or actor, although their art forms share some elements. Their commonalities will help us eventually to create a complete and *positive* definition of bertsolaritza.

The Bertsolari Is Not a Simple Troubadour

Semantically, the word *troubadour* like the French verb *trouvère* and the Italian word *trovare* is derived from the medieval Latin verb *tropare*, and has much in common with the Spanish verbs *hallar* and *encontrar* and the Latin verb *invenire*. In the same way that this Latin word came to mean to invent or to create, the verb *trovar* also means to create in a literary sense. In other words, it is the art of composing verses and their melodies. The troubadour composes poems that will later be heard by the public as song.

Unlike the minstrel, the troubadour created his own poetry and was also socially and intellectually superior. It seems that troubadourism originated in southeast France around the eleventh century at a time when that area of Europe had adopted a feudal political structure. It was there that the langue d'oc (the language of the common people) was deemed worthy of being the official language for lyric poetry and was destined for the highest social classes. Troubadour poetry exhibits certain characteristics that reflect the specific historical and political situations of the time. The courts of the feudal lords were extremely important in Provençal lyric poetry. The troubadour, a professional poet, had close ties with the feudal court where he lived and worked. Although he sometimes sang for the common people, that was not his primary job. His mission was to delight a small and select group at court.

A man's love for a woman was a common theme of troubadour poetry. The celebrated woman was usually the wife of the *dominus*, or feudal lord, and had to be a married woman. Unmarried maidens were not considered to have sufficient status because they did not possess property. Songs of courtly love exalted the kindness, beauty, and nobility of the ladies of the court. On some occasions, the troubadour utilized other themes. In his poetry, he defined the political views of his feudal lord and attacked the opposing side or renounced unfit practices or abuses. *Sirventès*, the genre of Provençal poetic composition of a political and moral nature, emerged in the same way. Another genre called *tenso* also existed. It consisted of two troubadours disputing themes that could range from true love to such subjects as flatulence or whether a woman was more attractive from the waist up or from the waist down.[3]

The technique of troubadour poetry was complicated. The rhyme had to be rigorously consonant because assonant rhyme was considered to be of poor quality. There are very few known exceptions in Provençal poetry. The troubadour also had to match the melodies to the lyrics according to metrical and rhythmic rules. This involvement of music demanded that an artist possess an adequate education, one that could not be replaced by innate qualities such as a good ear. Because of this, the troubadour had to pursue a series of studies to master this difficult technique. Additionally, the troubadour might improvise verses. While improvisation was not commonplace, the ability to improvise was held in high esteem.

The similarities between the feudal troubadour and the bertsolari are obvious. The etymology of the words *trovar* and *trovador* suit the Basque artist well. The bertsolari creates in a literary sense by fitting lyrics to music. Both artists compose poetry in song form meant for listening rather than to be read. However, the term *poet* or *poeta culto* does not exactly apply to either artist. In the Middle Ages, this term was reserved exclusively for the educated poet who wrote in Latin. The Basques too, distinguish between *olerkari*, the educated poet who writes verses, and bertsolari, the folk-poet who sings improvised verse. However, there are marked differences between the troubadour and the bertsolari:

1. The ultimate goal of improvised bertsolaritza is not the creation of complicated consonant rhyme, although it is a highly regarded element in competitions like the *txapelketak*. However, consonant rhyme is very important to bertsolari stylists, who preserve their own compositions in writing.

2. Another formal difference is the preparation of music. All that the Basque artist needs, to comply easily with the requirements of a public performance, is a good ear and a love for the art. On the other hand, as a *conditio sine qua non*, he must possess a talent for quick, spontaneous, and natural improvisation that flows from his lips like water from a spring.

3. Unlike the select minority or upper class of feudal society who listened to the troubadour's song, the bertsolari's audience is the common working people. Historically, these people were Basque speakers from small towns and fishing villages. Today, bertsolaritza

also attracts young skilled workers and even university students in industrial zones.

4. Different themes are employed in bertsolaritza. Love, which was a common theme in the Middle Ages, is not as popular at present. Sociopolitical and cultural themes are the most common today and are of great interest to this minority nation in the process of recovering its autochthonous values.

The Bertsolari Is Not a Minstrel

The word *minstrel* is difficult to define because its meaning varies according to historical periods and cultural settings. Many kinds of minstrels existed in the Middle Ages, including clowns, acrobats, tightrope walkers, and buffoons. For this discussion, however, we will focus only on the literary singing minstrel who acted as the troubadour's assistant. The minstrel did not compose poetry as did the troubadour; he sang the verses written by others. He performed a service for the troubadour by singing his verses and providing musical accompaniment. The minstrel was an indispensable assistant. Without him, the troubadour would not be a recognized artist. Minstrels were hired or appointed by feudal lords or troubadours. The minstrel's primary mission was to delight his audience through song and music. Toward the end of the Middle Ages court minstrels began to exclude songs from their acts, and their trade became that of simple buffoon.

There are clear differences between the minstrel and the bertsolari. The Basque artist creates his own poetry and serves only his audience. He does not need any musical instrument. The bertsolari depends solely on his voice. At times the bertsolari also aims to delight his audience and frequently performs at folk festivals. However, unlike the minstrel, he is the presenter and creator of his own poetry.

The Bertsolari Is Not an Educated Poet

The Basque language clearly distinguishes the olerkari from the bertsolari. Their different types of poetry comprise two different fields and are not two divisions of a single art form.

The literary expression of the olerkari depends on writing, whereas the bertsolari's oral literary expression requires only song. As a folk-poet, the bertsolari does not concern himself primarily with consonant rhymes or painstaking poetic techniques. For example, enjambment, so common in written poetry, is not found in bertsolaritza. With regard to the marriage of music and text, the norm of modern bertsolaritza is that each syllable of a word corresponds to one musical note.

Most bertsolariak of the twentieth century have been illiterate. They have depended on people who know how to write to record the verses they create orally. Creation and performance are simultaneous in bertsolaritza. The Basque artist must improvise in front of an audience and does not have time to rework the words. He has only a few seconds to choose a melody, rhythm, and the rhyme of the last line to compose a verse orally. His art is like a river that flows by the listener only once and can never return to its origin. Written culture was never an essential element for these bertsolariak. Even today, despite the involvement of college-educated bertsolariak, this art form is still conceived orally. Very few of these artists are engaged in cultivating written poetry. Even the *bertso jarriak* (written verses) of these artists are considered oral literary expressions because of the techniques used in their creation. The public also has always preferred this improvised oral form. Around 1930, at the height of the renaissance of Basque literature, no more than five hundred copies were printed of any one book of poetry. However, oral literary expressions remained popular. Bertsolariak performances were very widely attended.

Other palpable differences exist between the bertsolariak and modern poets. Modern poetry makes use of free verse, attempts to create essays, forces forms of expression to fit, and sometimes creates irrational images. Bertsolaritza, on the other hand, always follows traditional norms. Surrealistic images and enjambments have no place here, and metaphors are traditional.

The Bertsolari Is More Than a Mere Songster

Song is one of the most integral elements of bertsolaritza. There could not be improvised verse without music and song. Melody marks the rhythm of the verse for the bertsolari. However, melody is not as important in bertsolaritza as it is in opera, where the music is essential and more important than the lyrics. In opera lyrics can at times be a mere pretext for an exhibition of *bel canto* and an opportunity for the singer to showcase the voice.

For the Basque artist lyrics are more important than music. Consequently, the bertsolari is more poet than songster. His final goal is not to invent new music, but rather, to create beautiful verse with the help of music. The Basque artist sings to transmit a message and not to demonstrate his voice or interpret a musical score. A salient characteristic of the bertsolari's Basque music is the simplicity of the melody, in which each note corresponds to one syllable. This notion will be examined later on.

The role of the audience is also important. The public does more than listen passively. The listener actively participates by mentally creating verses simultaneously with the bertsolari.

The Bertsolari Is Not an Actor

Both the opera singer and the actor perform scripts written by others, and both recite memorized literary fragments. They enact scores and scripts conceived by someone else and have little freedom to improvise. The strength of their performance lies in their talent for literally interpreting their roles. The bertsolari and the actor share only one thing—they both express their ideas with words.

POSITIVE DEFINITION

Having considered what the bertsolari performer is not and the corresponding negative and exclusionary definitions, it will be easier to present a positive one to describe the nature of bertsolaritza. Xabier Amuriza, twice bertsolari champion and specialist, defines the most important elements of bertsolaritza as "herriaren kantuzko hitza" (the sung word of the people), and expressed this idea in verse:

> Neurriz eta errimaz kantatzea hitza horra hor zer kirol
> mota den bertsolaritza.[4]
>
> Bertsolaritza is a kind of sport that involves singing
> lyrics with rhythm and rhyme.

The concepts of community, song, lyrics, rhythm, rhyme, and entertainment are very important. Bertsolaritza is a form of artistic expression that involves intense mental exercise and creative and rewarding work. It is performed in the gymnasium of the mind where one thinks as one sings, and improvises without pausing to correct errors.

Technically, bertsolaritza is a Basque genre of oral improvised poetry created by folk-poets for an audience. Without an audience the bertsolari would have no reason to perform. The following description of the bertsolari, which is analogous to a photograph taken during a public performance and focused on the physical demeanor of the artist in a moment of tension, helps explain the concept:

> His beret is tilted to one side and he holds his hands behind his
> back. He looks into the great void and from a tumultuous rush
> of words searches for the right ones. He must reflect and sing in-
> stantly, choosing the most beautiful phrases. In the midst of the
> pressure created by that void, [he must] be sharp and quick in
> [his] creation.[5]

CONSTITUENT ELEMENTS

The formal characteristics of bertsolaritza are rhythm, rhyme, song, and improvisation. The roles of themes and the audience are also important, and will be examined later.

Verse Models

The fundamental unity of poetic improvisation is contained in the verse. The bertsolari improvises with the support of a melody that provides the metrical pattern and rhythm for each section. As soon as he chooses his melody, the bertsolari already knows what type of verse he will create, its various possibilities for poetic discourse, and the emotional tone that he will set with the melody.

Thus, short verses that have few rhymes and lines with few syllables offer greater possibilities for narrative and poignant dialectic formats. These verses conform most easily to epic poetry and subtle reasoning. On the other hand, long verses containing more than four rhymes and multisyllabic lines convey lyricism and dramatization, and are more suitable for the bertsolari when he is singing under the pressure of an anticipated intense climax. In Juan Mari Lekuona's *Ahozko euskal literatura*, I count more than thirty types of verses used in bertsolaritza. The thirty models are classified into seven groups, according to the distinct types of rhyme that each offers.

The main model (*nagusia*) of the first group is composed of hemistiches of ten plus eight syllables in the rhymed lines: 10/8 A.[6] The minor model (*txikia*) contains hemistiches of seven plus six syllables in the rhymed lines: 7/6 A. The classical model, however, consists of hemistiches of eight plus seven syllables: 8/7 A.

The second group is characterized by an abundance of rhymes. One model features nine rhymes (*bederatzi puntukoa*), while others have eight (*zortzi puntukoa*), or six (*sei puntukoa*). These are lines of single rhymes and uneven numbers of syllables.

There is also a group of verses called couplets (*koplak*). Couplets contain two rhyming lines of eight syllables combined with hemistiches as in the main model: 8A 8A 10/8A. There exists another group of verses made up of short lines, combining the models examined up to this point. These verses are characterized by short lines containing a different rhyme, thus causing a new acoustical rhythmic sensation. There is another group in which the lines all rhyme and contain the same number of syllables. Finally, there are unique verse models with different structures that arise when autochthonous lyrics are set to non-Basque or nontraditional Basque melodies. These melodies are usually Basque versions of popular songs.

Given the scope of this monograph, a detailed study of the verse and rhyme of each model is impractical. However, it is possible to describe the five most frequently used models in bertsolaritza: (1) *zortziko handia* consists of eight long lines; (2) *zortziko txikia* consists of eight short lines; (3) *hamarreko handia* consists of ten long lines; (4) *hamarreko txikia*, features ten short lines; and (5) *bederatzi puntuko bertsoa* is a verse of fourteen lines with nine obligatory rhymes.

Zortziko Handia

The zortziko handia verse type has eight lines. The odd-numbered lines consist of ten syllables and need not rhyme. On the other hand, its even-numbered lines consist of eight syllables and must rhyme. The caesura usually follows the fifth syllable. The traditional model is five plus five syllables for odd-numbered lines and five plus three for even lines. This is one of the most frequently used verse models because, along with zortziko txikia, it is the model used in *bertso-paperak* (written verses). It was the appearance of bertso-paperak in the nineteenth century that made possible the transmission of oral poetry. All bertsolariak use this model with relative ease and feel very comfortable singing it.

An example of zortziko handia is the verse of the legendary and comical bertsolari Joxe Manuel Lujanbio, alias "Txirrita" (1860–1936). This confirmed bachelor improvised the following verse at the 1936 txapelketa at seventy-six years of age, a few months before his death:

> Zenbat errezo egin izan det
> nere denboran elizan,
> ta pozik nago ikusirikan
> pakian nola gabiltzan.
> Ni naizen bezin kobarderikan
> inor ezin leike izan
> semeak gerra ez joateatik
> mutil zar gelditu nintzan.[7]

> I have said many prayers
> during my time spent in church
> and I am happy to see
> that we are at peace.
> No one could be
> as cowardly as I
> I have remained a bachelor
> so my sons would not go to war.

Zortziko Txikia

The uneven lines in zortziko txikia have seven syllables and the even lines have six. None of these lines contain a caesura. This type of verse is not conducive to long descriptions or great detail because by definition it has short (txikia) lines. It is difficult to create good descriptions with so few words. Zortziko txikia allows for expression of many feelings and employs the major or minor key to support the feeling being expressed. Its rhythm gives the verse a special liveliness. The following example of this type of verse was improvised by Xabier Amuriza in the txapelketa of 1980. The rhymed words *noiz, goiz, inoiz,* and *arrazoiz* were assigned to him:

> Euskalerrian libre
> izan ginan inoiz,
> orain esklabo gaude
> indarren arrazoiz;
> berriz libre gerade
> baina ez dakit noiz,
> beintzat ezta izango
> zuek naiz bezain goiz.[8]

> We were once free
> in the Basque Country
> now we are slaves
> by force;
> we will be free again
> but I do not know when,
> at least it will not be
> as soon as you would like.

Hamarreko Handia

The odd lines in hamarreko handia contain ten syllables and the even ones have eight. This model is used for intense subjects or long descriptions. Hamarreko handia is also appropriate for greetings and farewells. José Luis Gorrotxategi (1945-   ) used this model in a verse he improvised during the opening ceremonies of the 1980 txapelketa, a literary contest in which the best bertsolariak demonstrate their talents in front of a large audience and a panel of judges. While the verse was not an outstanding example of technique, it was very appropriate for the bertsolari's greetings to the residents of Donostia; the people of the Basque Country, in general; the previous champion, Manuel Olaizola, alias "Uztapide"; and the daughter of Pello Mari Otaño, alias "Katarro" (1857-1910), who had traveled from Argentina to attend the championship:

> Lendabiziko agur ta erdi
> Balda'tik Donostia'ri,

eta ondoren besarkada bat
Euskalerri guztiari;
ta berezi txapeldun degun
Uztapide aundiari,
Arjentina'tik Donostiara
etorri dan izarrari
ementxe bertso-entzule dugun
Otaño'ren alabari.[9]

First of all a greeting
from Balda to Donostia,
then a hug
for all of the Basque Country;
and especially
to the grand champion, Uztapide,
and to the star that has come
to Donostia from Argentina.
We have Otaño's daughter
Here to listen to verses.

Hamarreko Txikia

The odd lines in hamarreko txikia have seven syllables and do not have to rhyme. The even lines, on the other hand, have six syllables and must rhyme. The joyous or sad feelings evoked by this verse depend on the major or minor tone of the melody. The following representative verse by Uztapide is entitled "Ama" (Mother). He improvised this classic verse at the 1962 txapelketa and dedicated it to his deceased mother:

Amak eman ziraden
lenengo bularra,
andik artua nuen
bertsotako indarra,
geroztik biotzera
datorkit su-garra,
egunsentia joan zan,
laister illunabarra,
gero ta beerago
Uztapide zarra.[10]

My mother nursed me
for the first time at her bosom,
from there I received
the aptitude for versemaking,
from then on my heart
has known burning passion,

the dawn has departed,
twilight approaches rapidly,
old Uztapide
going more downhill every day.

Bederatzi Puntuko Bertsoa

The verse *bederatzi puntuko bertsoa* is made up of four-
teen lines and nine rhymes that must occur in lines 2, 4, 6, 8, 9, 10, 11, 12, and
14. The other lines (1, 3, 5, 7, and 13) do not have to rhyme. Odd-numbered
lines contain seven syllables and even lines contain six as in short verses (*txi-
kiak*). However, lines 4 and 14 have only five syllables, setting this model apart
from the others described above.

As we have mentioned, this verse is extremely complicated. It is perhaps,
the most difficult to improvise. Past bertsolariak, including Fernando Amezke-
tarra (1764-1823), frequently used this model. However, at the beginning of
the twentieth century it began to disappear. Many of the greatest bertsolariak,
such as Txirrita and Uztapide, seldom made use of it. At the 1967 txapelketa, a
special award was designated for the artist who could use the bederatzi pun-
tuko bertsoa with the most skill. No one won because none of the ten contes-
tants was willing to attempt this type of verse. On another occasion, during a
preliminary round of the Gipuzkoa txapelketa held in Eibar, the bertsolariak
again declined to use this verse.

During the four national competitions held in the 1960s, this verse was
rarely selected, and then only to demonstrate that it still existed. Today, how-
ever, several artists, including Angel Peñagarikano (1957-   ), use the verse
often and feel very comfortable with it. Others, such as Jon Lopategi (1934-   ),
Xabier Amuriza, and Jon Enbeita (1950-   ) improvise with it successfully. The
verse that follows is a good example of the bederatzi puntuko bertsoa impro-
vised by Francisco Petrirena, alias "Xenpelar" (1835-1869), about an old cow a
friend bought at a fair in Hernani. The number of syllables and rhymes for each
line are indicated below.

	1	2	3	4	5	6	7
1.	Be-	gi	bat	i-	tsu-	a	du,
2.	a-	dar	bi-	yak	mo-	*tzak,*	
3.	Kri-	sa-	llu-	a	di-	ru-	di
4.	a-	ren	ko-	ko-	*tzak;*		
5.	i-	ka-	ra-	tu-	tzen	gai-	tu
6.	ez-	tu-	la-	ren	o-	*tsak,*	
7.	bur-	la-	ka	a-	si	zaiz-	ka
8.	e-	li-	za-	tik	on-	*tzak;*	
9.	Sa-	no	dauz-		ka	or-	*tzak,*
10.	a-	gi-	ñak	zo-	rro-	*tzak,*	
11.	tris-	tu-	ra	bi-	o-	*tzak,*	

12. dan-	tzan	da-	bil	o-	*tzak;*	
13. Es-	ti-	yo	o-	nik	e-	gin
14. le-	ku	a-	rro-	*tzak.*[11]		

1. She has one blind eye
2. two broken horns,
3. that cow's face
4. looks like an oil lamp;
5. the sound of her cough
6. scares us,
7. she is mocking
8. the owls from the church;
9. her teeth are healthy,
10. her molars are sharp,
11. her heart is sad,
12. she shivers with cold . . .
13. she has not adjusted well
14. to her new environment.

Rhymes

Rhyme is based on the similarity and harmony of sounds. However, the concept of Basque rhyme differs from Spanish rhyme. In Spanish versification, rhyme occurs when two words sound the same from the last accented vowel to the ends of the words. Pertinent to this study are the differences between consonant and assonant rhymes. Assonant rhymes have similar vowel sounds from the last accented vowel to the ends of the words. For example, *leche, vete.* In addition to similar vowels, consonant rhymes have the same consonants. For example *Méndez, Meléndez.* In Basque rhymes (*puntuak*), the elements for Spanish rhyme are present. However, additional components may be introduced. Rhyme does not begin with the last accented vowel but rather consists of graphemes in the last syllable of a line. Rhyme begins at the end of the word and extends backwards (right to left) to the previous clause. This usually results in a homophony of the last three syllables of a line. Since the last syllable in a catalectic line is frequently a suffix (article, postposition), which is repeated in all rhymes of the verse, Basque rhymes generally require that similar phonemes begin at the end of the rhyming lexeme of each line starting with the suffix. In rare cases, rhyme occurs only in the suffix. For an example of this, see model A below.

Rhymes that are award winners have greater numbers of like phonemes. The more like phonemes a rhyme shares, the more highly regarded it is, although a bertsolari needs only to rhyme one phoneme at the end of a line. The following models serve as a classification of rhymes.

1. *Model A*: homophony of suffixes
   gizonA—etxeA
   zokoTIK—zeruTIK

2. *Model B*: rhyme of one phoneme of the last syllable of the lexeme preceding the suffix.
   gizoNA—esaNA

3. *Model C*: rhyme of two or more phonemes of the last syllable preceding the suffix.
   gizONA—ONA
   giZONA—oSONA

4. *Model D*: rhyme of one phoneme of the penultimate syllable of a lexeme preceding the suffix.
   gIZONA—hITZ ONA

5. *Model E*: rhyme of two or more phonemes of the penultimate syllable of a lexeme preceding the suffix.
   GIZONA—aGITZ ONA

6. *Model F*: rhyme from the antepenultimate syllable preceding the suffix.
   dA GIZONA—AGITZ ONA

Other Rhyme Types

It is uncommon to find assonant rhymes in bertsolaritza. When assonance occurs it appears as alliteration. Rhyming vowels are added to the penultimate and antepenultimate syllables of the lines in models B and C. For example:

Ni askotan bezela
tabernAN NENGUAN,
neskazar oiei esan
nioTEN lENGUAN
jantzi ori ona da
denborA BErUAN
baina ez ilbeltzian
eta ABENdUAN;
gaixuak otzak ilko
zaituztE NEGUAN.[12]

Like many other times
that I was at the tavern,
I told those old maids
the last time [I was there]
That outfit is good
for hot weather
but not for January

and December;
poor things, the cold will
kill you in the winter.

The occurrence of the last -AN is not considered part of the rhyme because it is a repeated suffix. The five highlighted words share only one grapheme, -U- which precedes the suffix -AN. There is a pattern in three of these words containing the pattern -ENGU: nENGU, lENGU, and NEGU (metathesis), and a similar sound as in abENDUAN. On the other hand, the -E- of bERUAN is an assonant rhyme. The remaining assonant rhymes are

1. tabernAn   nENGUAN
   denborA   BE rUAN
                ABEndUAN
2. nioTEN   LENGUAN
      TE   NE GUAN

The above demonstrates that in addition to like graphemes in all of the lines, there are also other interesting phonetic similarities. Some of these consist of consonant rhyme while others have assonant rhyme. Both types are mixed freely, providing a verse with an interesting display of alliteration on both the consonant and the assonant levels. This type of rhyme is extremely difficult to improvise or to compose. Homophony of metrical cadences is fundamental to oral poets.

Centers dedicated to teaching the art of bertsolaritza have published the following rhyming guidelines:[13]

1. Words ending in a vowel must be preceded by the same consonant.
   gazta — festa
   gabe — hobe

2. Diphthongs may stand alone as rhymes:
   jai — lasai
   goi — morroi

3. When consonants l, n, r, s, z, ts, and tz end a word, they must be preceded by the same vowel, although some consonants may be slightly different. For example, s and z, and ts and tz, are considered to be the same sounds.
   epel—sabel
   ados—gatoz
   hots—zorrotz

4. When two words have the same suffix, the preceding syllable of both words should be the same or similar. Using the suffixes rik and an, we get the following examples:
   sasirik—ikusirik
   etxean—atzean

5. Excessive effort in searching for complicated rhymes should be

avoided. However, it is very important to pair grammatically different words. For example:

> jarri (verb) — sarri (adverb)
> larri (adjective) — harri (noun)

6. In competitions, complicated rhymes are preferred and scored more highly than simple rhymes. For example:

> di*zuna* — egin*k*i*zuna*

Simple and extremely easy rhymes such as those composed of the verb forms *tzen*, *tu*, and *du* receive lower scores. For example:

bizi*tzen* — buka*tzen*

jarrai*tu* — luza*tu*

isil*du* — amil*du*

Each bertsolari establishes his own rules, some giving more importance to rhyme than do others. This evolves according to the times, geography, bertsolaritza schools, and other cultural factors. Thus, more skilled stylists demonstrate their mastery in this area. Earlier bertsolariak were more intuitive about the magical elements in the creation of rhymes than are their modern counterparts, who, rather, view these guidelines as aesthetic postulates to help them create more polished verses.

Music and Song

The French writer François Arouet (1694–1778) described the Basques as "these people who dwell or rather, leap about at the foot of the Pyrenees and who are called the Basques or Vascons."[14] This definition is incomplete, however, because it does not include the Basques' aptitude for music, one of the most salient characteristics of their culture. The Basques are immersed in music from birth. Every large town in the Basque Country has a choir and a dance troupe. Their talent for music and oral literary expressions is well known.

Basque composer Augustín González Acilu wrote that Basque music, as such, does not exist without Basque lyrics because music is a universal language.[15] However, it is evident that when Basques hear one of their country's folk songs, they recognize it as their own — something that belongs to them. Basque writer Carmelo de Echegaray (1865–1925) described this sentiment in the following way:

> No matter where we may hear Basque music, even the least sensitive of ears recognizes that it is ours, even though it may be a piece we have never heard before. It is the family likeness, the seal of the Basque race, that makes us immediately realize that this music that delights our senses and lifts our spirits belongs to us because it is characteristic of our motherland.[16]

The Basques have created a unique music with its own personality. To what degree this music is original is unclear. While it is difficult to assess how much it has been affected by external influences, it is evident they have indeed existed. It is also not surprising when one considers the fact that the Basque Country has closely coexisted with other cultures. In spite of this, outside influence on Basque music has not been as great as previously believed. Basque musicologist and writer José Antonio Arana has stated: "Today, modern music collections indicate that foreign influences have never had a significant effect on our folk songs."[17]

The Basques' musical originality lies in their extraordinary ability to copy others and to infuse each piece with a Basque flair. Even when using foreign elements, the Basque transforms the music with his unique character.

Basque folk songs merit a brief examination because they are so closely tied to bertsolaritza. Today the Basque Country boasts a rich legacy of folk music because of the patient, consistent work of specialists such as Jean Dominique Julien Sallaberry (1837-1903); José Antonio of Donostia, alias "Padre Donostia"; Resurrección María de Azkue; and others. This popular music has been a valuable resource for bertsolariak in creating their performances. A close relationship exists between the folk music of the Basque culture and its folk poetry because all of the poetry is sung.

Basque folk poetry has traditionally been melodic. Melody prevails over all other elements except lyrics. It is also syllabic—each syllable corresponds to one musical note. The use of syllables is the basis of Basque metrics and greatly facilitates the work of the bertsolari. Knowing how to fit music to lyrics is essential to this complicated art form. Basque music is not melismatic like Gregorian chant, in which one syllable may correspond to several musical notes. Gregorian chant was composed for singing Latin texts, which contained both short and long syllables. This division between types of syllables does not occur in the Basque language, at least not for musical purposes.

Another characteristic of Basque music is the occurrence of the minor key. When compared with other European folk traditions, there is a relatively high number of Basque songs composed in a minor key.

Lyrics prevail over music in bertsolaritza because the main concern is that the audience understand the message. Consequently, melodies are usually simple. One could say that, at times, the bertsolariak seem to recite rather than sing. The accompanying melodies are usually popular and of older origin. Melody serves as the foundation of the bertsolari's improvised poetry. Recently, music has become even more important in bertsolaritza. A verse without music, or one poorly sung, loses much of its charm. Half a century ago, most artists only used a half dozen melodies. In the 1965 txapelketa twenty-six different melodies were sung. In 1982, however, there were forty-two different melodies, eight of which had never been heard before.[18]

Variety of melodies is very important. The bertsolari who uses the same melodies becomes monotonous and runs the risk of boring the audience. As a result, artists try to avoid repetition. No two bertsolariak sing a given melody in exactly the same way; each contributes personal variations. Even a bertsolari singing the same melody twice may introduce minor variations. The contest judges are also concerned about melodic variety. Since bertsolaritza is a form of entertainment, the judges at times offer special awards for artists who contribute new melodies.

The appropriate tonal relationship between melody and lyrics is also critical. Joyful topics should be accompanied by lively melodies. At funerals only sad melodies in a minor key are employed. A good example of this occurred at the funeral of Uztapide. About fifty of his bertsolari friends attended the services and each one improvised a verse. Twenty-one different melodies were sung, all melancholy, in accordance with the ceremony.[19]

Slow melodies are more suited for certain situations. When a bertsolari is confronted with a difficult subject and anticipates problems, he can take advantage of slow melodies such as "Urrundik," "Xarmangarria," and "Maritxu nora zoaz" to help his performance. Whether he chooses a slow traditional melody or a modern one, the bertsolari strives to convey the appropriate melodic message to the Basque people.

Improvisation

Improvisation is the most distinctive characteristic of bertsolaritza. As an oral literary expression, improvisation does not rely on written texts or previously prepared formulas. Bertsolaritza originated in a language very rich in suffixes. Thus it is the very nature of Euskara that gives the Basque verse its unique character. Bertsolaritza is not concerned merely with the ability of an artist to say original things, but rather with a performer's quick and elegant delivery of verses. The originality of bertsolaritza lies in the way verses are created, through improvisation involving simultaneous creation and performance. In Euskara this kind of improvisation is described as *bapateko bertsoak* (verses improvised on the spot). According to Xabier Amuriza, spontaneous improvisation is simply "grabbing life as it goes by. Seizing life and moving forward with it."[20]

At competitive performances the moderator may assign a subject, melody, rhyme, and rhythm to the bertsolari. The moderator acts as a bridge between the bertsolari, the judges, and the audience. Sometimes the beginning of the verse is provided and the bertsolari must complete the rest without delay. At other times neither melody nor rhymes are assigned and the artist must choose them himself. His ability to respond immediately is critical. Upon receiving his assignment, the artist has two or three seconds to choose a melody and create the last line of the verse.

Rhyme is the foundation upon which the artistic edifice of the verse is constructed. To facilitate the construction of verses, the bertsolari employs a special technique referred to in Basque as "amaia da hasera, atzekoz aurrera" (the end is the beginning, from back to front). This philosophic principle maintains that what comes last is foremost in our thoughts, although it may be the final thing to be carried out. The last line must be the most important and the cleverest so that it has a strong impact and achieves its intended effect. The bertsolari strives to summarize all of his thoughts in the last line to win the audience's applause.

Upon establishing his premise, the bertsolari begins to sing as he reflects on the material he will need to complete the rest of the verse. The remaining lines should complement the last one and be logical and coherent. The bertsolari has only a few seconds to perform all of these operations. This type of improvisation, unlike written poetry, does not allow for pauses, interruptions, or corrections.

The element of uncertainty in improvisation extends to subjects as well. The assigned subjects may range from historical events to something currently happening in the square where the performance is taking place. Thus, the artist runs a risk, the danger of making an error in front of a large audience. The improvisational performance is like the death-defying leap of a trapeze artist, where there is no safety net to save his life should he make a potentially fatal error. A bertsolari's errors will be noticed on the recorded taping of the contest or will be reflected in the judges' notes, which are later evaluated. This setting produces such anxiety that it even affects the most skilled bertsolariak, like Uztapide, and keeps them awake for nights before a competition.

Improvisation is what bertsolaritza is all about. As we shall see later in greater detail, this kind of improvisation is different from that of similar literary expressions found in the Irish, Galician, or Welsh cultures. The improvisation of the Serbian bards, with their extraordinary memories, is also different because they use formulas and set phrases. Such formulas are never used in bertsolaritza because they are not well received by the audience. In using them a bertsolari may even lose points in competitions with strict judges.

Audience

Bertsolaritza was defined earlier as the sung word of the people ("herriaren kantuzko hitza"). The word people (*herri*) in the definition indicates the importance of the community's role in this collective expression of oral literature. The bertsolari is the principal agent and plays an essential part. However, this improvised literature is not created privately on paper; it requires an active audience. Bertsolaritza is a collaborative effort performed *with* and *in front of* the community. Therefore, members of the audience are not simple spectators; they are active participants. Bertsolaritza is public entertainment and, like a sporting event, cannot be carried out in an empty stadium behind closed gates.

The improvisation performance for an audience is defined in Basque as "jendeaurreko bertsolaritza" (bertsolaritza before the people). This literary manifestation exists because of the community. Although the verses usually do not include a refrain, one is sometimes added so that the audience can participate by repeating the last line with the bertsolari. The Basque artist does not sing at home. He needs a challenge that he cannot find within his family. According to Xabier Amuriza: "I feel no need to sing at home . . . I soon found out I was not the only one [to feel this way]."[21]

Bertsolaritza is a collective art form that creates a bond between the artist and a large family of enthusiasts. The bertsolari needs an audience to create just as a plant requires water and nutrients to bear fruit. The family of enthusiasts has its own dynamics. The bertsolari who becomes a member of this family realizes that improvising for a large audience is a risky venture. The audience applies a great deal of pressure on the artist to perform. The bertsolari experiences unpleasant moments. Most artists feel their greatest degree of nervousness just before a performance. Some very good bertsolariak have retired from competition because they could not bear their preperformance anxiety.

A twofold interaction exists between the bertsolari and the audience. The bertsolari is the qualified representative of the community, a guide, and a would-be priest who sometimes reproaches the people. He is the shepherd who defends his flock—the Basque Country and its culture—and their freedom from enemies. In turn, the community has certain expectations of the bertsolari. As a monitor of problems that affect his countrymen, he must be attentive to everything that is happening in all of the Basque Country. He must use a variety of subjects and explore those that his audience requests. Such was the case with Gipuzkoan bertsolari Joxe Zapirain (1873-1957), who felt obliged to repeat the story of his wife's death. He hesitated at first because he did not want to sadden his audience, but ended up singing the story to satisfy the crowd.[22]

Sometimes one hears the expression "herria bertsolaria" (versemaking people). To truly understand this artistic movement one must realize the importance of active audience participation. Zavala once said: "Anyone who does not mingle with the public and observe people the way the bertsolari does cannot easily comprehend how important bertsolaritza is to the Basques."[23] At some point in their lives, many Basques attempt to improvise verses. Many more are able to create them if they are given more time to do so. However, they may not be good enough to perform in public.

The audience actively participates. Thanks to the listeners' applause, the bertsolari feels at home among a family sharing Euskara as a common language. The Basque artist appreciates a knowledgeable audience that applauds his wit and the literary beauty of his verses, but also criticizes his errors. It is in this kind of setting that the bertsolari surrenders more passionately to his art form. The worst experience for a bertsolari is a cold and indifferent audience. When this occurs the performance session ends quickly.

For at least the last two centuries, bertsolaritza was created and preserved mostly by men from Gipuzkoa. It was a pastime for night owls who spent long hours in taverns and in hard-cider shops. The presence of women was practically prohibited in these establishments. The same atmosphere pervaded performances at handball courts or in public squares. The *etxeko andre* (housewife) stayed at home with her children while their father went to listen to the bertsolariak.

This type of sociological conditioning is changing drastically. The audience today in the public square is much different from that of twenty-five years ago. Then 90 percent of enthusiasts were adult men. Today a large number of spectators, perhaps 80 percent, are young people of both sexes who do not live in rural areas.

Themes

One of the greatest challenges of bertsolaritza is choosing an appropriate subject that may be developed and embellished properly.[24] In theory, any type of subject is valid. Xabier Amuriza describes this idea in verse:

We sing of what is happening around us,
about life and about death,
analyzing and summarizing
all aspects of life in the Basque Country.[25]

Traditionally, bertsolariak have improvised verses with religious and historical themes as well as different aspects of daily life, such as sports, culture, social relations, nature, God, death, the world, and love.

Religion and History

Although the Basque Country was not Christianized until the eleventh century, the Basques are a very religious people. Consequently, it is not surprising that religious subjects abound in bertsolaritza. They include the eternal truths of the Catholic creed (death, judgment, hell, heaven); the catechistic truths, such as the ten commandments and the seven sacraments; biblical subjects, such as the birth and passion of Christ, the Virgin Mary (referred to by her different Basque names: Begoña, Aránzazu, Itziar, etc.); the lives of the saints like Saint Genevieve;[26] the missions; and the Lenten sermons of rural areas of the Basque Country. Popular historical subjects include Basque emigration to the Americas, the Napoleonic wars, and in particular the two Carlist (1833-1839 and 1872-1878) wars that devastated the Basque Country in the nineteenth century.

Daily Life

As the qualified representative of the community, the bertsolari must concern himself with the different aspects of daily life. The sporting and competitive nature of the Basques is manifested in rural sports and inspired by work activities on land and at sea. Bertsolaritza echoes these sports, using as themes oxen trials, stone lifting and dragging, wood chopping, grass-cutting competitions, and regattas.

The botanical and zoological world, trees and birds (especially the nightingale and the kinglet), the whale, and the Breton cow were once popular subjects for bertsolariak. Relationships between master and servant, boss and laborer, courtship and marriage were also frequent themes.

Today, political and cultural subjects affecting the Basque people often arise: the end of the Franco regime, the independence movement, ETA, new political parties, the Basque autonomy statute, entrance into the European Common Market, the Basque university, Euskara, violence, torture, the civil guard, prisons, drugs, and gay and lesbian rights.

A brief comparative study of the 1982 txapelketa and the four competitions that took place during the Franco regime in the sixties demonstrates the political and religious change that has occurred in the Basque Country. Some of the subjects assigned in the 1960, 1962, 1965, and 1967 txapelketak serve as reference points for comparison. In these four contests, the themes were taken from real life, but did not directly portray politics in the Basque Country because many topics were censored. During the Franco dictatorship it was very dangerous to deal with political issues. It was easier to use themes that did not challenge Spanish morale or unity.

1960   The following occupational subjects appeared: laborer, handball player and soccer player, physician and healer, priest of a large parish and priest of a small one.

1962   The following subjects arose: the three Magi, Pope John XXIII's illness, a landlord and a renter in a small village, the apostles, and matters of peace, work, love, health, youth, friendship, family, and so on.

1965   Themes included Basque handball, the use of Euskara in the liturgy, the emigration of workers to Germany, the origin of human life, and the gypsy healer.

1967   Subjects included the purchase of a casket for a person who was destined to die soon, a young hitchhiker, the abandonment of the Basque farms, the miniskirt, a guitar player, African natives cooking the bertsolari Mattin in a cauldron, and Euskara. It is evident that during this decade the bertsolari sang like a bird in a cage, without any freedom. There were few opportunities for reviving the Basque cultural spirit because people feared government reprisals. For example, when moderator Alfonso Irigoien assigned the subject of Euskara to Nafarroan bertsolari Mikel Arozamena (1930–1976) as a subject, the artist simply limited himself to expressing his wish for its survival.

1982   In contrast to all the foregoing, a competition section was entitled kartzelako gaia (the subject of imprisonment).[27] Other sections were directly related to political matters: relations between Russia and the United States (Yuri Andropov and

Ronald Reagan), the nuclear arms race, obligatory military service, and the like.

Even when dealing with nonpolitical subjects, most bertsolariak seized the opportunity to attack and condemn the Spanish right wing (as represented by Manuel Fraga Iribarne) and the Socialists and Communists (in particular Felipe González and Santiago Carrillo), referring to them as *etsaiak*, or enemies of the Basque Country.

The change of attitude with regard to subjects and the ways of dealing with them may also be observed in the area of religion. By the end of the 1960s, there was a wave of unprecedented secularization in the Basque Country. The reorganizational ideas of Vatican II had been put into practice, and this initiated a worldly trend. Great seminaries emptied out and today remain as monuments to a past religious spirit. The slogan "Jaungoikoa eta lege zarra" (God and the old laws) was replaced with the cry of "Euskaltzaleen Jainkoa hil behar dugu" (We must kill the God of the Basques). The theocratic society, in which the church had played such a crucial role during Franco's dictatorship, was transformed into one that separated religious believers from Basque nationalists. According to ethnologist Julio Caro Baroja: "It can be said with confidence that of all the coercive forces active in modern society, the Catholic church was the most powerful at that time." [28]

Religious subjects were discernible in all four of the previously discussed txapelketak held during the Franco regime. The word *God* was used frequently and with great respect. At times it even became commonplace to use *God* in the verses. For example, Jon Mugartegi mentioned God in three consecutive verses and declared himself a friend of the priests. Today religious themes are less popular.

This attitude change is also evident in aspects of morality. The Jansenist influence was very strong in the Basque Country. It is not surprising that Saint Cyran (1581-1643), Jansen's closest associate, was Basque. Some topics, such as sex, were taboo until just a few years ago. Many of the changes in Basque society are also reflected in bertsolaritza.

In the 1965 txapelketa Xalbador was asked to describe the talents a bertsolari should possess. He indicated purity of words, among others. Xalbador would have had a difficult time accepting the type of verses created in the exchange between Xabier Amuriza and Angel Peñagarikano during the elimination round in Durango in 1982, in which the audience understood such double entendres as "panderoa, iturri automatikoa, plumeroa, busti nere florerua, uxola." [29]

In summary, in an improvised performance no one knows what subjects will be assigned and consequently there are no rehearsals. The bertsolari must be prepared to develop verses on any subject, including the most unusual or unexpected. In the performance section called *ofizioak* (occupations) the bertsolari may have to defend the occupation that his opponent holds in real life. [30] Sometimes even more surprising situations arise. On one occasion, moderator José María Aranalde (1933-   ) assigned the subject of divorce. Manuel Lasarte

(1927–   ), who had not lived with his wife for six years, was obliged to create verses against divorce.

Qualities of a Bertsolari

In addition to the ability to undertake risks in improvising verse, there are other minimum prerequisites the Basque artist must meet before he can be considered a bertsolari. He should have a mastery of Euskara, a love for the art form, creativity and imagination, sensitivity and responsiveness to his audience, and self-confidence. Three other fundamental qualities are also critical: a very strong memory and quick mental reflexes; a sense of humor and irony; and public presence (*plaza gizona*).

Memory and Mental Reflexes

Bertsolaritza entails quick thinking, speed of composition, and a talent for performance. Memory plays a very important role in this process. Without a good memory the bertsolari is lost. As we have seen, some verses are quite long, as in bederatzi puntuko bertsoa (fourteen lines). Simple poetic improvisation is not sufficient. The artist must remember everything that is said by the other bertsolariak and, as a result, memory is critical. This is particularly true in the txapelketa section called ofizioak in which two bertsolariak debate. Their task is twofold: they must pay attention to their opponent while they mentally create an appropriate response.

Traditionally, the bertsolari was concerned only that the end of his verse be exceptional, in order to deliver a coup de theater. Today, that is not enough. A bertsolari is normally required to improvise three verses. Consequently, he must structure his message in a logical way, giving it an introduction, a body, and a conclusion. The bertsolari must mentally prepare the last line as he elaborates his artistic composition. He must be able to express himself with poetic beauty. The fact that he is a folk poet does not exempt him from that requirement. Folk expression entails the search for images, or the use of comparisons, idioms, proverbs, and sayings that abound in the Basque language and add color. There is always the danger that, after deciding on the final rhyme, the bertsolari might forget it. This is why bertsolaritza requires a good memory and a rare mental agility that Xalbador describes as "izpirituz bizi ernea izan" (to be very awake in spirit).[31]

Humor and Irony

Bertsolaritza is a festive event, a pastime, and a form of public entertainment. The audience pays an admission fee to attend large competitions and expects poetically beautiful and entertaining performances.

Basque humor in bertsolaritza is effectively conveyed through two expressions: *adarra jo* (to pull someone's leg) and *ziria sartu* (to goad someone). There are various types of humor. There is witty humor, which makes an audience smile. Mattin Treku, alias "Mattin" (1916-1981), and José Miguel Iztueta, alias "Lazkao Txiki" (1926-1993), used this kind of humor without having to improvise a verse. Their physical expressions alone created laughter because the audience was sure the performance would be enjoyable. There is another type of Basque humor that is very subtle and profound. Such bertsolariak as Xalbador, Manuel Lasarte, and Uztapide, among others, maintain a serious façade and make the listener think in order to discern the humor.

In general, Basques are timid by nature. They use humor and irony as a defense mechanism against the embarrassment and shyness they feel. Sometimes they use the kind of black humor that is found in the writings of Jon Mirande (1925-1972) and Dominique Peillen (1932-   ). This humor is therapeutic medicine for the bertsolari, because it helps him forget all of his problems.

Bertsolaritza is a collective art form and entertainment in which broad permissiveness exists. A bertsolari is allowed to say things he would not be able to say in ordinary conversation. He may even joke about the church and the clergy, subjects that are traditionally treated with a great deal of respect. This oral literary art provides an escape from social repression. The naturalness of expression found among small children is present in bertsolaritza. Xabier Amuriza defines this free expression as *biluzik jartzia* (undressing in front of the audience).[32]

The audience understands that silly things, funny jokes, and irony are permitted. If something turns out a bit on the impertinent side, the bertsolari is forgiven; it is not always easy to say what one would like to. The improviser is like the town crier who airs matters publicly and jokingly criticizes what is wrong.

Humor helps the artist conquer his fear, which is especially intense at the beginning of a performance. The bertsolari's task is difficult because he must sing in verse and reveal his soul in public. As a consequence, most bertsolariak began their training by performing in the corner of a tavern or during the night vigils of Saint Agate, taking advantage of the anonymity and protection of the benevolence of friends.[33] Before entering the public arena of the square, the bertsolari must prepare himself. Most artists have something to eat and drink a few glasses of wine. Although wine does not clear the head, it provides some of the boldness needed to be witty.

Showmanship

The Basque artist must effectively present himself in front of an audience and project self-confidence. He must have a good ear for music, a good voice, and stage presence. A good ear is paramount because without it the bertsolari would be lost. This is a quality that can be improved with time and practice.[34] Voice is not as important as an ear for music, but a bertsolari with little voice or a poor one forfeits a great deal in sung verses. However, there were two extraordinary bertsolariak who rarely performed for an audience because they had weak voices; they were more widely known for their written verses: Indalecio Bizkarrondo, alias "Bilintx" (1831–1876), and Pello Mari Otaño. The latter was known as "Katarro" (cold) because of his poor voice.

The bertsolari should also imitate the actor's stage presence, but not his movements, and remain still before the microphone. Men like Jon Azpillaga (1935–   ) and Xabier Amuriza are worthy of the title plaza gizona, because they possess all three important qualities. Others, such as Jon Mugartegi (1933–   ), lose much of their extraordinary quality in this category because of poor health and timidity. To be an outstanding bertsolari, one must possess many qualities that are found only among a small circle of people.

CHAPTER THREE

Bertsolaritza

Performance Types

One of the first milestones in bertsolaritza occurred in a challenge between two bertsolariak in 1801. Since then there have been four types of performances: challenges, performances at folk festivals, floral games, and txapelketak (competitions).

CHALLENGES

Challenges were usually carried out between two bertsolariak or two pairs of bertsolariak. These challenges were very important in the nineteenth century, but have since disappeared completely. They lasted about two hours, and the bertsolariak were free to choose rhymes, rhythms, and subjects. A panel of three judges was chosen by the bertsolariak and the town mayor, who could serve as one of the judges if he desired. Wagers were made. Challenges were treated like sporting events where all the details were worked out in advance: location, date, amount of bets, and so on. However, the subjects to be dealt with were unknown. As in a boxing match, each competitor kept his combative strategy a secret. The weapons consisted of dialectics of rhymed and sung words.

The most famous challenge of the nineteenth century took place at the handball court in Billabona (Gipuzkoa). It was historically important because of the expertise of the contestants, the panel of judges, the amount of money wagered, and the size of the crowd that attended the event. Historian and folklorist Juan Ignacio Iztueta (1767–1845) gives us a more detailed account in his book *Guipuzkoako dantzak* (Dances of Gipuzkoa). The bertsolariak were Zabala from Amezketa and José Joakin Erroizena, alias "Txabalategi," from Hernani, both considered among the best at the time. More than four thousand people witnessed the challenge. Since there were no railroads or automobiles, this great gathering of humanity demonstrates the large following that bertsolaritza had in Gipuzkoa. Five ounces of gold were wagered, a considerable amount in those days. Zabala chose the legendary Fernando Amezketarra, considered the greatest bertsolari of his time, as a judge; Txabalategi, in turn, selected the sacristan from Aizarna; and the mayor of Billabona chose Father José Mendizabal to serve in his place.

Unfortunately, Iztueta does not give an account of all the verses that were heard that day. However, we do have a record of those that the judges improvised at the end of the performance. One of these verses informs us that the judges were unable to decide which of the two bertsolariak had performed the best; both contestants had given exceptional artistic performances. The judges opted to accept the audience's decision to declare a tie. Fernando Amezketarra described the event in this way:

> Nic gogoan naucana,
> Zuc dezu itzeguin:
> Utzi bear ditugu,
> Biac berdin berdin;
> Guipuzcoa guziac
> Ar-dezan atseguin.[1]

> You have put into words
> what I was thinking;
> that we should
> call a complete tie
> so that all of Gipuzkoa
> will be pleased.

Iztueta describes another challenge between two bertsolariak pairs representing different Gipuzkoan towns: Zabala and Fernando Bengoetxea (1764–1823), from Amezketa; and Txabalategi and Altamira from Tolosa. This event lasted all evening. The exceptional quality of their verses obliged the bertsolariak to continue improvising until midnight. According to Iztueta, the audience was reluctant to leave the plaza, even though it was very late.[2]

FOLK FESTIVALS

Performances at folk festivals have been and continue to be the most common for bertsolariak. These artistic presentations are intended for entertainment rather than competition. The object is not to see who is the best bertsolari, but rather to amuse the audience and enjoy the festivities with it. In this setting, the bertsolari does not experience the tension of competition, because there are no judges. In most cases, there is no *gai-jartzaile* (moderator) to impose the conditions of the performance. Bertsolariak particularly enjoy the folk festival because it gives them a greater degree of freedom to control their pace, time, themes, and so on. This type of bertsolaritza is very important in the social life of Basque-speaking communities.

Unlike txapelketak, these performances do not require as much technique and allow the bertsolari to develop a closer relationship with the audience. In these events no time restrictions are placed on the artist; the performance simply ends when the audience feels satisfied.

It is difficult to estimate how long such a performance should last. Its length depends considerably on the number of participants. If there is only one bertsolari, the performance is quite short, approximately half an hour. The ideal performance includes a pair of bertsolariak, who create a dialectical exchange and debate. The artists compete against each other and against themselves, thereby producing the proper dynamics for two bertsolariak. A performance of this nature normally lasts an hour. Sometimes three bertsolariak participate, although this is not an ideal number. Uztapide is quoted in his biography as having stated that three "is not a good number for the improvisation of Basque verse."[3] In such cases, a different relationship is established among the artists, and the performance could last for two hours.

The length of bertsolaritza performances at folk festivals is influenced by several factors. Although it is difficult to establish precise rules, some general principles are followed. The artist must literally nurture his audience without boring them. He must surrender himself to his public and thoroughly satisfy them with a beautiful performance. This is the most effective way to attract followers and assure that they will return in the future. Extremely long performances may tire an audience, and while rare they are not unheard of. Basarri commented:

> It has often been said in the north of the Basque Country that we commit a harmful error in performances of bertsolaritza. These sessions are too long. . . . Such excess is boring to the audience. That is what happened in Sara.[4]

In order to avoid this type of problem, bertsolariak arrive a few hours in advance in the town in which they are expected to perform, in order to inform themselves on local issues. This also makes them more prepared to deal with topics that may arise. Performances usually begin with these local themes and, after twenty minutes or half an hour, move on to more general topics.

FLORAL GAMES

The first floral games (lorejaiak) were organized by Antoine d'Abbadie (1810-1897) in the northern Basque Country in 1853. In later years these games were also celebrated in the south. The lorejaiak included various activities: award ceremonies, Basque dance contests, livestock competitions, and even literary readings that usually centered on poetry.

Antoine d'Abbadie was born in Dublin, Ireland, of an exiled Basque father and an Irish mother. He was considered Zuberoan because of his father. He had also developed a friendship with his compatriot, the romantic Augustin Chaho (1810-1858). D'Abbadie was an intrepid traveler, astronomer, naturalist, and founding member of the Académie de Sciences de Paris. After eleven years in Africa, he returned to the Basque Country in 1849. He arrived with the intention of sponsoring a Basque literary revival after the Basque Country's defeat in the first Carlist War and the loss of liberty to Spain.[5]

The cultural and literary milieu was very weak in the Basque Country at the time. D'Abbadie attempted to establish a Basque language department at the seminary in Baiona, but his plans were rejected. The Basques were in the midst of a hostile environment, in which even seminarians were prohibited from speaking Euskara among themselves. More than half a century had passed under the rule of the French Republic, which sought to abolish the Basque language.

It was in this climate that d'Abbadie became the main promoter of the floral games and Basque culture. His early efforts were very simple, beginning with coordination of a handball game in 1851 and the first floral games in 1853. The main attraction of the latter was a Basque poetry competition featuring Basque emigration to America as its theme. Etxahun presented a poem in this contest but did not receive an award. The first- and second-place prizes were awarded to two priests. Etxahun felt humiliated and criticized both the judges and the winners.

Antoine d'Abbadie later broadened his efforts to include the southern Basque Country and thus paved the way for the literary renaissance of the works of José de Manterola (1849-1884) in Gipuzkoa and Sabino Arana (1865-1903) in Bizkaia. After 1877 there were numerous literary competitions organized by the Council on Floral Games. These contests declined somewhat at the beginning of the twentieth century and disappeared altogether during the seven-year dictatorship (1923-1930) of Miguel Primo de Rivera.

Contests of improvised verse with a panel of judges were always a part of the floral games. These bertsolaritza performances were very popular until the Spanish Civil War (1936-1939). The most sought-after bertsolariak for these events were José Elizegi, alias "Pello Errota" (1840-1919), and Txirrita. Unlike the two txapelketak that were celebrated only in Donostia, the floral games were held in the most important towns of Gipuzkoa and Bizkaia.

TXAPELKETAK

The contest known in Euskara as txapelketa is a rather modern phenomenon. It was first celebrated, as we know it today, in 1935 as the first "Day of the Bertsolari." It is an artistic and literary show in which the audience is entertained and delights in the beauty of improvised verse. A txapelketa is an all-day event, a festival unto itself. Most of the well-known bertsolariak of the Basque Country participate. There is a panel of judges, and an official known as the gai-jartzaile (moderator) whose role is to assign subjects, rhymes, rhythms, and melodies. In these contests the artist's relationship with the audience is not as close as at folk festival performances, because the bertsolari must remain very focused and is preoccupied with his presentation. The txapelketa is a public competition. The bertsolariak hardly speak to one another. They must concentrate fully on their artistic material. Bizkaian bertsolari Deunoro Sardui (1934-) offers this metaphor: "When a bertsolari performs at a village festival he brings firewood that he has gathered along with him to make a fire. In competitions, on the other hand, he must go to the forest to search for firewood." [6]

The audience is larger at the txapelketak. During the months preceding the competition, several elimination rounds are held in different towns. The txapelketa itself always takes place in Donostia. A committee of organizers is responsible for choosing the panel of judges and the moderator, establishing the rules, and choosing the verse themes. The txapelketak from 1962 to 1982 were organized by Euskaltzaindia (the Academy of the Basque Language). Since the 1986 txapelketa, however, the bertsolariak themselves have chosen the organizing committee. There were no txapelketak from 1982 to 1986.

Bertsolaritza has historically involved challenges and competitions as well as art and entertainment. Xabier Amuriza views bertsolaritza as a game and describes it as *kirol nazionala*, or a national sport. Recently, certain traditional aspects of bertsolaritza have been questioned, and its classification as game and sport have been rejected. Anthropologist Joseba Zulaika addresses this subject in a short essay entitled *Bertsolarien Jokoa eta Jolasa* (Entertainment and Games of the Bertsolariak, 1985). He compares the concepts *jolas* and *joko* (entertainment) with that of kirol (game or sport). Zulaika concludes that the competitiveness that exists today in txapelketak is an aberration of bertsolaritza and is damaging to this literary art form. Competition has its place in games and sports but not in bertsolaritza because it is neither game nor sport, but rather art and entertainment.

The formal aspect of this artistic expression (rhyme, rhythm, caesura, etc.)

is measurable. However, other aspects such as the grace and spirit of a verse cannot be measured. These elements are like a sudden wind that passes by and cannot be captured. A verse can still possess literary beauty in spite of errors like *poto egin* (repetition of a rhyme in the same verse) or the use of nonconsonant rhyme. Today bertsolaritza is becoming a competition in which judges quickly evaluate the quality of verses using numbered score cards. According to Zulaika, judges can measure the beauty of a sculpture, but not the spirit or artistic quality of an improvised verse.

While I disagree with the general focus of his thesis, I believe Zulaika's work contains many valid assertions and some useful suggestions for the future direction of the artistic bertsolaritza phenomenon. There is no doubt that a verse may be very beautiful in spite of its lack of complicated consonant rhymes. It is also true that it is extremely difficult to evaluate the literary worth of a verse in a few seconds. However, I do not agree that txapelketak, as they exist today, are an aberration of the authentic foundation of bertsolaritza. Txapelketak are one of the most original forms of bertsolaritza in spite of the obstacles and difficulties faced by the Basque artist. Historically, txapelketak have attracted thousands of enthusiasts. As a consequence of their popularity, bertsolaritza is becoming an institution and reaching very high artistic levels.

Amuriza's thoughts about bertsolaritza as sport and game are very appropriate: "Bertsolaritza is art and the Basque people throughout history have assigned a sense of game to it. Bertsolaritza is not only that, but also that, or at least that."[7]

A brief analysis of the nine national txapelketak—those that took place in 1935, 1936, 1960, 1962, 1965, 1967, 1980, 1982, and 1986—will help give us a better understanding of the nature of the txapelketa.

The 1935 Txapelketa

The 1935 championship took place on January 20, in Donostia at the Poxpolin Theater, which is located in the basement of the former Casino Kursaal. The following distinguished individuals were the judges: José de Aristimuño, alias "Aitzol" (1896-1936);[8] Manuel Lekuona; dramatist Toribio Alzaga (1861-1941); and musician José María Olaizola. The three-hour performance took place in the morning. Of the twenty bertsolariak who participated, seventeen were from Gipuzkoa, two from Bizkaia (Esteban Uriarte [1894-1947] and Abarrategi), and one (Mattin from Senpere) was from Lapurdi. A young Basarri was unanimously declared the winner and received an award of one hundred pesetas. His verse "Uso zuri bat" (A white dove) was among the best.[9] Txirrita also stood out for his humor with his verse "Larogei urte gainean ditut" (I am almost eighty years old).[10]

The criteria for the evaluation of verses were creativity, imagination, inspiration, rhythms, rhymes, and appropriate treatment of themes. The highest possible score was twenty. The txapelketa was divided into four sections: free melodies and themes, assigned melodies and themes, assigned first line (the bertsolari had to finish the verse as soon as he was given an opening line), and occupations, in which two bertsolariak demonstrated their proficiency by challenging one another verbally.

The 1936 Txapelketa

Txirrita was the champion of the 1936 txapelketa and a young Uztapide was awarded second place. The competition was held at the Victoria Eugenia Theater on January 19. Ten bertsolariak competed, mostly from Gipuzkoa. Bizkaia was not represented at all. This was Txirrita's last txapelketa; he died later the same year. The previous year's champion, Basarri, took part in the competition by acting as moderator.

The 1960 Txapelketa

The Spanish Civil War contributed to the disappearance of the Basque cultural renaissance. Many of the writers and bertsolariak who remained in the Basque Country were imprisoned or confined to labor camps. At that time Basque culture went underground. During the first decade of Franco's dictatorship only one book was published in the Basque language. It was a religious poem, *Arantzazu euskal sinismenaren poema* (Aranzazu poem of Basque faith) by the Franciscan Salbatore Mitxelena (1919-1965). Twenty-two years passed without any official competitions or txapelketak, until two provincial contests were held in Bizkaia in 1958 and 1959 as elimination rounds for the national finals to be held in Donostia. Later, Nafarroa began to hold elimination rounds in Lekunberri and Elizondo. In Gipuzkoa the eight best bertsolariak were invited to compete. After winning an elimination competition in Eibar on November 8, 1959, Uztapide and Joaquín Mitxelena (1924-1988) became finalists along with Xalbador and Mattin, the invited representatives from the northern Basque Country.

The Academy of the Basque Language served as *euskaltzaleak* (Basque enthusiasts) in organizing the 1960 txapelketa. The panel of judges was composed of eleven new members chosen from among writers and specialists of bertsolaritza. This competition was the first in which a tape recorder was used to help evaluate the verses. Basarri was chosen as the winner. Since he was the champion of the 1935 txapelketa, Basarri did not have to perform in the morning rounds and reserved his performance for the finals in the afternoon. He won the txapelketa with only thirteen verses.

The 1962 Txapelketa

In June of 1962 regional elimination rounds were held again in preparation for the final round, which was celebrated on December 30 in Donostia's Astoria Theater. It was a great public success. The finalists were J. Zabaleta and Mikel Arozamena from Nafarroa, Lazkao Txiki from Gipuzkoa, Xalbador and Mattin from Iparralde, and Jon Lopategi from Bizkaia. They were joined by Basarri and Uztapide, former champion and finalist, respectively, from the previous txapelketa.

Basarri, Uztapide, Xalbador, and Lazkao Txiki competed in the morning session. Uztapide and Basarri emerged as the finalists, and Uztapide won—much to the surprise of many. Basarri was unhappy with the decision of the judges and refused to participate again in a txapelketa—in spite of the fact that he was only forty-nine years old. The judges' deliberation, through a process of secret balloting, lasted exactly twelve minutes. The secret ballot maintained each judge's freedom of choice and eliminated influences to favor one finalist over the other. The voting resulted in eight judges favoring Uztapide, two Basarri.

The 1965 Txapelketa

Uztapide emerged victorious again in the 1965 txapelketa, winning his second *txapela* (a beret is the prize for this event). This txapelketa was conducted in the same manner as the previous ones, with a change of location as the only difference. The 1965 event was celebrated at the Anoeta ball court. There were 115 bertsolariak competing besides Mattin and Xalbador, 71 Gipuzkoans, 26 Bizkaians, and 16 Nafarroans. In the afternoon session, four bertsolariak competed, one of whom would be selected to face Uztapide. They were Xalbador, Lazkao Txiki, Mitxelena, and Mattin. In the final round it was Lazkao Txiki against Uztapide. Upon winning the championship, Uztapide thanked everyone by creating a verse that was filled with humor. There were no major innovations in this txapelketa, as there had been in others.

The 1967 Txapelketa

The 1967 txapelketa was held in Donostia on June 12. It is sadly notable because the audience disapprovingly whistled at Xalbador's performance for no apparent reason.[11] As in the previous txapelketa, when he had proved himself to be an exceptional bertsolari, he maintained his composure by stoically accepting the unjust offense of his audience. His humble reaction immediately changed the whistling into more than five minutes of applause. In great part, this jeering was due to the fact that many Gipuzkoans did not correctly understand Xalbador's use of language.

This incident is interesting because it illustrates the circumstances that may lead to some of the problems in bertsolaritza, such as dialectal discrepancies and provincialism. A series of events occurred that contributed to the audience's outbursts. Uztapide, as the previous champion, did not have to perform until the last round in the afternoon, and as a consequence did not participate in any of the elimination rounds. The nine finalists from the morning session were Lazkao Txiki, Xalbador, Jon Lopategi, José Luis Gorrotxategi, Arozamena, Txomin Garmendia (1934–   ), Jon Mugartegi, Bautista Madariaga (1926–   ), and Mattin. Of these contestants, only the first four won the right to participate in the afternoon events. The majority of the audience wanted a bertsolari from the south to compete with Uztapide, but the judges chose Xalbador as his match, thus causing some members of the audience to protest vehemently. In spite of this, the elderly Uztapide won the champion's beret for the third time. Xalbador won second place and also received the award for the bertsolari who improvised the best verse.

The dialectal problem that arises when an audience is unable to understand the language of the bertsolariak is gradually being resolved over time with frequent audience contact and use of the unified Basque language. Xalbador's use of the Behe-nafarrera dialect was excellent, but difficult for most people to understand. One must consider the historical fact that the Pyrenees and the frontier between the French and the Spanish states have served as barriers to mutual linguistic comprehension among Basques.[12] The beginnings of bertsolaritza were very difficult because artists from the north and the south were mixed together in a performance. Uztapide demonstrated this point in his account of the French Basque Harriet during the 1936 txapelketa: "At that time we did not understand Harriet well."[13]

Another problem affecting bertsolaritza is partisanship. Spectators always want a bertsolari from their province to win. While this is understandable to a certain point, it can become excessive. This competitive desire manifested itself in the 1986 txapelketa, as well.[14] According to Uztapide this incident was the reason (although not the only one, in my opinion) that there were no more txapelketak until 1980. The other factors contributing to the twelve-year silence prior to the 1980 txapelketa were the political repressions that had increased during the Franco years, and the ETA (Euskadi Ta Askatasuna) guerrilla activities, its armed struggle, and the organization's first fatal confrontations.[15] While bertsolaritza did not completely disappear, prohibitions were imposed on it as a consequence of the political unrest, and the txapelketak were no longer held.[16]

The 1980 Txapelketa

In 1980, five years after Franco's death, a txapelketa was organized by the Academy of the Basque Language. The academy did not hold widely competitive elimination rounds, but simply chose the sixteen most qualified bertsolariak.

This txapelketa marked the beginning of a new period in bertsolaritza, comparable to the innovation spurred by Basarri in 1935. The presence of new bertsolariak, such as Xabier Amuriza and Jon Enbeita, caused bertsolaritza to take a new course. The changes were noteworthy: new melodies, more artistically elaborated rhymes, a higher level of cultural sophistication, use of the unified Basque dialect, and a greater degree of freedom in dealing with sociopolitical themes. Hence, a new form of bertsolaritza was born from this movement.

The sixteen bertsolariak chosen by the academy to compete in two elimination rounds in Arrasate (Gipuzkoa) and Gernika (Bizkaia) were reduced to eight finalists: Txomin Garmendia, Angel Larrañaga (1947-), José Luis Gorrotxategi, and Patxi Etxebarria (1930-) from Gipuzkoa; Xabier Amuriza, Jon Azpillaga, and Jon Enbeita from Bizkaia; and Emmanuel Sein, alias "Xanpun" (1928-), from Lapurdi. A panel of ten judges established the following criteria for evaluating the verses:

1. treatment: handling of subjects with depth and beauty;
2. language: use of beautiful and poetic forms;
3. structure: verses following a logical pattern (i.e., introduction, body, conclusion); and
4. rhythms and rhymes: avoidance of serious errors like poto egin.

In general verses were of very high quality, especially some of those by Xabier Amuriza, which will be analyzed later. For the first time in txapelketa history, the champion's beret left Gipuzkoa and was awarded to Amuriza from Bizkaia. Amuriza also won a special award for the bertsolari who used the greatest number of new melodies. Jon Enbeita, another Bizkaian, was awarded second place.

The 1982 Txapelketa

Xabier Amuriza won the champion's beret for the second time and Jon Lopategi was the second-place winner in 1982. An important change took place in the four years between 1982 and 1986. The bertsolariak as a group acquired a great deal of power and established a formal organization. They became the new organizers of the txapelketak, a function previously controlled by the academy.

The 1986 Txapelketa

The 1986 txapelketa took place at the Donostia velodrome in Anoeta on March 23. Although this competition did not contribute anything new in an artistic sense, it was innovative in the organization of the competition, the selection of artists, and the evaluation process. This trend is gradually becoming formalized.

After the 1982 txapelketa, there was discontent among the bertsolariak because of the attitudes of the academy, the entity responsible for organizing the six previous competitions. The bertsolariak, as a group, wanted to participate in the process of selecting the panel of judges. They presented to the academy the following five conditions for reform:

1. Lengthen the admission period for the next txapelketa, which would take place in 1986.
2. Create a committee to organize the txapelketak.
3. Open the committee to any bertsolari who wished to participate, to avoid the restriction in the number of participants that occurred in the 1982 txapelketa.
4. Establish a diverse panel of judges with ten members from the academy and five from the group of bertsolariak and permit the group of performers to choose ten members from this pool to form the panel of judges for a given performance.
5. Require the judges to evaluate without delay the literary beauty of the verses using numbered score cards as is common practice in many sporting events.

When the academy accepted only the first three conditions and rejected the last two, the bertsolariak decided to organize the next txapelketa themselves. They created an organizational committee made up of bertsolaritza enthusiasts and specialists. The 1986 txapelketa produced outstanding results:

1. Very good organization in spite of the complex nature of the different competitions.
2. Extraordinary public attendance. It was calculated that between eight thousand and ten thousand people attended. Since the Balda handball court used in the 1982 txapelketa was not large enough to accommodate the great number of enthusiasts, the committee used the spacious velodrome in Anoeta instead.
3. The highest attendance by young people, both in the audience and as participants. Among the young bertsolariak Andoni Egaña, Jon Sarasua, Xabier Pérez, alias "Euskitze" (1966-   ), Luis Otamendi (1947-   ), Anton and Josu Arriola (brothers); and Ireneo Ajuria (1946-   ) were especially outstanding.
4. Araba as host of the competition. Araba is the Basque province with the smallest number of Basque speakers. This demonstrates the kind of interest that bertsolaritza is awakening in all areas of the Basque Country.
5. The first performance by a woman, Cristina Mardaraz (1948-   ) from the province of Bizkaia, in a national txapelketa. Although she did not reach the final phase, she is proof that change is currently taking place. Today many young people attend special schools to learn the art of bertsolaritza.

Some of the subjects covered in this txapelketa indicate that bertsolaritza now addresses the problems facing the Basque people: drugs, rebellious youth, ecology, opposition to military service, NATO.

The 1986 txapelketa was conducted in two phases. The first included all bertsolariak who were interested in participating; there were a total of seventy-one artists. Six finalists were chosen to join Xabier Amuriza (the previous champion) and Jon Lopategi (second-place winner) in forming the final groups. The event lasted four hours. Since the scoring was made public, we know how many points each contestant obtained. The champion, Sebastián Lizaso of Gipuzkoa, scored 1,867 points. Second place went to Jon Lopategi, with a total of 1,850 points. The scores of the remaining contestants were Xabier Amuriza, 1,846; Jon Enbeita, 1,835; Iñaki Murua, 1,812; Andoni Egaña, 1,809; Jon Sarasua, 1,804; and Angel Peñagarikano, 1,790.

The Gai-Jartzaile

Before ending this section on txapelketak it is important to explain the role of the gai-jartzaile, who is the intermediary between the artist and the audience. His role is significant as an ancillary figure who should not overshadow the bertsolari. The role of the moderator is a recent addition to this multisecular movement and appeared for the first time in the 1935 txapelketa. A moderator is not really necessary when bertsolariak perform at folk festivals. However, his presence at competitions such as txapelketak has become indispensable.

In earlier years the bertsolariak had greater freedom, and their verses were more spontaneous. They usually performed from the balcony of the town hall or on a stage set up in a handball court. Today everything is programmed, especially in the txapelketak. The structure of one composition is almost identical to that of the next, and the moderator's role is strictly limited to reading the rules established by the commission empowered to assign the themes.

Many bertsolariak have begun to express their weariness and the disillusionment they feel over the lack of freedom in versemaking when working with certain moderators. The gai-jartzaile's duty is to inform the bertsolari about problems in the town where he is to perform, or in a txapelketa, by simply pointing out the conditions to the contestants and then disappearing from the scene. The protagonists of this artistic art form are the bertsolariak and the audience. At times performances are mediocre because the moderator does not limit himself to this secondary role. The bertsolariak today prefer to work with more freedom, especially outside the competitive setting. Their message is one of freedom, and a moderator who does not perform his task well creates a false and artificial atmosphere, one that is detrimental to the performance. In large competitions moderators are usually chosen carefully and there is no danger of this occurring. However, in small village festivals a fan may act as moderator, and this may be harmful to the spontaneous and improvised nature of this literary expression. The txapelketa serves as the forum for national competitions of bertsolaritza and is responsible for the prosperity of this artistic phenomenon of Basque oral folk literature.

DIFFERENT BERTSOLARITZA VERSE TYPES

Bertso Jarriak

Even though verse improvisation is the most important characteristic of bertsolaritza, bertso jarriak (also known as bertsopaperak) are an offshoot of the same literary phenomenon. Bertso jarriak (written verses) reached a peak in popularity during the time of Xenpelar and were very important during the nineteenth and the first half of the twentieth centuries. These verse types are not classified as written and refined literature, although they appear in written form. The mental process of the literate poet and the bertsolari are very different, as are the ways in which they deal with themes and the techniques they employ. The fact that an uneducated bertsolari may have dictated his oral creation to someone else so that it could be transcribed does not mean that his verses should be categorized as written literature. Since these verses are fundamentally improvised, they belong to the genre of oral literature. Bertsolariak use essentially the same technique in the jarriak as they do in their improvised verses, although they are conceived differently and the bertsolari has more time to reshape the verses. According to Juan Mari Lekuona:

> One must point out the fact that from the literary-technical point of view, there are no great differences between the two procedures. They use the same resources in terms of language, metrics, poetic structure, dynamics of thought, and cultural features, etc. If we compare them from a strictly literary aspect, both types of bertsolaritza (improvised and written) are practically the same thing.[17]

The bertso jarriak tradition has been very rich, and through it the literary art of such great bertsolariak as Bilintx and Xenpelar has been preserved. All bertsolariak who consider themselves to be good should master both forms as did Etxahun, Xenpelar, Juan José Alkain, alias "Udarregi" (1829-1895), Txirrita, Pello Errota, and later Basarri, Xalbador, and Amuriza among others. In general, the subjects of written verse are more serious than those of improvised bertsolaritza. At first artists took these verses to publishers, who printed them on rough pages. The verses were later edited in *Bertsolariyak*, a magazine edited by Juan José Makazaga (1887-1963).[18]

It is said that each time Udarregi improvised a new verse, he went up to his farmhouse attic and scratched a mark on the old walls to keep track of the number he had created. When he had gathered enough verses to compose a poem, he asked the village sacristan to transcribe them and sent them to the publisher for publication. This type of verse was also known as *bertso berriak* (new verses). Some bertsolariak, including Pello Errota and Txirrita, have earned money by composing them. This practice has gradually become commonplace.

One name that stands out among the poets who sold bertso berriak is Eusebio Mugertza, alias "Mendaro Txirristaka" (1874–1955). He was a popular bohemian figure who earned his living selling his own verses, as well as those of Xenpelar, Pello Errota, Txirrita, and others. He was a mediocre folk poet who lacked the versifying skill, but he had great inspiration in writing about simple and everyday things. He is especially remembered for the humor of his verses. At times he composed verses partly in Euskara and partly in Spanish.[19] He was a chronicler of his time, narrating such historic events as the Cuban (1898) and the African (1923) wars. Clad in a long black smock, in the old Basque tradition, he went from town to town, especially in Gipuzkoa, traveling through Tolosa, Urretxu, Hernani, and Azpeitia. The papers he sold were the best gift a village woman could buy at the market for her husband, who would sing the verses during the long winter evenings at the farmhouse.

Kopla Zaharrak

In the discussion of Basque oral literature, it is also appropriate to describe the kopla zaharrak (old couplets), a genre that is related to bertsolaritza. Critics of Basque literature do not agree about whether they are part of the same literary phenomenon, even though both consist of sung verse. According to Manuel Lekuona the kopla zaharrak are part of the old tradition of bertsolaritza. However, Pierre Lafitte (1901–1985) and Xabier Amuriza do not agree. Amuriza maintains that while the *koplariak* (couplet singers) improvised to some extent, their improvisation was not as pure as that of bertsolariak. The kopla (couplet) is a short verse that contains two or, at the most, three rhymes. These three-rhyme verses are traditional throughout the Basque Country and have special characteristics in Bizkaia. Unlike the bertsolari, the *koplari* is like a short-distance runner. The differences between the two art forms are clear. Apart from their short form, koplak are intended to be sung and accompanied by such Basque musical instruments as the *alboka* (horn), *dulzaina* (flute), and *trikitixa* (accordion). Many couplets serve as background music for dancing and feature livelier melodies and faster rhythms than those found in bertsolaritza.

An interesting and unique characteristic of the koplak is their apparent lack of logic. In contrast with bertsolaritza, in which verses must be logically structured (beginning, middle, end), the koplak exhibit a lack of logical sequence and unity. There is no coherent relationship between the ideas and the images presented. The relationship that does exist in koplak is simply an acoustical one. The following well-known kopla serves as a good example:

Eder zeruan izarra
errekaldean lizarra.
Etxe ontako nagusi jaunak
urre gorriz du bizarra.[20]

The beautiful star in the sky
and the ash tree by the creek
The owner of this house
has a golden beard.

The words *izarra* (star), *lizarra* (ash tree), and *bizarra* (beard) share only a musical connection, which is produced by the rhyme. This phonic relationship partly makes up for the lack of a logical connection between the two parts of the verse, thereby creating a new relationship that assures internal unity. Another peculiarity evident in this verse is the occurrence of only one verb with many images.

The tradition of kopla zaharrak is an important part of Basque folk literature and has been appreciated by many Basque writers and folklorists such as Resurrección María de Azkue, Orixe, and Gabriel Aresti (1933-1975). "Berreterretxe kantoria" (The song of Berreterretxe), a famous song dating back to the fifteenth century, also exhibits this lack of logical connection between the two parts of the poem's first verse.

Haltzak ez du bihotzik
ez gaztanberak ezurrik;
enian uste erraiten ziela
aitunen semek gezurrik.[21]

The alder tree does not have a heart
nor does curd have bones.
He never believed that
noblemen lied.

It is interesting to note that writer Gabriel Aresti was a much better poet than a bertsolari or a koplari. Early in his career, when he tried imitating the refined poetry of José Mari Agirre, alias "Lizardi" (1896-1933), he quickly discovered the rich tradition of folk poetry and concentrated on imitating it instead.

The characteristic absence of logic that occurs in the koplak is also displayed in the well-known folk song "Goiko mendian" (On the tall mountain):

Goiko mendian elurra dago
errekaldean izotza.
Neu zeugandik aske nagota
pozik daukat biotza.[22]

There is snow on the tall mountain
and ice in the ravine.
My heart rejoices
to be free of you.

The logical, rational unity found in syllogism is not present in the koplak. However, we must keep in mind that syllogism pertains to philosophy, where reason prevails, while the koplak may be classified as poetry. In poetry, communication of imagery prevails over the power of reason. The essence of the koplak is poetical, in which imagination and sentiment play a principal role.

In his book *Euskalerriaren yakintza* (1959), folklorist and renowned writer Resurrección María de Azkue presents us with koplak, entitled "Ikusi nuenean" (When I saw her), most likely from "Arta zuriketak." Here the poet takes a young lover and uses many images to describe her. Sometimes these images are of a delicate nature, and at others they are full of hyperbolic expressions that inspire laughter. The following kopla has been reproduced with the author's original spelling:

1. Ikusi nuenean nik zure begia,
   iruditu zitzaidan, maitea, ampolai gorria.

2. Ikusi nuenean nik zure okotza,
   iruditu zitzaidan, maitea, gaztaña-lokotsa.

3. Ikusi nuenean nik zure sudurra,
   iruditu zitzaidan, maite, lukainka-muturra.

4. Ikusi nuenean nik zure agoa,
   iruditu zitzaidan, maitea, karabi-zuloa.

5. Ikusi nuenean nik zure belarria,
   iruditu zitzaidan, maitea, azaren orria.[23]

1. When I saw your eye,
   it reminded me, dear, of a red cherry.

2. When I saw your chin,
   It reminded me, dear, of a prickly chestnut burr.

3. When I saw your nose,
   It reminded me, dear, of the end of a sausage.

4. When I saw your mouth,
   It reminded me, dear, of the opening of a lime oven.

5. When I saw your ear,
   it reminded me, dear, of a leaf of cabbage.

The Basques have been great enthusiasts of spontaneous short verses. To them the creation of verse is like a game that does not end until the imagination is exhausted. Orixe, for example, added another six verses to "Ikusi nuenean." Using more humorous comparisons, he describes an old maid: "Her bristly hair resembles a witch's broom; her forehead, a frying pan; her brow, livestock; her breasts, charcoal pyres; her hips, Mount Azpiroz; and her legs, twisted goat's horns."[24]

CHAPTER FOUR

The Basque Language
and Bertsolaritza

The Basque language is the instrument with which the bertsolari creates a work of art. The *Diccionario de la lengua española* informally defines the word *vascuence* (Spanish for Euskara) as that which is so confusing and obscure that it cannot be understood.[1] However, for Basques in general and especially for bertsolariak, Euskara is a very intimate and beautiful language. Many bertsolariak have paid fines (e.g, Jon Azpillaga and Jon Lopategi), served jail sentences (e.g, Balendin Enbeita, Txomin Garmendia, Joxe Lizaso, and Xabier Amuriza), been exiled (e.g., Basarri), and suffered other abuses in defense of it. Bertsolariak have always been the most zealous advocates of their language and are conscious of their role as its guardians:

Gu gera izkuntza maitagarria bizirik gorde degunak.[2]

We are the ones who have maintained our dear language alive.

Most bertsolariak of the nineteenth century did not have an opportunity to attend school, and during the first half of this century these artists received only a very elementary education:

Gure kolegiuak sagardotegiak [3]

Our schools [were] the cider shops.

Notwithstanding, these men were highly skilled artists who had complete mastery of their language. Although they sometimes did not follow grammatical rules, grammarians depended on them. Bertsolaritza has been the coffer in which the treasure of the age-old tongue of the Basques has been preserved. The more than two hundred volumes of Antonio Zavala's collection, *Auspoa*, serve as examples of a language rich in locutions, idiomatic expressions, plays on words, and the pure idioms used by these bertsolariak.

The Euskara spoken by nineteenth-century bertsolariak was full of Spanish words. This was not unique to Basque improvisers but rather was characteristic of all Basque speakers of the time, who were simply reflecting their cultural environment. Even the best catechisms of parishes throughout the Basque Country suffered from what Miguel de Unamuno (1864-1936) called a "foreign influence." It was thought that Basque sounded more elegant, sonorous, and solemn when a few foreign words (Spanish words in particular) were sprinkled about.

There were two types of Euskara, the purely popular variety spoken privately among friends, and the eloquent type used in public and in the church. We find examples of some of these foreign words, such as *prezisamente* and *señaladamente* in the verses of Txirrita and Udarregi.

In addition to their roles as promoters and defenders, most bertsolariak, especially the younger ones, are also pioneers and architects of the unified Basque dialect. Older bertsolariak, such as Basarri and Uztapide in the south and Xalbador and Mattin in the north of the Basque Country, initiated the unification process, perhaps without even realizing it. Today's young artists, including Jon Lopategi, Xabier Amuriza, and Jon Enbeita, are the strongest proponents of the unification of the language and faithful followers of the reforms made by the Academy of the Basque Language. While dialectal diversity is very important, it has created many difficulties for the bertsolariak and an audience trying to understand the verses' messages.

As mentioned earlier, speed is an essential element in the composition of verses. But, how can artists manage a quick response if they do not totally understand one another? In recent years, in the small nation of the Basque Country, four major dialects have been employed in the art of bertsolaritza: Gipuzkoan, Bizkaian, Lapurdin, and Behe-nafarrera.

Gipuzkoan has traditionally been the most frequently used dialect in bertsolaritza because it was in this province that the literary phenomenon took root. There have been more bertsolariak from Gipuzkoa than from any other province. Bizkaian artists easily adapt to the Gipuzkoan dialect; however, there are no Gipuzkoan bertsolariak who improvise verse in Bizkaian. Language barriers are even more considerable when comparing dialects of the northern provinces with those of the southern provinces. Unified Basque was imposed as a solution to these problems and is now the medium of communication among Basques, even though it has its limitations. The widespread use of the unified dialect is due in large measure to its propagation by the bertsolariak.

Historically, the presence of different dialects did not pose a problem because bertsolariak rarely ventured out of their respective provinces. However, with modern means of transportation, these artists are now able to perform in several provinces of the Basque Country on the same day. There are more frequent performances than formerly, especially during the summer months. Txirrita and Pello Errota, the most famous bertsolariak of the early twentieth century, did not perform more than twenty times a year. Today most artists participate in one hundred performances or more annually, and in different provinces.[4] In view of this change, a common dialect that can be understood by all Basques has become a necessity.

At the present time the influence of a written form of the unified Basque language is becoming evident in bertsolaritza. There is little difference between the Basque spoken by some young bertsolariak and the unified dialect. Eighty percent of modern Basque literature is published in Euskara Batua (unified Basque). The unification of dialects is becoming a practical reality because of its widespread use at the Basque university and bertsolaritza schools and performances, among other factors. Unification is achieving goals that twenty-five years ago seemed very distant, if not unattainable. In 1960 Basarri stated: "Unfortunately, the unification of our language is farther away than we would like it to be."[5]

Both popular Euskara and its unified written counterpart have advantages and disadvantages in bertsolaritza. The suffixes, the ellipsis, and the verb are quite useful.

BASQUE SUFFIXES

Basque is a non-Indo-European language. Prepositions, while common in Romance languages, do not exist in Euskara. Nominal, adjectival, and verbal suffixes, however, are abundant. Verbal suffixes are applied to auxiliary verbs as well as to principal verbs. Causality, tense, finality, and so on, in subordinate clauses are generally indicated by the suffix of the auxiliary verb.

ELLIPSIS

An ellipsis consists of the omitting of one or more words necessary for correct grammatical structure while keeping the meaning of a sentence clear. It is a rhetorical form used to condense sentences and it adds beauty, color, clarity, and force. The ellipsis is important and is found in many languages, but is used frequently in Euskara in both prose and verse. The omitted word is usually a verb. If we compare Euskara with Spanish we see similar cases of ellipsis. The words that are commonly omitted are in brackets in the following examples:

Kaixo zer moduz [zagoz]?   ¿Qué tal [estás]?

[Ni] ondo eta zu [zer   [Yo estoy] bien y tú,
     moduz zagoz]?   ¿[cómo estás]?

It is common to find Basque verses with only one verb (as in kopla zaharrak) or with none at all.

VERB

One of the greatest challenges of the language for new students of Euskara is the verb, even though its structure is very logical. The verb is the backbone of the sentence and is usually placed at the end. In Basque there are synthetic and periphrastic verbs. The latter are compound verbs and are composed of main and auxiliary verbs. The auxiliary normally follows the main verb. However, word order in affirmative sentences may often change, especially in poetry, without altering the original meaning. The switching of word order is common practice, especially among Basques from the northern provinces.

Unlike the Spanish verb, in which infinitives may have one of only three endings (-ar, -er, -ir), Basque has a wide variety of verb endings such as "amai*tu*" (to finish), "sal*du*" (to sell), "eto*rri*" (to come), "esan" (to say), "ero*ri*" (to fall). These verbs may be abbreviated in some moods such as the subjunctive and the imperative. For example, the subjunctive "ikas . . . dezagun" (let us study) is derived from "ika*si*" (to learn) and the imperative "etor bedi" (have him come) is derived from "eto*rri*" (to come). All these techniques help the bertsolari with improvisation.

ARTICLE

Some elements of Basque grammar do not facilitate the bertsolari's task. Unlike the Romance languages or English, in Euskara the article changes greatly according to the noun number (singular or plural) and the nature of the verbs. The English article *the* has the Basque equivalents -a, -ak, -ek, and -ok formed by the article plus the ergative -k. Many Basque words are not used as they appear in the dictionary but are transformed by the articles that are attached as suffixes. For example, in the case of *gizon* (man):

gizona the man, singular subject of intransitive verb or singular direct object of transitive verb.

gizonak the men, singular subject of a transitive verb; plural direct object of a transitive verb; plural subject of an intransitive verb; plural subject of a transitive verb in western dialects.

gizonek the men, plural subject of a transitive verb.

gizonok the men, plural subject of a transitive verb when the speaker belongs to or is close to the reference group.

When one considers the great difficulty of rapid improvisation and the grammatical elements of Euskara, it is not surprising that errors are sometimes made in bertsolaritza. When a bertsolari performs alone, the session is brief and many mistakes can be avoided. However, performances are usually longer, and on many occasions the bertsolariak must perform two or three times daily during popular festivals. When as many as one hundred verses are improvised during a single performance, it is unrealistic to expect that all them will be of equal literary value. Xabier Amuriza relates that on occasion he goes home feeling as if he has been a circus clown and uses the word *pellokeria* (idiocy) to refer to the uneven episodes in his performances. He described one situation where he felt like a dog running away after stones had been thrown at it.[6]

There are two major errors, *poto egin* and *betelana*, that merit some discussion. Poto egin is the repetition of a word-rhyme with the same meaning in a single stanza. This is permitted only when words that are spelled alike and sound alike do not share the same meaning, as in *berri* (new, as an adjective) and *berri* (news, as a noun). The same holds true for the auxiliary verb *du* and for numerals. For example, in "Loriak udan intza bezela" (As the flower [loves] the dew in the summer), a famous verse by Bilintx, *bat* (the number one) is repeated four times as a rhyme. In such cases, this is not considered an error as long as the word is used as a suffix and the succeeding words are different:

Loriak udan intza bezela maite det dama gazte *bat*,
ari ainbeste nai diyotenik ez da munduan beste *bat*;
inoiz edo bein pasatzen badet ikusi gabe aste *bat*
biyotz guztira banatuzen zait alako gauza triste *bat*.[7]

As the flower loves the dew in the summer, I too, love a
    young lady;
there is no one in the world who loves her as much as I.
If I ever pass a week without seeing her,
my heart becomes engulfed in a melancholy shadow.

Betelana is another frequently committed error and is considered a very serious one. Basque grammar makes a clear distinction between *lana bete*, or completing the assigned task, and *betelana*, which is leaving a task unfinished. The latter implies the failure to approach a subject directly or properly. Sometimes the subject is indirectly addressed and at other times not at all. This may occur when the guidelines for structural development and logic (i.e., beginning, middle, end) are not followed. In such cases, the bertsolari is accused of speaking for the sake of not being silent, and his work is considered nothing more than filler material.

Even the greatest bertsolariak are susceptible to betelana. It is easy for an artist to digress from the assigned topic when he is unfamiliar with the subject matter. This happened in the 1962 txapelketa when the great champion Basarri finished his verse with the progress of the Basque language instead of the orphans of fishing villages, as he had been instructed.[8]

The same error sometimes occurs when bertsolariak perform in pairs and one of them fails to correctly follow the gist of the dialogue. These errors, among others, are evaluated and points are subtracted from a bertsolari's total scores.

PART II

The History of Bertsolaritza

CHAPTER FIVE

Origins of Bertsolaritza

Recorded history on bertsolaritza dates back to the nineteenth century. The available information about this artistic expression as it existed before then is sparse and limited. The problem becomes greater if we consider the evolution of bertsolaritza. We have analyzed the four types of performances that have been practiced since the nineteenth century, but what of the earlier performances? Did bertsolariak sing in competitions and at performances similar to the floral games or were there other forms of bertsolaritza, such as the paid mourner's improvisation, which will be examined later? Last, a question remains as to who were the protagonists of this art form. Until very recently, bertsolariak and enthusiasts of bertsolaritza were exclusively male. However, formerly there were also women who sang and improvised verses. All of these questions lead us to examine the origins and evolution of the phenomenon.

Manuel Lekuona dates the origin of bertsolaritza from the pastoral period:

> Of the four periods of humanity's social evolution, from hunting to pastoralism, from pastoralism to agriculture, and from agriculture to industrialism, the period which most easily lends itself to bertsolaritza is the pastoral period, 10,000 years ago. . . .

As we see, the art of bertsolaritza is definitely a product of pre-historic society.[1]

For Manuel Lekuona, the pastoral lifestyle is the most conducive for the development of improvised sung verse.[2] This viewpoint, which implies ancient origins for bertsolaritza, may be a likely and acceptable explanation, even though there are no historical or archaeological data to support it. Juan Mari Lekuona, a specialist in Basque oral literature maintains:

> It is obvious that we shall not begin to measure the antiquity of bertsolaritza in terms of years. It is more logical to isolate a period of civilization and analyze the possibilities that existed in it for the Basques to have begun and fostered the custom of improvising popular verse. If we refer to the different periods of civilization we see that humans progressed from hunter, to shepherd, to farmer, and finally to industrial worker. One can assert that the bertsolari establishes himself in the pastoral period and reflects a world of more ancient origin than that of the classics and employs literary forms older than those of Greek and Roman literature.[3]

As we progress from prehistoric times to the first written testimonies, we find in the Middle Ages limited and very incomplete written verses. These remnants provide only a glimpse of what bertsolaritza was like in the fourteenth and fifteenth centuries. Antonio Zavala writes: "It saddens the soul to think that centuries and centuries of bertsolaritza lie in darkness forever."[4]

These fragments are, nevertheless, important because they represent the most ancient records of Basque literature and provide us with some information about bertsolaritza. These written fragments may be classified as epic ballads and eresiak (songs that hired mourners improvised in verse when a loved one died). Both genres are considered venerable relics of Basque oral literature and are of great interest because of their dramatic and lyric character and the information they provide on improvised verse.

The most outstanding war ballads and epic poems (with translations and historical dates of events in parentheses) are "Peru Abendañoren Aieria" (Song of Aramayona, 1443), "Urruxolako gudu-kanta" (War song of Urrexola, 1388-1401), "Arrasate erre zuteneko koplak" (Couplets on the burning of Arrasate, 1488), and "Berreterretxe kantoria" (The song of Berreterretxe, 1434-1449). At the end of the fourteenth and the beginning of the fifteenth centuries, the Basque Country was ravaged by wars of sedition. Disputes over territory, property, and pasture boundaries were settled by warfare. The Ahaide Nagusiak were families representing the most important lineages and were supported by extended families in certain areas and local people who formed their bands. The Ahaide Nagusiak included the Oñacinos and Gamboinos in Gipuzkoa and Bizkaia and the Agramonteses and Beamonteses in Nafarroa. Relentless battles, fires, pillage, treason, and assassinations devastated the country and gave rise to the entire epic genre and the improvisation of sung verse.

Esteban Garibay was a chronicler who provided the most information on war ballads. During the sixteenth century, Garibay transcribed events of earlier centuries that had been passed down through oral tradition. The appearance of sung verses, in Garibay's transcription, represents the oldest written evidence that this phenomenon has been deeply rooted in the Basque Country since the fifteenth century. In the fifth part of the second book of his *Memorias*, Garibay states:

> After doña Emilia de Lastur had died in childbirth, it came to pass that her husband, Pedro García de Oro, wished to marry doña Marina de Arrazola with whom he had been previously infatuated. One of doña Emilia's sisters was very upset over this and traveled from Deba to Arrasate to sing the following dirge on the day of Emilia's last honors, as was the custom in those times:[5]

> Zer ete da andra erdiaen zauria?
> Sagar errea eta ardao zuria.
> Alabaia, kontrario da, Milia!:
> Azpian lur otza, gañean arria.

> Lastur'era bear dozu, Milia!
> Aita-yaunak eresten dau elia
> ama-andreak apainketan obia,
> ara bear dozu, Milia!

> Yausi da zerurean arria,
> aurkitu dau Lastur'en torre barria.
> edegi dio almeneari erdia . . .
> Lastur'era bear dozu, Milia!

> Arren! Ene andra Milia Lastur'ko!
> Peru Garzia'k egin deusku laburto:
> egin dau andra Marina Arrazola'ko.
> Ezkon bekio: bere idea dauko.[6]

> What is the wound of a woman who has given birth?
> A baked apple and red wine.
> But for you, oh Emilia! It has been the opposite
> the old earth below you, the tombstone above you.

> Oh Emilia! You must go to Lastur.
> Our dear father is bringing down the flock.
> Our dear mother is decorating your tombstone.
> Oh Emilia! You must go [there].

A stone has fallen from the sky,
it has struck the new tower of Lastur,
it has knocked down half of the merlons . . .
Oh Emilia you must go to Lastur!

Come! My lady Emilia of Lastur!
Pedro Garcia has behaved in a vile manner:
He has taken Marina de Arrazola as his wife.
Let him marry her, she is just like him.

Doña Sancha Ortiz, Pedro Garcia's sister, responded to the dirge by defending her brother and stating that the deceased had lived in a large house and had been the owner of many keys (a symbol of wealth):

Ez dauko Pero Garzia'k bearrik
ain gatx andia apukaduagatik;
zeruko mandatua izanik,
andrariok-ala kunpli-yasorik.
Gizon txiki sotil baten andra zan,
atearte zabalean oi zan,
giltza-porra andiaen yabe zan,
onra andi asko kunplidu yakan.[7]

It is not Pedro Garcia's obligation
to try to lessen such a terrible misfortune;
since it was an order from heaven
it must be carried out, and he must accept the marriage.
She was the wife of a strong little man,
she lived in a house with a wide gate,
she was the keeper of a great handful of keys,
she was greatly honored. [paraphrase]

The exact date of these dirges is not known, but they are undoubtedly from the first half of the fifteenth century. In them the two women attack each other through sung verse. According to Luis Michelena:

Eresiak were composed on such occasions as weddings and
funerals, and, according to numerous testimonies, were impro-
vised by women. Often they [the women] responded to each
other's verses, thereby creating debates much as modern bertso-
lariak do.[8]

Esteban Garibay's description does not portray the women as hired mourn-ers who composed dirges in order to make a living. Instead he offers an image of upper-class women who perhaps improvised verses as a social obligation to the deceased. It was a type of catharsis and a way to make peace with the dead. One of these women was doña Sancha Ochoa de Ozaeta. The burning of Arra-sate and the death of the lord of Butrón provoked her son to avenge his death.

Martín Bañez de Artazubiaga was assassinated in 1464, and his wife, doña Sancha, "raised a great cry of grief, as was customary in that century . . . and sang many dirges, which in Euskara are called *eresiyac*."[9] "Raised a great cry" and "sang dirges" refer to the singing of verses. Doña Sancha improvised verses about her husband's tragic death, and in them she sang about her loneliness and that of her children.

This phenomenon, in which women creatively improvise verse, is not exclusive to the Basque Country. We will see later that the Tuareg women of Africa also participate in this type of activity. An example of this poetic genre, similar to the one found in Basque culture, comes from Slavic culture and

> is to be found in the lamentations sung or recited by women during burial ceremonies. Structured on a pattern of incantations and questions, they varied according to the emotional improvisations of the mourners, who expressed their grief in language ranging from the most basic prose to lyricism of exquisite intensity.[10]

In the *Fuero de Vizcaya* (a book of legal charters), written in 1452, we find two sections that prohibit verse improvisation by women. From it we can deduce that verse improvisation was widespread within the Basque culture (because laws are not decreed for isolated cases). *Hiltariak* (hired mourners) were women who received money for weeping and singing verses at funerals. Laws prohibiting such activities were as follows:

> *Section 35 Law 6*   Concerning how mourning of the deceased may be carried out. . . . They ordered and decreed that from this day forward, when anyone dies in Bizkaia or outside its boundaries, at sea, on land, no citizen of any part of Bizkaia, flatland, village, or city is permitted to mourn by means of tearing one's hair, scratching one's face, uncovering one's head, singing, or wearing sack cloth under penalty of one thousand maravedís for each offense.[11]

The second law was directed at women known as *profazadas*. The word *profazo* means discredited and of bad reputation, and a *profazador* is a person who gossips and tries to cause quarrels between friends through rumors and deceit. The profazadas were women of ill repute who went from town to town selling their wares at fairs and markets. They also improvised and sang verses that were usually humorous and involved mockery. Their activities were illegal and at times punishable by deportation, as described in

> *Section 8 Law 1*   And concerning women, who are recognized as insolent troublemakers in their neighborhoods, and who invent couplets and ballads with the intention of defamatory libel [the fuero shall refer to them as profazadas].[12]

The Council of Trent was held in the midst of the Renaissance (1545) and greatly influenced the religious life of the Basque Country. The priest's Sunday sermon to some extent influenced the Basque way of life. The spirit of Saint Paul's phrase "mulieres taceant in Ecclesia" (let the women be silent in church) affected both religious and social circles in the Basque Country. Women were relegated to a lower social level. Improvisation as practiced by hired mourners and profazadas disappeared and was replaced by bertsolaritza, which thrived in the cider shops and had only men as its protagonists.

The role of these artists and the social context have changed over time. Although the new type of bertsolari did not follow in the footsteps of hired mourners or improvisers of war ballads, his art form was more similar to that of the profazadas. His mission remained to entertain people. When we trace the history of bertsolaritza, we encounter a very popular type of bertsolari who was well liked by the people although he was not socially accepted. He was the cider-shop bertsolari of the eighteenth century. Families were ashamed to claim such artists as their own because they were regarded as night owls and clowns.

This historical outline is brief because the available information is scant and the texts are incomplete. Our knowledge of nineteenth-century bertsolaritza is improved thanks to the precise information provided by Juan Ignacio Iztueta. Iztueta was born in Zaldibia (Gipuzkoa) and lived during parts of two centuries (the eighteenth and the nineteenth) of upheaval. In his youth he had a criminal record and was incarcerated. However, his past did not hinder him from later being named warden of the correctional prison of Donostia.

Iztueta interests us for many reasons. As a historian, folklorist, poet, and expert on bertsolaritza, he was one of the most important writers on Basque culture during the nineteenth century. He was an excellent observer of Gipuzkoan history, language, and legal institutions, and one of the very few lay writers of Basque literature. In spite of his humble origins and the fact that he was self-educated, he was a gifted writer of both prose and poetry. His poem "Kontxesiri" (To Kontxesi) is an excellent example of his poetic gifts.

Iztueta wrote *Guipuzcoaco provinciaren condaira edo historia* (History of the province of Gipuzkoa), which was published in 1847, two years after his death. This work is actually more ethnographic than historical in that it describes sheepherding, agriculture, animals, botany, statistics, customs, and the sports of his native province.

What interests us the most about Iztueta is his information on folklore and bertsolaritza. He was the first to provide a detailed written account of bertsolaritza, including the descriptions of contests in Billabona, Azpeitia, and Tolosa; the enthusiasm of the Gipuzkoan people for the art; and the respect or disrespect toward the authorities that bertsolariak aroused in the people.

Iztueta was also a *dantzari*, or Basque folk dancer, and was interested in all Basque folk expressions. His first book is titled *Guipuzcoaco dantza gogoangarrien condaira edo historia* (History of the memorable Gipuzkoan dances, 1824). In one of his chapters, "Izneurtulari edo bertsolarien jostaketa" (The diversion of versemakers or bertsolariak), Iztueta provides details that allow us to trace the history of bertsolaritza. He describes the contest held in Billabona and the great enthusiasm for improvisation of sung verse that was present in Gipuzkoa: "The Gipuzkoans have always possessed the ability to sing improvised verse well."[13]

It is fair to assume that bertsolaritza did not originate in 1801 with the emergence of the Billabona contest. The appearance of Fernando Amezketarra and other exceptional bertsolariak of his time could not be explained if bertsolaritza had not been widespread in Gipuzkoa. The fact that these artists were *escolatu-gabecoac* (illiterate) demonstrates the dedication of these folk poets and adds to the merit of the art form.

The presence of four thousand spectators at the Billabona contest also supports the widespread enthusiasm for bertsolaritza in the province of Gipuzkoa. It has been recorded that toward the middle of the nineteenth century the population of Gipuzkoa was 120,000; of these, 100,000 were monolingual Basque speakers.[14] When we consider the absence of modern means of communication, the sheer numbers of spectators present in the plaza of Billabona demonstrates how popular bertsolaritza was throughout Gipuzkoa.

This fact, however, should not lead us to believe that at the time bertsolaritza was widespread throughout the entire Basque Country. Different Basque provinces were known for their unique literary expressions. Zuberoa was known for its pastorale, Bizkaia for its kopla zaharrak, Nafarroa for its *romancero*. Gipuzkoa is considered the birthplace of bertsolaritza and continues to be the province that has produced the most and the best bertsolariak in the last two centuries. It is probable that the origin of bertsolaritza, like the origin of the Basque language itself, will remain a puzzle in spite of efforts to untangle the mystery.

CHAPTER SIX

Characteristics of

Great Bertsolariak

Now that we have briefly traced bertsolaritza from prehistoric times, the Middle Ages, and the nineteenth century, we will examine the characteristics of some of the most famous bertsolariak of the last two centuries. We will focus only on the most representative artists, because a more extensive study would be beyond the scope of this work. This discussion will serve as background for the short biographies on the four bertsolariak provided later.

PREROMANTICISM (1800-1839)

The preromantic period is known as the "Generation of Fernando Amezketarra" because of that bertsolari's great talent. Juan Ignacio Iztueta tells us that bertsolaritza had the support of local authorities in Amezketa, while in other Gipuzkoan towns bertsolariak were fined and even incarcerated.[1] As a consequence, a large bertsolaritza movement arose in the area of Amezketa. Even the parish priest improvised verses.

While our information is scanty regarding the few famous bertsolariak from the preromantic period, we do know something about the following versemakers: Gipuzkoans Fernando Amezketarra, Zabala, Txabalategi, and Altamira; the sacristan of Aizarna; the shepherd of Izuela, Augustín Arruti (1780-1837);[2] and the Nafarroan artist Juan Etxamendi, alias "Bordel" (1792-1879).[3]

Most bertsolariak of this period were illiterate and from rural areas. These men spoke the common language of the farmhouses and were not influenced by written literature or urban culture. Their bertsolaritza art form was essentially improvised. Bertso-paperak (written verses) did not have the vigor they would acquire in later years. Consequently, the main means of transmission depended on the collective memories of individual community members.

The bertsolaritza performances, which usually took place in taverns or cider shops, occurred without prior preparation. The contests that were held frequently to determine the best bertsolari had a panel of judges and were carefully planned.

Fernando Amezketarra (1764-1823)

Fernando Amezketarra was born in Amezketa (Gipuzkoa). He was the first great bertsolari to be recorded in history and was the most skilled improviser of his time. He was sharp-witted and, although he had no formal education, he possessed a natural talent for and cultural awareness of bertsolaritza.

Amezketarra was a shepherd and farm laborer. He occasionally worked in the copper mines in the Aralar Mountains. He did not own his farmhouse, but rented it, as did most rural Basques of the nineteenth century. Amezketarra's verses addressed the economic difficulties faced by laborers and their desires to overcome them.

Amezketarra's accounts in his jocular short stories and improvised verses made him a legend in the Basque Country. Unfortunately, his humorous side detracted from his exceptional talent as a bertsolari because the audience paid particular attention only to that aspect of his work. In all three of Juan Ignacio Iztueta's descriptions of bertsolaritza, he mentions Amezketarra in the famous contests of Billabona, Tolosa, and Azpeitia. In the last instance, Amezketarra's opponent did not even dare to appear before the audience, underscoring the magnitude of Amezketarra's reputation. Amezketarra also had a rare talent for improvising such difficult rhymes as the bederatzi puntuko bertsoa. On the hundredth anniversary of his death, a plaque, which partially describes Amezketarra's (referred to as Pernando) personality, was hung on the wall of the house where he was born. It bears the following inscription:

Pernando,
Amezketako bertsolari,
adimenez argi,

ezpañetan irri,
urkoari zirri,
jendearen jostagarri
ibilli zan erriz erri.[4]

Fernando,
Amezketa's bertsolari,
with sharp intelligence,
a smile on his lips,
harassing his neighbor,
the people's entertainment,
he went from town to town.

Amezketarra had extraordinary talent for improvising verses. The parish priest once asked him how three different persons existed in one divine presence. He quickly responded with the following:

Nola sinisten dedan
arrazoiarekin
orain esango diot
sagartxo batekin:
usai ta saborea
kolorearekin,
horra hiru jenero
gauza bat batekin.[5]

Since I believe [in God]
with reason,
I will now explain it
with a little apple:
smell and taste
with color,
there [you have] three different aspects
in a single thing.

ROMANTICISM

The period of romanticism is considered the golden age of improvised verse and bertso-paperak. It is referred to as "the generation of Xenpelar" because of his mastery of bertsolaritza. The period coincided chronologically with both Carlist wars, which left the Basque Country devastated economically and spiritually. Although Basque society continued to rely essentially on agriculture, industrialization, mechanization, and railroads appeared for the first time. The center of bertsolaritza shifted from Amezketa to the area of Errenteria and Oiartzun (Gipuzkoa).

Although contests continued in this period, they were not as important as in earlier times. In contrast, bertso-paperak became more common and the technique of improvisation was refined. New themes appeared, new melodies were created, the repertory of rhythms was enriched, and rules for rhyming were more closely observed.

The greatest bertsolariak of the period were Xenpelar, José María Iparragirre (1820-1881), Bilintx, Etxahun, and Joanes Otxalde, alias "Otxalde" (1814-1896).[6] Because means of communication between the north and the south of the Basque Country were not yet well established, in spite of their great talent, Etxahun from Zuberoa and Otxalde from Nafarroa Beherea remained unknown to enthusiasts from the southern provinces. Their art varied considerably from the norms traditionally observed by Gipuzkoan bertsolariak. Both of these northern artists were less concerned with quality of rhyme and enjoyed more freedom with regard to bertsolaritza's literary techniques.

Francisco Petrirena, Alias "Xenpelar" (1835-1869)

Xenpelar was an extraordinary improviser who greatly influenced bertsolaritza. However, he is best known for his bertso-paperak. Undoubtedly, he was the most accomplished bertsolari of the nineteenth century and was very famous and respected in the south of the Basque Country. Although he died at thirty-four, a saying arose during his lifetime that is still heard today: "bertso berriak, Xenpelarrek jarriak" (new verse by Xenpelar).

Xenpelar was born in Errenteria in a farmhouse called Senpelarre located near Oiartzun. As a child, he was not able to attend school. His family was so poor that they were forced to send him to another farmhouse, called Eula, as a servant.[7] These circumstances permitted little opportunity for instruction in bertsolaritza.

After Xenpelar married and had three children, his financial situation obligated him to leave his position at Eula to find work at a textile factory in Errenteria. He eventually became a supervisor. Xenpelar was a man of innate intelligence, a devout Christian with deep convictions, and a skilled, quiet worker.

Xenpelar was the first great bertsolari to be closely associated with the issue of the fueros.[8] After the death of Spanish king Fernando VII (1784-1833), the Basque Country suffered a period of restlessness because of the loss of the fueros and the general decline of freedom. Xenpelar felt that a great offense had been committed against the Basque provinces of Gipuzkoa, Bizkaia, and Araba when they lost the liberties that had been theirs historically. A growing trend toward industrialization occurred at the same time that rights were being taken away, which contributed to social and political problems.

Xenpelar was an advocate of statutory freedom and opposed Madrid's centralism. He was against the Spanish liberal politicians because they were enemies of religion. At the same time, he also opposed the Basques who favored war as a means of solving the problems resulting from the loss of their ancient rights.

In the midst of a difficult prewar atmosphere, Xenpelar wrote his famous verses "Ia guriak egin du" (We are on the verge of perishing). His verses were like predictions of a clairvoyant prophet. With vibrant, forceful words he condemned Madrid's violence and the war that accomplished nothing more than to turn brothers against one another. Unfortunately, the warnings of this popular poet were not heeded and the second Carlist War broke out three years after his death.

Many Basques, including Xenpelar, felt that the conflict over the Spanish throne, caused by the aspiring Don Carlos V de Borbón, was none of their business. They only became interested because this competitor for the throne spoke of defending the fueros:

> Gerra nai duan guziya . . .
> berari kendu biziya.
> Ez naiz ni gerraren
> baizik pakearen alde . . .
> Gu gera iru probintzi
> lengo legerik ez utzi
> oyeri firme eutsi
> naiz anka bana autsi.[9]

> Let all who want war . . .
> be killed.
> I am not in favor of war,
> but rather peace.
> We three provinces
> must not forget the old laws.
> Let us stand steadfast behind them
> even though they may break our legs. [paraphrase]

Xenpelar frequently employed the themes of religion (the lives of the saints and popular missions) and labor and social problems in his verses. Industrialization provoked a series of labor conflicts that were hitherto unknown. The hiring of French technicians and workers for the construction of the Irun-Madrid railroad created many problems that were reflected in Xenpelar's verses. The French workers were paid higher salaries than the Basques. Xenpelar protested:

> Jornalik aundienak
> frantzesak dauzkate.[10]

> The Frenchmen get
> the highest wages.

Humor is also a dominant characteristic in the poetry of Xenpelar. He had a special gift for competing and debating and often used humor and irony in his verses. In analyzing the different rhythm patterns of his most famous verses, on the buying and selling of a Breton cow, we have become familiar with his imagination, humor, satire, and irony. He often made use of hyperbole and comparison.

His poetic strength lies in the technique of his style. Xenpelar was always recognized as a sharp and concise bertsolari. He founded a prestigious school in Gipuzkoa that is known for the special emphasis placed on the formal and technical aspects of versemaking. Xenpelar excelled in this dimension of bertsolaritza as no other artist has.

Xenpelar's often idiosyncratic rhythm creations were products of deliberate and profound reflections and his ability to employ the five rhythmic models discussed earlier. He frequently used those consisting of eight lines, both long (10/8) and short (7/6). However, he did not limit himself to them. His innovative spirit propelled him to search constantly for new rhythms and different versemaking techniques.

His rhymes were carefully created so that they were never mediocre. In this respect, traditional Gipuzkoan style differs greatly from that of Etxahun and other northern bertsolariak. For example:

1. In his verses about the Breton cow, Xenpelar made use of complicated and sophisticated rhymes such as -OTZAK and -ARRAK.

2. When he used gerunds, he was not satisfied with the rhyme of the last syllable -TZEN; rather, he began rhyming from the preceding syllables: BILTZEN—iBILTZEN.

3. The inclination to use complicated rhymes is present throughout his works. He never paired -EAN with -AN. Nor did he ever use the rhyme -IA. Instead, he looked for a consonant that preceded these vowels, -LIA.

The few small grammatical errors that are found in Xenpelar's verses can be attributed more to the faulty memories of his recounters or to random error than to Xenpelar's ignorance. For example: "*Zugaz* akordatzen naiz" should read "Zutaz" (I remember you).

His music and melodies were generally lighthearted and dancelike. It is likely that some melodies said to be Xenpelar's were not really composed by him. They may simply have been popular at the time. Xenpelar possessed an extraordinary talent for improvisation and always created his verses by singing rather than by counting syllables (on his fingers or by any other means), as is attributed to other bertsolariak. He even composed bertso jarriak by singing them. Someone else later transcribed them on paper.

Xenpelar was referred to in Euskara as *eskolatu gabea*, or unlearned, as were many other bertsolariak, such as Fernando Amezketarra and Pello Errota. However, Xenpelar differed from these other bertsolariak in that he did not confine himself to rural themes. Instead, he became a more worldly bertsolari in the tradition of Bilintx.

José María Iparragirre (1820-1881)

José María Iparragirre was a wandering bohemian, reminiscent of the medieval bards. He was not as prominent as Xenpelar because he was not a great improviser. He was, however, a born adventurer. He was hot-blooded and possessed a vivid imagination. His life, like his art, was different from that of bertsolariak who were rooted in a particular province. He rebelled against everything that involved discipline and method. He voiced the sentiments of an ancient and rural people who possessed little formal education.

Iparragirre considered himself more of a songster than a bertsolari: "Kantari pasatzen det nik beti eguna" (I spend my days singing constantly).[11] Apparently, his talent for improvisation was not very great. On one occasion, when Xenpelar challenged him to improvise verses in front of an audience, he did not appear for the event.[12]

Iparragirre was born in Urretxu (Gipuzkoa). When he was thirteen years old his parents sent him to Gasteiz to study humanities; but soon after that, they moved to Madrid and he went with them. That same year, the first Carlist War broke out. One morning the adolescent Iparragirre told his mother he was going to school, and as he himself relates he took to his heels and ran away from home. He reappeared in the Basque Country and enlisted as a volunteer in the Carlist forces. His desire was to defend the fueros and Basque liberty. He served as honorary guard to the aspiring regent Don Carlos V de Borbón.

The historical agreement of Bergara was enacted after the Carlists' defeat and was symbolized by an embrace between the liberal general Baldomero Espartero and the Carlist Rafael Maroto. Even though the wording of the agreement respected the Basque fueros, in reality it was a betrayal by the central power in Madrid because it included the caveat "without damage to the constitutional unity of the monarchy," which later served to suppress Basque liberty.[13] Consequently, many Basques were forced to seek exile after the defeat of the Carlists. Young Iparragirre, who had not yet turned twenty, found himself among the exiled.

Iparragirre escaped to France where he learned the language and studied solfeggio and voice.[14] He read the works of romantic authors such as François René de Chateaubriand (1768-1848) and Alphonse de Lamartine (1790-1869). The year 1848 was crucial for France and for Europe as the entire continent trembled with revolutionary spirit. The people of Europe, thirsting for freedom and propelled by romantic notions, welcomed the concept of nationality as a means of combating tyranny. The people also demanded public instruction and universal suffrage. As a consequence of public uprisings, there were assassinations, deportations, and incarcerations. Napoleon III (1808-1873) completely suppressed democracy and freedom. Iparragirre was detained in Toulouse for sympathizing with the revolutionaries because he was caught singing the "Marseillaise." He was deported from the country when they learned he was a foreigner.

Iparragirre then moved to England, arriving in London at the height of the Victorian period. The World's Fair took place in 1851 and Iparragirre played the guitar for an Italian theater company. At the time Manuel Mazarredo (1807–1857), a centralist general from Bilbo, was visiting London and arranged special permission for Iparragirre to return to Spain. After twelve years of exile he was finally reunited with his family.

In 1853 Basque protests against Madrid's government were frequent because of the Basques' frustrations with the political situation.[15] Iparragirre once again found himself in an environment of protest. He was in Madrid when Basque students demanded the return to the conditions that existed prior to the law of 1839, which stripped the Basques of many of their liberties. The words *fueros*, *freedom*, and *Gernika* were on the lips of most Basques. However, the centralist government in Madrid did not comprehend the suffering felt in the Basque Country.

In the midst of this frustration Iparragirre exchanged his rifle for a guitar and set out to do battle through song. He composed his famous work "Gernikako arbola" (The tree of Gernika), which he sang for the first time accompanied by another Basque on piano at the San Luis, a Madrid cafeteria. The verses of this song overflowed with veneration, generosity, freedom, universality, peace, and brotherhood. The song is a solemn zortziko (5/8 rhythm), almost religious in tone. The political climate of strife and conflict of the time made it the hymn of Basque liberty. It is not, however, the Basque "Marseillaise," as many have mistakenly claimed.

Iparragirre returned with his guitar to the Basque Country singing "Gernikako arbola" and lifted the spirits of many Basques. He achieved the perfect marriage of music and lyrics. His simple poetry was naive, romantic, sentimental, and possessed an authentic quality. No other poetic composition by a bertsolari penetrated the soul of the Basques like Iparragirre's song.

In spite of its message of brotherhood and peace, the song was declared dangerous, and Iparragirre was incarcerated in Tolosa. During his time in prison he composed "Nere amak baleki" (If my mother knew) in which he speaks of his time in jail, his deportation from the Basque Country, and his wanderings in foreign lands.[16]

After prison he traveled around Santander and northern Spain and visited Portugal. However, he returned to the Basque Country once again after this second exile. Upon his return he composed the famous verses "Nere maitearentzat" (For my beloved), best known for the words of the first line "Ume eder bat ikusi nuen" (I saw a beautiful child).[17] Around this time he fell in love with Angela Querejeta, who was nineteen years his junior, and they decided to get married. When Iparragirre encountered several bureaucratic problems, they moved to Latin America and lived there for nineteen years.

On August 29, 1858, they set sail from Baiona to Buenos Aires. They were warmly welcomed by the Basque community of Buenos Aires and were married shortly afterwards. From there they continued to Montevideo where Iparragirre found work as a shepherd. However, either because his sense of liberty was so pronounced or his desire to work was so weak, when his sheep escaped from the fold he did not concern himself. Instead, he claimed that animals had the right to live in freedom, too.[18]

Even as his flock became smaller, his family continued to grow until they had eight children. After his failure at the ranch, he opened a bar in Montevideo and named it Gernikako Arbola (after his famous song). However, he tended to spend the day singing instead of working. Because of his easygoing and generous spirit, he also failed in this business and was forced to return to sheepherding. This time he went to Río de la Plata, where he remained for several years. The Basque community did not hear anything from him and there were even rumors that he had died.[19]

After the Carlists' defeat in the second war, King Alfonso XII totally suppressed the few Basque freedoms that remained. When Iparragirre received word of this, his blood began to boil again. With the assistance of the Basques of the Laurak Bat (The Four Are One) society of Buenos Aires and the four Basque provincial councils, he was able to return to the Basque Country. He left his family behind and never saw them again. Before departure in 1877, he sang his verses "Jaungoikoa eta arbola" (God and the tree) in the Colón Theater of Buenos Aires.[20] These verses demonstrated his desire to live in peace.

In 1878 he disembarked in Bordeaux and upon arrival in Hendaye, he sang his famous verses "Nere etorrera lur maiteari" (My arrival to my beloved land).[21] When he saw the mountains of his dear Basque land, he knelt down and kissed the ground of his ancestors. He sang at the Teatro Price in Madrid that same year, but his baritone voice was not as strong as it had been in earlier years. Iparragirre's career as an artist was ending. The four provincial councils and several writers, including José de Manterola and Arturo Campión (1859-1937), awarded him a retirement pension. He died on April 6, 1881, and fulfilled the wish he had so often sung of:

> Jaunari eskatzen diot
> grazia emateko
> nere lur maite ontan
> ezurrak uzteko.[22]

> I pray that God
> grant me the grace
> of leaving my bones
> in this my beloved land.

His life story and his literary art remain in twenty-seven poetic compositions, some of which are immortal. His most famous works include "Gernikako arbola," "Kantari euskalduna" (The Basque bard), "Nere amak baleki," "Nere maitearentzat," "Agur euskal erriari" (Good-bye Basque Country), "Nere etorrera lur maiteari," and "Ezkongaietan."

Iparragirre's favorite themes were liberty, love of the Basque Country, and the ancient language of his ancestors. Unlike Xenpelar, who spoke always of three Basque provinces, Iparragirre made references to the four provinces including Nafarroa:

> Bat da gure izarra,
> bat gure bandera:
> esan beti Laurak-bat
> izan nai degula.[23]

> One is our star,
> one is our flag:
> Always say that we wish to be
> the four in one.

Iparragirre's style did not always follow the rules of aesthetics. He sometimes used colloquialisms and, on occasion, he even sacrificed correct grammar for poetic beauty. For example he once said: "Zibillak esan *naute*" instead of "Zibillak esan *didate*" (The civil guards have told me), the grammatically correct choice.

Miguel de Unamuno said of Iparragirre:

> In Iparragirre there is more feeling than imagination; his fame can be attributed as much to chance, and the time in which he related his work, as to his intrinsic merit. He was a poet due to his circumstances, and more than a poet, he was a musician.[24]

His best verses as a bertsolari perhaps come from "Ezkongaietan." These verses are sharp, humorous, and full of irony. At times the influence of the Bizkaian dialect is evident (as in his use of the word *bearra*, which means work only in Bizkaian), something not found in the verses of Gipuzkoan bertsolariak. In general, Iparragirre did not use a great variety of rhythms and rhymes. The rhythms he most frequently used were the zortziko handia and txikia (verses composed of eight lines with 10/8 and 7/6 syllables, respectively).

He used popular melodies for his first poems, including "Zugana manuela" (2/4 rhythm) and "Nere maitearentzat" (6/8 rhythm). Later he used the 5/8 rhythm, which was very common in the Basque Country. His melodies were well known and are frequently used today. Many of the melodies used, especially in "Ezkongaietan" and "Nere etorrera lur maiteari," are very beautiful. Iparragirre was the first bertsolari to use musical interludes in his verses.

Indalecio Bizkarrondo, Alias "Bilintx" (1831–1876)

The two most revered romantic bertsolariak in the Basque Country were José María Iparragirre and Bilintx. Iparragirre sang of the tragic suffering of his beloved Euskal Herria, which was on the verge of disappearing as a result of the loss of the fueros. Bilintx, on the other hand, sang of love, especially unrequited love, like no one else could.

Nineteenth-century Basque society was divided by the Carlist wars. Most Basques supported Don Carlos V de Borbón, but there were also many liberals, and Bilintx was one of them. The bertsolariak were divided along political lines: some were liberals and others were Carlists, but no one in these two groups was a Basque nationalist. However, there were some nationalists who were not interested in the conflict involving Don Carlos's bid for the throne, but followed him because he promised to honor the fueros. Bilintx enlisted as a volunteer in the battalion of the fourth company. Rather than fighting at the front, his duty was to remain in the villages to defend them against the enemy. The Carlists captured a large part of Gipuzkoa and bombed its capital.

Bilintx was born on April 30, 1831, in Donostia. His life was marked by tragedy. As a child he fell from the third floor of a building thereby acquiring a sunken chin and a disfigured face. As a consequence, he was known by the nickname "Moko" (beak). On another occasion, he was gored by a bull and nearly died.

When Bilintx was thirty-eight years old he married Nicolasa Erkizia. They had three children. He was a loving husband and an affectionate father, kind, honest, friendly, funny, loved by everyone, and resigned to all the calamities in his life. He was a carpenter by trade and also worked as doorman at the Teatro Viejo in Donostia where, with his wife's help, he sold newspapers and tobacco. He said that life "had given him many hard blows as if he were a rebellious donkey." Sometime during the early 1870s, eight thousand reales were stolen from him, which was quite a large sum of money at the time. On January 20, 1876, during the holiday honoring the patron saint of Donostia, Bilintx was at home when a grenade launched by Carlists went through his window and severely wounded him in both legs. He died of gangrene six months later, on July 21, 1876.[25] He was buried in the cemetery of Polloe in Donostia.

Although thirty-five of Bilintx's compositions have been preserved, many of his verses have been lost, perhaps forever. The works that we do possess are extant because of José de Manterola's interest and efforts.[26] Manterola saw Bilintx as a great folk poet and was able to salvage part of his work.

Bilintx's greatest weakness was his extreme modesty. It appears that he did not believe that his verses were of any value and did not want them published. On the other hand, this may have been a response to the conditions during the civil war that discouraged many poets from signing their verses for fear of persecution. There had never before been so much poetry about a war. Poets on both sides avoided signing their works so they could be published anonymously. Both of these reasons may explain the limited number of works attributed to Bilintx; however, the little we do have is enough to establish him as a great popular poet. When Miguel de Unamuno was asked to evaluate Basque poetry of the nineteenth century he wrote: "We may also say that we have two and a half poets: Iparragirre and Bilintx."[27]

Bilintx had little formal education, but he was blessed with a thirst for culture and great artistic sensitivity. He was an easily inspired poet of deep feelings and refinement. He was born to love. Nearly all of his poems reflect his kind and gentle character, the simpleness of his soul, and the purity of his feelings.

Bilintx's friends, José de Manterola and Benito Jamar, appreciated his great talent and acquainted him with the European poetic movements.[28] Bilintx, thirsty for poetic art, enthusiastically assimilated them. When Benito Jamar read to him the verses by German poet Heinrich Heine (1797-1856) that had been translated into Spanish, Bilintx listened eagerly. On his own, Bilintx read the works of Gustavo Bécquer (1836-1870), Ramón de Campoamor (1817-1901), and Antonio Trueba from Bilbo (1819-1889). He also wrote in Spanish as a correspondent for the Madrid newspaper *La Correspondencia de España*.

Even though Bilintx was a bertsolari, he was also a worldly and educated poet. Some people believe that his famous composition entitled "Domingo Kanpaña" was not improvised.[29] This raises a question about the degree to which Bilintx was an improvising bertsolari. There is no doubt that he was a great bertsolari of bertso jarriak. His written work is of extraordinary quality and occupies an important place in romantic bertsolaritza of the nineteenth century.

Bilintx certainly considered himself a bertsolari, as the following incident demonstrates. There was a female bertsolari named Joxepa who lived in Hondarribia. She was famous because Bilintx mentioned her in a verse. According to Bilintx she had no equal in all of the Basque Country. Apparently, though, she did not think very highly of him as a bertsolari from what he tells us in the following lines:

> Ni bertxolariya naiz
> bañan det aditu
> ez nitzaizula zuri
> ala iruritu.[30]

> I am a bertsolari
> but I have heard
> that you do not
> consider me as such.

Bilintx did know how to improvise. As an improviser he did not rank as high as Fernando Amezketarra, Xenpelar, Pello Errota, or Txirrita. This is due in part to two factors working against him: poor physical appearance and, therefore, poor stage presence; and a weak voice. As discussed earlier, these two factors are important for a bertsolari. He shared the same misfortune as Pello Mari Otaño, who was nicknamed "Katarro" (cold) because he had a poor voice. Both could have been great improvisers, but are known essentially for their written verses because they often avoided public performances. Another factor contributing to Bilintx's reputation as a bertsolari who wrote more than he performed is the fact that his improvised verses were not collected and consequently have been lost.

The thirty-five works that have been preserved include "Domingo Kanpaña," "Juana Bixenta Olabe," "Izazu nitzaz kupira," "¡Ja, jai!," and "Potajiarena." The themes he most frequently used involved love, morals, and ethics.

His love poems and humorous compositions made Bilintx famous. His love poems have a sweet, melancholy tone and a sad and doleful air. They reflect a soul lacerated by pain. The love in his verses is tinged with sadness because it is unrequited. He sang of love with more tenderness than anyone in the nineteenth century. His romantic heart opened wide and longed for love, affection, and friendship—a rare quality in earlier Basque writers. He wrote his love poems in the first person. Love was his inspiration in "Kontxesirentzat" (For Kontxesi), "Beti zutaz pensatzen" (Always thinking of you), "Juramentua" (The promise), "¡Ja, jai!" (No way!), and "Izazu nitzaz kupira" (Have mercy on me).

Humor, satire, and sarcasm are often present in "Domingo Kanpaña," "Zaldi baten bizitza" (The life of a horse), and "Potajiarena" (About porridge). This last poem deals with the humor of a Basque priest with a voracious appetite, but in no way reflects any type of anticlericalism in Bilintx's work. Although he did not portray himself as being as religious as Xenpelar, Urretxindor, or Xalbador, Bilintx was a man of deep Christian convictions.

Finally, his moral and ethical traits are evident in his verses "Pobriaren suertia" (The luck of the poor) and "Juana Bixenta Olabe." In the latter, a cunning notary tries to take advantage sexually of a village woman but is unable to overcome her dignified resistance. Later he repents and asks for her forgiveness. She agrees if he promises not to repeat his behavior. At that moment their roles are reversed: the young woman takes the role of judge and the notary becomes confused. He reveals his intentions to marry her and she agrees, but says that she must ask her mother's permission first. At the end they are married and Bilintx delivers a moral. In "Pobriaren suertia" he paints a painful picture of a poor man. Society lashes out at him in the form of those who see him and do not take pity, but rather flee from him or insult him.

Bilintx's style reflects the influence of earlier bertsolariak. He also learned a great deal from Spanish poets. However, his style was unique and Basque. In his own way he revised bertsolaritza according to the norms of the language spoken in Donostia and that of the literary movement of Donostia during the last third of the nineteenth century. His Euskara reflected phonetic peculiarities found in the language spoken by the common people of Donostia at that time. Examples include "Joshemari" (José María), "biyotza" (heart), and "janariya" (food). He also used many non-Basque words. However, his Euskara was refined and delicate. His images were beautiful and his verses were correctly constructed. Poetry came to him naturally and he composed verses effortlessly, propelled by a natural need to create.

Bilintx crafted verses in a very personal way that was sweet, gentle, and human. Verses came to him like song to a bird. Since he was a bertsolari *esko-*

latua, or educated in versemaking, his technique in both rhythm and rhyme was excellent. His written verses were very elaborate. He frequently used the rhythm pattern of zortziko txikia, the verse type of eight lines and 7/6 syllables. On rare occasions he used very long verses consisting of 15, 30, 40, or more lines. This practice was later adopted by Pello Mari Otaño, but never became very popular. Many bertsolariak, including Xenpelar and Txirrita, did not use this type of verse.

After Bilintx was fatally wounded in 1876, Madrid journalist M. Curros Enríquez wrote the following lines in the *Imparcial*, which offer even more proof that Bilintx's fame extended beyond the Pyrenees: "In Donostia we have an eminently popular poet. He is a native of this country, not extremely educated, but gifted with a precious talent."[31]

At the time of his death, the fueros also disappeared in spite of opposition from Basque representatives in Madrid's parliament.[32] Even though he held liberal ideas, and it was often the case that those with such ideas were nontraditional, Bilintx knew how to exalt the Basque language like very few could. His work in this field was appreciated by nationalistic bertsolariak including Pello Mari Otaño. The following words describe their regard and love for Bilintx:

> Gu aren aurrean gaude
> beti belauniko.
> Emendik joan zan baña
> ezta beñere ilko.[33]

> We remain here before him
> forever on bent knees.
> He is gone
> but he will never die.

PRERENAISSANCE (1876-1935)

The prerenaissance of bertsolaritza had a long transitional period that started at the end of the second Carlist War and lasted until the beginning of modern bertsolaritza. This period essentially developed around five central figures: Udarregi, Pello Errota, Txirrita, Urretxindor, and Pello Mari Otaño. However, there were also other very talented bertsolariak in this period, including Joxe Bernardo Otaño (1842-1912); Juan Lujanbio, alias "Saiburu" (1874-1954); Mattin from Senpere; Eusebio Eizmendi, alias "Txapel" (1893-1969);[34] and Akilino Izagirre, alias "Zepai" (1906-1971).[35] It was during this time period that the challenges between two artists disappeared, while bertso-paperak flourished.

New cultural events, such as the floral games emerged. The best bertsolariak competed in these contests, which forced artists to leave their native provinces and thereby extended bertsolaritza throughout the Basque Country.

Sessions in which more than four artists improvised began to gain in popularity. These events promoted improvisation because they obligated the bertsolari to create verses spontaneously before a panel of judges who made decisions and rewarded the best artist. The hometowns of Pello Errota and Pello Mari Otaño, Asteasu and Zizurkil (Gipuzkoa), respectively, became the new centers of bertsolaritza.

Basque society underwent a great change, especially in Bizkaia and Gipuzkoa, as a result of industrialization and Sabino Arana's newly created modern nationalism. Many bertsolariak, especially Pello Mari Otaño and Urretxindor, reflected this political change in their verses. Basque culture acquired new strength with two very different sources of artistic dispersion. One of these sources was created by José de Manterola in Donostia. The other was created by Sabino Arana in Bilbo. Bertsolaritza never declined in Gipuzkoa; however, the linguistic purism created by Sabino Arana conditioned and somewhat devalued the traditional bertsolaritza of the Gipuzkoan school.

Juan José Alkain, Alias "Udarregi" (1829–1895)

Udarregi was born to a family of poor laborers in Usurbil (Gipuzkoa). When his father, Juan Miguel Alkain, was sixty years old he was forced to emigrate to Buenos Aires in search of work, but he had no luck and made no money. He returned to the Basque Country where he had left his family and died at the age of ninety. He knew how to create verses, as we see in the following example in which he describes his journey to Argentina:

> Sosik baneuka Euskalerrira
> joango nitzake ostera,
> zer estadutan arkitzen naizen
> korputza erakustera.
> Familiya daukat urruti
> andriak ez nau erruki
> izurratu nau ederki! [36]

> If I had money I would go back to the Basque Country again,
> to show what a state
> my body is in.
> My family is far away,
> my wife has no compassion for me.
> She has really made me miserable. [paraphrase]

His son Udarregi began to improvise verses at an early age, like most bertsolariak. He became famous when he was older, primarily as a result of his participation in a contest that was part of the 1889 floral games organized by Antoine d'Abbadie in Azpeitia.

Udarregi was illiterate. He admitted (in a verse he wrote that is reproduced in Antonio Zavala's book about him) that the cider shops had been the school where he learned the art of bertsolaritza. We also know that he needed a sacristan to transcribe the verses he improvised. For paper, he used the old walls of the farmhouse attic, where he made a mark for each verse he composed.

He wrote many bertso-paperak, but he is especially famous for improvising. He was an authentic plaza gizona, always eager to perform for an audience. His main secret was the difficult rhythm pattern called bederatzi puntuko bertsoa. Zavala's *Azpeitiko premiyoaren bertsoak* (Verses from the Azpeitia award), contains seventy-two of Udarregi's verses composed in this complicated rhythm.[37]

His Euskara contained a surprising number of words of Spanish origin, such as *señaladamente*, *malamente*, and *pesadunbría*. He undoubtedly used these words to demonstrate his sophistication. At that time it was believed that using Spanish words gave Basque a special sonority. Many of these words are no longer used in bertsolaritza. At the end of the nineteenth century Udarregi was criticized by proponents of linguistic purity for using non-Basque words.

Udarregi's verses centered around traditional themes of the period, and in this respect he did not demonstrate much originality. His verses about a pilgrimage to Rome by a large group of Basques wanting to visit Pope Leo XIII varied slightly. He also focused attention on the suffering brought about by the Carlist Wars.

José Elizegi, Alias "Pello Errota" (1840–1919)

Pello Errota was the most clever bertsolari of his time. It is difficult to recognize this poor illiterate miller as the great bertsolari from Asteasu (Gipuzkoa) from a photograph we have of him. He possessed great ingenuity and a refined sense of humor, and was loved for his simplicity and humility. He was not ashamed to admit his lack of formal education to anyone:

> Orain astera guaz
> predikadoriak
> beñere kolejiyuan
> ibilli gabiak.[38]

> Now we will begin
> preachers
> who never went to school.

Pello Errota performed publicly many times in town squares, at festivals, and at the floral games. He was more suited for improvisation than for written verses and shone in public because of his mental quickness, witty humor, and ability to express his ideas clearly with few words. Udarregi recognized Pello Errota's superiority:

Lau probintzi oyetan
ori da jueza.[39]

In these four provinces
he is the authority.

He had the reputation of being a skilled bertsolari and was highly respected. His name was well known across the oceans and his voice extended to Latin America. When he was asked by the Basque community in Argentina to perform there, he went and spent ten months. He sadly described the loss of religious faith among many Basques in Argentina, in contrast with those in his hometown. His favorite themes included the description of Gipuzkoan rural life: work, religion, pastimes, and the hard times brought about by the second Carlist War.

Although he did not excel in written verse as did Xenpelar and Txirrita, bertsolaritza was his vocation. He improvised verse upon request and specialized in matters of the heart. Technically, he did not contribute anything new to the old school of Gipuzkoan bertsolaritza, but he was extraordinary in the field of improvisation.

Joxe Manuel Lujanbio, Alias "Txirrita" (1860–1936)

We finish our discussion of famous Gipuzkoan folk poets of the twentieth century with Txirrita, who is considered the patriarch of classical bertsolaritza. Txirrita was born on August 14, 1860, in the Ereñozu district of Hernani (Gipuzkoa) in a farmhouse called Latzezar. He spent most of his life at Txirrita, a farmhouse in Errenteria. During the last years of his life he lived at his nephew's farmhouse, Gazteluene, in Alza (Gipuzkoa). He died on June 3, 1936, when he was seventy-six years old.

Txirrita performed for the first time in his own town square when he was thirteen years old. Unlike his contemporary bertsolariak, he did not travel from town to town. Although he only performed in fifteen to twenty places each year, he participated in five to six bertsolaritza sessions a day. Txirrita was a bertsolari twenty-four hours a day. After performing in the plazas he spent the night improvising verses and drinking hard cider with his friends until the barrel ran dry.

As a bertsolari his style was a mixture of Fernando Amezketarra's extraordinary sense of humor and José María Iparragirre's sociable nature. He dressed in the traditional style, with a long smock and Basque beret. Toward the end of his life he used two canes to get around. He was a stonemason by vocation, but his real profession was bertsolaritza. He totally and unconditionally dedicated himself to being an artist, and he never retired from his role as a bertsolari.

He did not exhibit the same kind of diligence in stonemasonry. His maxim in his stonemasonry job was "sweet idleness" because he lacked dedication and was in the habit of living at other people's expense. As a young man he forfeited his right as firstborn to inherit the farmhouse and land that were lawfully his. He wandered from town to town without any money in his pockets, but was happy and full of cheer. He was always willing to improvise a verse in exchange for a drink of hard cider. He enjoyed betting, challenges, and rural sports. His friend Pello Errota described him as follows:

> Bestek ematen dirua eran
> berak ditunak gastatu
> aizkenerako gelditu oi da
> nun illundu an ostatu.[40]

> He spends the money that people give him
> and his own money drinking.
> Finally, he ends up
> wherever the night catches up with him. [paraphrase]

He was a born improviser, but he was also very talented as a writer of bertso-paperak. Antonio Zavala dedicated five volumes to him in his collection *Auspoa*.[41] The title of one of these illustrates the wealth of Txirrita's art: *Ustu ezin zan ganbara* (The attic that couldn't be emptied). Many of his written verses have been collected in a book by Juan José Makazaga called *Bertsolariyak*. Each week Txirrita wrote twelve to fourteen verses, most of which were specifically requested and provided him with money. Sometimes he even received requests from individuals in the north of the Basque Country.[42] The themes of these requested verses generally revolved around family problems, separations between spouses, and love relationships that disintegrated because of economic interests. In his verses Txirrita criticized and satirized the guilty parties. On some occasions, he had to respond to his own verses, because the "victims" of these satires asked him to write rebuttals.

Txirrita used a wide variety of themes. So much attention has been focused on his humorous side and his vagabond lifestyle that he has not been taken seriously. The truth is, however, that he was a chronicler of the times in which he lived because he described historical events and the Basque Country's sociopolitical situation. If there had been chroniclers and journalists like Txirrita prior to his time, there would not be so many gaps in the history of the Basque Country.

Txirrita sang of the loss of freedoms in the Basque Country with the revocation of the fueros, the war between the Romans and the Cantabrians, the Spanish-American War (1898), World War I, and the assassination of Spanish minister Antonio Cánovas del Castillo (1897). He also wrote about sports events (regattas and the boxing match between the Basque boxer Paulino Uzkudun and the world champion Joe Louis), religious events (Adam and Eve, the missions of Goizueta, the pope, the lives of the saints, the supposed apparitions of the Virgin in Ezkioga, Gipuzkoa), and social events (strikes in the port at Pasaia and Basque emigration to America).

The Roman-Cantabrian War

Txirrita provides us with so many details about the Roman-Cantabrian war it was as if he had been there personally. He maintained that the Cantabrians were Basques who were fighting for their freedom.[43] Although this is what was traditionally believed, in reality the Basques lived peacefully with the Romans for many centuries. It is also true that many Basques made up part of the Roman legions. We must recognize that bertsolariak are not modern historians who meticulously examine historical data. They are simply spokesmen for their people and sing of their beliefs. Txirrita also spoke of the seven provinces of the Basque Country.

The Assassination of Antonio Cánovas del Castillo

Txirrita's life was deeply affected by the defeat of the Basques in the second Carlist War and the subsequent loss of freedoms. In 1876, when Txirrita was sixteen years old, a decree was issued by Antonio Cánovas, the Spanish president at the time, that totally abolished the Basque fueros. Cánovas was assassinated at the Saint Agate hot springs in Arrasate (Gipuzkoa). The majority of teachers in the Basque school system were Castilians who persecuted speakers of the Basque language by punishing students who spoke in Euskara. This practice was criticized by Juan Ignacio Iztueta as early as the beginning of the nineteenth century. It was also condemned later by Urretxindor and Xalbador. Txirrita strongly condemned the punishments to which Basque children were subjected:

> Eskola erderazkuak
> maisu geienak kastillanuak . . .
> itz bat euskeraz aditzen bada
> autsi biarrik kaskuak.[44]

> The schools are in Spanish,
> most of the teachers are Castilian
> if they hear a word of Euskara
> they rap [the children] on the head.

Txirrita's patriotism is evident in the harsh attitude he maintained toward Cánovas even after his death. He did not utter his name while he was alive, but after Cánovas's death, Txirrita no longer feared any repercussions and harshly attacked him for annihilating Basque liberties. He used the word *galdu* (to lose) five times in a ten-line verse:

> Il da Canovas, fuera Canovas
> pikaro gaizki eziya
> galdu zituen gari-zelaiak
> gallendu zaio sasiya;

galdu zituen ipar garbiyak
gallendu trumoi nasiya,
galdu zituen fueruak eta
Jaungoikuaren graziya,
galdu zituen bizilekuak,
galdu du bere biziya.[45]

Cánovas is dead, out with Cánovas,
ill-bred villain,
he destroyed the wheat fields,
he vanquished the thistles;
he banished the clean breezes,
he brought turbulent torment,
he eliminated our fueros
and the grace of God,
he destroyed our homes
he lost his life.

Txirrita's idea of nationalism did not include the independence of the Basque Country, as proposed by Urretxindor. He did, however, believe in constantly defending the fueros.

Beste gauzarik ez dugu eskatzen:
biba lengo fuero zarrak.[46]

We ask for only one thing:
Long live the old fueros from before!

The Spanish-American War

Txirrita condemned the Spanish-American War for two reasons. Under a provision in the fueros that had previously been honored by the Spanish kings, Basques were not obligated to fight any war outside their own territory.[47] Military service was not obligatory as it now is:

Lenago etzan kintik tiratzen
gure sor-leku maitian.[48]

Before, they didn't call us to the service
in our dear homeland.

When Basque liberties disappeared, however, because of the revocation of the fueros, military service became mandatory. Many young Basque soldiers lost their lives in the Spanish-American War, a conflict that was of no concern to the Basque people:

Zenbait amaren seme onradu
Cuba'n sartu zan lurpian;
guraso askok negar egin du . . .

geinak lutuz jantzi giñaden
Kantabriya'ko partian.[49]

How many mothers' sons
were buried in Cuba,
many parents wept . . .
most of us were dressed in mourning
in the Cantabrian region.

He also condemned the war because it seemed that rich families used their
wealth to exempt their sons from serving in the military:

Aberats askok pagatzen
zuen soldadu juan zenbait pobre.[50]

Many rich people paid
[while] the poor went as soldiers.

World War I (1914-1918)

Txirrita confessed to being a supporter of the Allies.
He praised French marshal Ferdinand Foch (1851-1929), who in his opinion
deserved a statue, as well as the Americans and the English. He provided many
details about World War I. He related a story that a German told him about the
kaiser's ruling Paris, he described the power of German submarines and zep-
pelins, and he spoke about the French bravery at Verdun.[51]

Social Issues

As mentioned earlier, Txirrita was an unskilled
stonemason. In his verses he described labor problems and social vindication.
He spoke of the proletariat and the dock workers' strike in Pasajes Ancho
(Gipuzkoa) from a new perspective. During the 1919 strike, workers from Oiar-
tzun protested that they were not being hired. Txirrita complained about a
Basque contractor who spoke Euskara but hired non-Basque workers rather
than Basques:

Biba euskera!, maiz oju egin
kastillanuak ekarri.[52]

Always shouting, "Long live Euskara!,"
but hiring Castilians.

Txirrita was endowed with a great deal of natural talent although he could
not read or write. He knew only a few words in Spanish and used them to lend
sonority to his verses, as had Udarregi. Txirrita's bertsolaritza followed in the
tradition of Xenpelar. They both based their art on Basque oral poetry. This was

their source of inspiration. There is no trace of written tradition or any connection with written literature in Txirrita's work because he was completely illiterate. The cider shops were the only schools he was able to attend, as had been the case for Udarregi and Pello Errota. Txirrita was a villager and never identified himself with the city.

Most of his verses are written in zortziko handia (10/8) and txikia (7/6). He also used ten-line-verses, but avoided the complicated bederatzi puntuko bertsoa. As mentioned earlier, Txirrita was a narrator and chronicler, and he needed these verses to describe events without restrictions. In addition, his poems are generally long, consisting of twelve to twenty-one verses, an adequate number to deal with the extensive themes he wished to narrate.

On the surface, his verses seem simple, and that is where his uniqueness lies. Txirrita created verses as if he were speaking, without forcing vocabulary or syntax. One verse followed another as if they were waves at sea. The poet Gabriel Aresti described Txirrita's popularity by stating that "he is not the greatest bertsolari, but he is the most 'bertsolari-ish' of all bertsolariak."[53]

Txirrita stands out for his humor, his quickness, and his mastery of this literary art. In addition to being a chronicler, he was like a photographer who created an instant image, a portrait of a person or a situation with just a few words.

The Basque language served as the perfect instrument for his art. He mastered Euskara without ever having attended school. In everyday conversation he always used Basque words, but when improvising verses in public he sometimes turned to words of Spanish origin, for example *amigo, aturditurik* (from *aturdir*, or to stun), and *prezisamente*. This practice was a reflection of the Basque culture in which he lived. One only has to look through Basque prayer books of the period, for example, to see that Basque was peppered with non-Basque words. Txirrita was an apologist for his language:

> Gau eta egun nere buruan
> bueltaka dabilt euskera
> jaio ta iru urte baño len
> ikasi nuen izkera;
> altxa gogotik kuidado gabe,
> gu zure kontra ezgera,
> lenago maite izan zaitugu
> ta oraiñ ez guaz uztera.[54]

> Day and night,
> in my head Euskara goes round and round.
> I learned the language
> before I turned three.
> Unwillingly and unexpectedly it emerges.
> We aren't against you,
> we loved you before,
> and we won't abandon you now.

Txirrita's mastery of Euskara was accompanied by a refined sense of humor. His verses dedicated to the Irun-Madrid railroad train are exceptional. He personifies inanimate objects and describes a dialogue between the steam boiler and the boiling water it holds inside.[55]

Humor is one of the most important characteristics of Txirrita's style. Txirrita and Pello Errota once made fun of each other in a public performance. It was well known that Txirrita was a confirmed bachelor. With this in mind, Pello Errota commented with irony about Txirrita's recent visit with his girl-friend in which she gave him two shirts. In turn, Txirrita responded by pointing out that the humble miller, Pello Errota, was poor:

> Pello Errota: Dudarik gabe egina dio
> andregaiari bisita
> oso dotore etorri zaigu
> bi alkondara jantzita.
>
> Without a doubt he has
> visited his girlfriend.
> He has come to us dressed elegantly wearing
> two shirts.
>
> Txirrita: Bi alkandora ekarri ditut
> bat eraztia aztuta
> Pellok bi nola jantziko ditu
> bat besterikan eztuta.[56]
>
> I'm wearing two shirts
> because I forgot to take one off.
> How could Pello wear two [shirts]
> if he only has one.

Sometimes Txirrita's style was dramatic. He could be stern when a situation called for it and would thus echo the feelings of the people, who did not forget the injustices or abuses of power. For example, a soldier by the name of Diostegi murdered a shepherd in the hills of Hernani in 1885. The body was found, but the courts could do nothing about Diostegi because he was a soldier. As years went by Diostegi became so old and feeble that he needed two canes to get around. He lived alone and abandoned and had to beg in order to survive. This was the only revenge of a people that could not find justice. One day the old soldier found himself face to face with Txirrita in a tavern. Txirrita's normally jovial disposition turned dark, and he became a judge who relentlessly condemned the criminal. He delivered two verse lines like two hard blows:

> Beste munduan ikusiko du
> emen hil zuen artzaya . . .
> Zu baño gizon formalagoa zan
> zuk il zenduen artzaya.[57]

In the next world he will see
the shepherd he killed here . . .
He was a more honest man than you,
the shepherd you murdered.

Kepa Enbeita, Alias "Urretxindor" (1878-1942)

Urretxindor was the first great bertsolari born in
Bizkaia. Although bertsolaritza was never as widespread in this province as it
was in Gipuzkoa, the birth of this art form in Bizkaia was not merely an at-
tempt to copy its neighboring province. There were precedents: the verses of
the war canticles from the Middle Ages, which were written in the Bizkaian
dialect; and the Bizkaian art of versemaking associated with the kopla zaha-
rrak. In some regions of Bizkaia, including Arratia and Txorierri, there has
always been a strong tradition of singing kopla zaharrak with the tambourine
and accordion. The practice has survived with more vigor in Bizkaia than in
other provinces. On the other hand, the long verse known as zortziko handia,
which is frequently used in Gipuzkoa, was completely unknown in Bizkaia. It
was Urretxindor who introduced this verse type in his home province.

Urretxindor was born in a farmhouse called Usparitxa in the Areatza zone
of Muxika (Bizkaia). As a child he attended the local school, but soon had
to abandon his studies because the teacher severely punished the children for
speaking Euskara. One day, after young Kepa was punished, he threw the ring
he was forced to wear—the symbol used to identify a naughty child—onto the
roof of the parish church and never again returned to school. From that point
on, nature was his classroom. He was brought up in a family with seven chil-
dren that earned its living from farming and basketry.

Urretxindor was known for his kindness, religious faith, and his Basque
patriotism. In 1919 he fell ill with a lung condition and had to travel to Bias-
teri (Araba) every year thereafter to convalesce. The beginning of the civil
war found him there. In 1939 he returned to his farmhouse; he died there on
December 12, 1942.

Urretxindor's enthusiasm for bertsolaritza was inherited and passed down
by him. His father, brothers, sons, and grandsons were bertsolariak, but he was
the most famous and admired member of the family.[58] His artistic contributions
can be divided into two periods.

First Period (1897–1904)

While he was still quite young Urretxindor became
a plaza gizona and participated in many competitions. When he was nineteen
he was awarded second place in the Durango contest, and in 1903 he won a
very important contest held in Las Arenas-Getxo (Bizkaia). The latter marked

his coming of age as a bertsolari because he performed with such great artists as Txirrita, Pello Errota, Frantses-Txikia, and Aizarna. No one ever thought a Bizkaian would be able to compete with the Gipuzkoan bertsolariak. His victory and his later works make him worthy of his title as the first great Bizkaian bertsolari.[59]

During this period, Urretxindor was known as a great improviser who used his Bizkaian dialect well, both vocabulary and verb forms. He was very popular, spontaneous, and full of creativity. Dressed in his traditional black pants, beret, and white shirt, he was recognized throughout the Basque Country. The quality of his verses entitled "Bei zarren bertsuak" (Verses dedicated to an old cow) is sufficiently high to distinguish him as an outstanding spontaneous improviser.[60]

Second Period (1905–1936)

In later years, Urretxindor strayed to a great extent from traditional bertsolaritza. His role as an improviser diminished as his art evolved. He aspired to transcend the boundaries of bertsolaritza to become an olerkari. In reality, he remained in an intermediate area that critic and writer Santiago Onaindia (1909–) refers to as *oleskari*.[61]

Urretxindor's artistic evolution was brought about by his friendship with the town doctor, Juan Bautista Arrospide, who had been friends with Sabino Arana, the founder of modern Basque nationalism.[62] The linguistic and political revolution led by Sabino Arana was a revelation for the young bertsolari.[63] The new standards for spelling, the creation of new words, lexical purity, and the elimination of words of non-Basque origin affected Urretxindor's improvised bertsolaritza, causing him to become an atypical bertsolari with a slightly artificial quality to his verses.

The political ideas of Sabino Arana and the possibility of an autonomous and independent Basque Country also affected Urretxindor. As a bertsolari, he dedicated himself to the service of the Partido Nacionalista Vasco (also referred to as PNV, the Basque Nationalist Party). He actively participated in meetings with such politicians as José Antonio Agirre, president of the Basque Country, and educated poets like Esteban Urkiaga, alias "Lauaxeta" (1905-1937). Urretxindor's presence charged the spirits of those nationalists who looked forward to a Christian and independent Euskadi. Other nationalist groups that sympathized with the PNV listened to Urretxindor with fervor and sometimes hoisted him onto their shoulders like a victorious bullfighter. All of this made him spokesperson of the cultural and political movement and of the literary renaissance of that time. With his beautiful voice, he enthralled people as he spoke of the beauty of Euskara and of the benefits of a free nation. Urretxindor transmitted culture that was in turn cultivated by the people of the Basque Country.

Among Urretxindor's many strengths was the fact that he added a new dimension to bertsolaritza by taking it out of the cider shops and taverns and placing it in the public squares, theaters, and performance halls. The young Basarri was also active in the movement to transform bertsolaritza into a source of culture for the common people. Urretxindor was so involved in this new movement that he practically abandoned improvisation at festivals. On the rare occasions that he did participate in these events, he was accompanied by Esteban Uriarte, Basarri, and his son Balendin. Urretxindor did not enter the 1935 or 1936 txapelketak. He did, however, write poetry on a weekly basis for Basque magazines, including *Aberri, Ekin, Euzkadi, Euzkerea, Gure Herria, Jaungoiko-Zale,* and *Karmen'go Argia.*

The Basque Country itself was one of his favorite themes. "Urretxindor" means nightingale and, in truth, he was like a bird that never stopped singing for forty years. He sang of rural life, the traditional problems facing the Basque Country, nature, his homeland, his language, and the writers who had glorified it. He also delved into the modern problems of Euskal Herria. As a bertsolari, Urretxindor is considered the spokesperson of his generation.

Homeland

For Urretxindor, the homeland did not consist of three provinces, as it had for Xenpelar. He also disagreed with Iparragirre, who saw the Basque Country as the union of the four southern provinces. Urretxindor saw Euskal Herria as seven provinces that formed a nation. His most famous patriotic poems include "Abesti abertzalia" (Patriotic song), "Aberrijaren ziñopea" (Patriotic oath), "Ai, ze ederra" (How beautiful), "Beste ames bat . . ." (Another dream . . .), and "Il zan Aberrija biztuteko" (To revive the dead homeland). In these verses his political beliefs are clearly displayed and mirror the ideology of Sabino Arana. Through his poetry, Urretxindor communicates the idea that in the past the Basque people were free, and their representatives met beneath the tree of Gernika to govern their country in accordance with the fueros and ancient customs. Euskadi had been recently stripped of its freedom. Sabino Arana shook the Basque people from their state of political lethargy. He was the Basque Country's chosen son and his death was Euskadi's darkest day. However, Arana's death did not cause the Basques to lose hope in his message of freedom for the Basque Country.

Nature

Urretxindor carefully observed nature from his farmhouse and found poetic inspiration in its smallest details. He even described the onomatopoeic sounds of a bird's trill: "txorrotxioka . . . txiroliroli . . . urrugurruka." [64] He was enamored of the beautiful landscape of Euskadi:

> Aran, baso ta mendijak,
> zugazti, zelai, aitz, iturriak
> landa ta lorategijak,
> solo ederrak arto ta gari [65]

Valleys, forests, and mountains
orchards, meadows, rocks, fountains
fields and flower beds
beautiful gardens, corn and wheat.

The Basque Language

Euskara should be the language of the Basque country—it is the most beautiful flower in that lovely garden. Other languages are useful, but for the Basques, Euskara is superior. Urretxindor felt optimistic that enemies would never be able to destroy this ancient language. He dedicated some ten poems to his native tongue. A person born in the Basque Country who does not speak Euskara is considered a foreigner. Euskara was Urretxindor's great love:

Nire maitia Euzkerea da
beti nabil bere bila.[66]

Euskara is my love
I am always searching for her.

Basque Writers

Basque writers have played a key role in maintaining and honoring Euskara. Urretxindor identified the following writers as being very important: Pablo Pedro Astarloa (1752-1806); Emeterio Arrese (1869-1954); Lizardi; Isaac López Mendizabal (1879-1977); and Ebaista Bustintza, alias "Kirikiño" (1866-1929).

An important ingredient in Urretxindor's style was his use of images. He used them often and with great success. His versemaking technique was free of errors. He used familiar rhythms like zortziko handia and txikia and bederatzi puntuko bertsoa as well as new ones: 7/5, 7/7, 8/6, and 8/8 (where the first figure indicates the number of syllables in odd lines and the second figure indicates the number of syllables in even lines). Some of his melodies were popular tunes, some were revised versions of melodies borrowed from Xenpelar and Bilintx, and others were original creations. He used his own melodies mostly with verses of 8 and 10 lines. He employed approximately twenty-five different melodies when improvising.

At the time of his death his fame extended to Latin America. The great Argentine poet Leopoldo Lugones (1874-1938) dedicated the following poem to Urretxindor:[67]

I salute the free bard Pedro de Enbeita the Basque . . .
I salute him in remembrance of the homeland worthy of
    all glory.
I salute him in remembrance of the fruit of the tree of Gernika,

I salute him in remembrance of the fuero of honor and justice,
Pedro de Enbeita, the Basque! Long live liberty! [68]

RENAISSANCE (1935-1968)

Traditional bertsolaritza disappeared with the death
of Txirrita shortly before the Spanish Civil War. The public's attitude about
bertsolaritza was changing during this time. Requirements for themes, tech-
nique, and language were becoming stricter. The txapelketak of 1935 and 1936
became a part of the cultural renaissance. Aitzol, Manuel Lekuona, and Juan
José Makazaga were instrumental in educating the public about the new di-
rection of bertsolaritza.

Bertsolaritza was no longer practiced in the cider shops; instead, perfor-
mances could be found in such new public arenas as plazas, handball courts,
theaters, movie houses, and churches. At this time bertsolariak also began to
use the media: radio, books, magazines, and newspapers. More culture and
knowledge spread through these media. New techniques and a greater variety
of melodies emerged.

Although there were no breakthroughs in bertso-paperak during this
period, improvisation reached great heights. Txapelketak became popular per-
formance events because they were brief and well organized.

Ignacio Eizmendi, Alias "Basarri" (1913-   )

Basarri was born on November 27, 1913, in Granada-
Erreka, a farmhouse in Errezil (Gipuzkoa), where he lived until he was six
years old. When he started school, he resided in Azpeitia for two years. He later
moved to Zarauz with his family where he has since lived except for three years
during the Spanish Civil War and the time he spent in exile. His parents opened
a bar, the Azken Portu, in Zarauz, which was frequented by many bertsolariak
including Frantses-Txikia and Juan Ignacio Goikoetxea, alias "Gaztelu" (1908-
1986).[69] His father also enjoyed singing the verses of the old bertsolariak. By the
time he was ten years old he knew many popular verses and melodies. Basarri
performed for the first time at a very young age in the plaza of Zestoa. He was
nervous and not at all convinced that he wanted to be there.

By the time he was twelve years old he concluded that Txirrita's type of
bertsolaritza did not fit into the modern world. The young Basarri hoped to
elevate this form of literary art to a more prestigious level. Bertsolaritza had
fallen into disregard among most Basques. Bertsolariak were too often viewed
as crude buffoons who made people laugh. The case of Frantses-Txikia, who
lived in an alcoholic stupor and was found dead at the side of a road, only
served to reinforce that negative image.

Basarri was influenced by two bertsolariak in particular. He adopted Pello Mari Otaño as a role model because of his bertso jarriak. In Basarri's opinion Otaño never wrote a bad verse. His other role model was Urretxindor, with whom he performed on several occasions. From him he learned the art of plaza-gizona, patriotism, and the necessity of varying themes and performance locations. He also learned how to deal with themes in a concise manner from Urretxindor, who never composed a dishonest or unfair verse. The respect enjoyed by modern bertsolariak is in great part due to Basarri's efforts to restore prestige to the art form. Modern bertsolariak, in general, follow the guidelines Basarri established.

The 1935 txapelketa marked a crossroads in bertsolaritza and revealed a new style different from that of the aging Txirrita. The trend was much more than a shifting of performances from the cider shops to theaters. Radical changes were occurring. Txirrita represented Basque culture during a period of decline, while Basarri was the spokesperson for a new culture on the verge of birth. Basarri, who was twenty-one at the time, won first prize in this contest, while Txirrita, at seventy-six years of age, ranked fifth.

The cultural change represented by Basarri required that a bertsolari study, read books, and use sources for obtaining information. Basarri began to write for *Zeruko Argia* when he was eighteen. He later wrote for other magazines and Basque newspapers including *Euzkadi, Argia, Eguna,* and *El Día*. He was the bertsolari who made the greatest contributions toward restoring improvised bertsolaritza. His influence was very important throughout the renaissance period.

The Basque cultural renaissance was drastically shortened by the Spanish Civil War. Basarri enlisted as a soldier in the Loiola battalion. When the war was over he left Bizkaia and went first to Santander, and later to France. During his exile in France he worked in Landes. Upon his return to the Basque Country he was punished and assigned to a labor battalion, with duty in Miranda, Madrid, Oiartzun, Palencia, and Melilla. He finally obtained his liberty and was able to return to Zarauz after a six-year absence.

The decade following the war was extremely hard on Basque culture because of Franco's relentless dictatorship. During these difficult years artistic spontaneity was crippled by censorship and fear of reprisal. No one was permitted to address a political subject in public. One of Basarri's friends was quoted as saying: "Kristalezko eskaileran ibiltzen jakin behar dik" (You have to know how to climb a glass staircase).[70]

Under these delicate circumstances it appeared that some aspects of Basque culture hid as if in catacombs, while other aspects were forced into exile. It was during this time that the team of Basarri and Uztapide generated great enthusiasm for bertsolaritza among the Basque people. Their performances became an integral part of local festivals throughout the Basque Country.

Basarri also developed his skills in journalism, his favorite hobby for forty years. He began writing for the newspapers *La Voz de España* and *Diario Vasco,* covering Basque rural sports, bertsolaritza events, and sports wagers. He combined this work with his job as a radio announcer. For thirty years Basarri was able to broadcast in Euskara on Gipuzkoan radio stations. In a period when Euskara was heard mainly in church, Basarri found a way to give de facto language lessons on the radio using a popular Euskara that was spontaneous and refined, in spite of the dictatorship. The Basque people, especially in Gipuzkoa, awaited these broadcasts like they waited for rain in the summer.

His love of reading, his good memory, and his excellent library served him well in his endeavors.[71] Basarri was able to attend school for only a very short time, but he learned on his own because he was eager for culture and education. These circumstances helped him adapt to the demands of modern times.

When he failed to win the 1962 txapelketa, Basarri decided not to participate in any more contests. He did, however, compete in 1968 in another competition for bertsolariak called "bertsolariak first prize," which he and Xalbador won. Basarri currently channels his energies into writing and has published the following collections of poetry: *Ataño III* (1949), *Basarriren bertso-sorta* (Collection of poems by Basarri, 1950), *Kantari nator* (My songbook, 1960), *Laugarren txinpartak* (Fourth poetry book, 1966), *Sortu zaizkidanak* (My creations, 1973), *Kezka giroan* (Amidst troubled times, 1983), and *Bertsolaritzari buruz* (About bertsolaritza, 1984).

His thoughts about bertsolaritza, Euskara, and Basque culture are revealed to us in these books and in his journalistic work. He regards the Basque farmhouse as the bastion of the Basque language and traditional Basque values. Basarri has always sung the praises of the *baserri* (Basque farmhouse). It was no accident that he chose Basarri as his nickname:

> Euskal baserri aintzagarriak,
> gure oñarri lerdenak . . .
> gure izkuntzaren gordetzallerik
> bikañen da sendoenak . . .
> O, kaletarroak, txapela erantzi
> iñoiz mendira joatean,
> baserri zabal urtez jantziak
> aurrez aurre ikustean.[72]

> Glorious Basque farmhouses
> our splendid foundation . . .
> the most excellent and enduring
> guardians of our language . . .
> O, countrymen, take off your beret in respect
> whenever you go to the mountains
> and see the farmhouses
> before you, shrouded in time.

Maintaining these beliefs, Basarri's views on the future of Euskara, bertsolaritza, *ikastolak* (Basque schools), and bertsolaritza schools clash with those of many of the younger generation. Basarri is conservative because of his age and generation. He makes several valid points when he maintains that bertsolariak must think *in* Basque and think *as* Basques and must possess certain innate qualities to be true performers. He attributes the decline of traditional Euskara to the influences of industrialization. However, his views on other subjects are limited. He is pessimistic about the future of the Basque language, the work that is being carried out in schools of bertsolaritza, and the relevance of Euskara Batua. In this respect he is holding onto the traditional values of the past, rather than facing the challenges of modern life.

Basarri is a natural-born bertsolari and although he is accomplished, he is not a learned poet. When he was a young man he came to the realization that the refined poetry of Lizardi and Lauaxeta rarely reached the general public. He opted for bertsolaritza because it was a popular poetry for the rural community, unpretentious, and did not require a great deal of formal education. Basarri is an accomplished teacher of bertsolaritza with a specific goal—to be understood and to communicate a message to the community:

> If there is anything that is deeply rooted among us, it is, without a doubt, bertsolaritza. I prefer not composing verses to composing them in such a way that they would prove incomprehensible to the community.[73]

One of his most outstanding talents is the ability to maintain the thread of the story in his verses. He is a great narrator who never exhausts a topic. At festival performances he also proves to be an excellent competitor. He is skilled at preparing the groundwork so that his opponent can easily follow the discourse. Uztapide, Xalbador, and Jon Azpillaga have followed his example.

Basarri is a serious and very humane bertsolari. He refrains from using satire or rough language. In his work one can detect the influence of forty years of dictatorship, during which he had to perform a balancing act similar to that of a circus trapeze artist. He expounds without being unpleasant, narrates without being offensive, and describes without being abrasive. Instead of criticizing, he prefers to exalt the beauty of Euskara and Basque country life. This is the world that provided him with themes for his art. Basarri was never comfortable with political topics. He suffered a great deal when he was forced to work with them.

Basarri is very conscientious about the techniques he uses in his verses. There is generally no betelana (empty verse lacking in logic) in his work. He embellishes his verses well with images and comparisons, clearly focusing on the themes and carefully choosing the details. He usually averages ten to twelve verses to develop a theme.

Manuel Olaizola, Alias "Uztapide" (1909–1983)

In this century perhaps no bertsolari has been as much loved by the people and by other artists as the Gipuzkoan Uztapide. His humility and unpretentious manner were attractive. Xalbador once called Uztapide the best friend he had in his lifetime.[74] Uztapide was a sensitive, honest, and kind man. He was shy by nature and appeared somewhat reserved during morning performances. He felt more relaxed and open during the afternoon sessions. On an artistic level, to date he has been the only bertsolari to win three national txapelketak: 1962, 1965, and 1967. In 1980 he was very ill and was unable to compete in the competition won by Xabier Amuriza. Uztapide was born on May 10, 1909, in a farmhouse bearing the name Uztapide in Zestoa (Gipuzkoa). He began to improvise verses at a very early age and had his first public performance at the 1936 txapelketa, where he took second place even though he deserved first.[75]

The Spanish Civil War broke out that same year, and Uztapide found himself at the battlefront. After the conflict ended he began to improvise verses again. For twenty-six years he was the inseparable friend of Basarri, and together they traveled throughout the Basque Country. Uztapide established himself as a folk poet, singer of nature, lover of Euskara, and proponent of the small nation that refused to disappear.

The 1962 txapelketa was Uztapide's rite of passage as a bertsolari. At that time Basarri was considered the indisputable champion. His work was culturally superior to all other bertsolariak and no one dared to strip him of the champion's beret. However, on this occasion Uztapide gave a magnificent performance and won the competition. He later went on to win two more times. He also participated in all manner of contests and competitions, thereby enhancing festivals and fomenting interest in bertsolaritza. While performing at the handball court of Anoeta in Donostia on May 10, 1972, Uztapide experienced a small stroke that left him unable to speak. In spite of three attempts to continue singing, he finally had to withdraw. He later recovered the ability to speak. During the last decade of his life he merely existed, unable to lead a normal life or perform as a bertsolari. He died on June 8, 1983, and many Basques grieved his death as the loss of a family member. With Uztapide's demise, the Basque Country lost one of its greatest ambassadors of popular culture. Posthumously Euskaltzaindia named him as an honorary member, not for his erudition or academic achievements, but rather for the exceptional contribution he made to oral and popular literature.

Uztapide's written work is a poor reflection of his skill as an improviser. He always defined himself as an artist of improvisation. Unfortunately many of his improvised verses were not recorded and no trace of them remains. He did, however, leave behind three books. Two of them are written in verse: *Noizbait* (At last, 1964), and *Sasoia joan da gero* (In the autumn of life, 1976). His memoirs, *Lengo egunak gogoan* (Remembering past days, 1975) are written in prose. Uztapide was not a man of much formal education, but the prose in his book demonstrates that he had a talent for words and was a great narrator. He used his native Gipuzkoan dialect to create a rich and detailed writing style. His text is filled with many idioms, witticisms, images, and analogies.

In *Sasoia joan da gero* Uztapide demonstrated that, in addition to being an improviser, he was also a *bertso-jartzaile*, or creator of written popular verse. Since he was ill when he wrote the book, it does not reflect his best work.

Repetition of certain ideas is evident and some parts are artistically weaker than others. Even so, this book is the product of an extraordinary bertsolari.

The fact that Uztapide was a folk artist is fundamental to his style. Nature and the older bertsolariak were his teachers. In spite of his solemn demeanor, he had a good sense of humor. The influence of traditional forms is evident in his humor. He inspired genuine laughter without using potentially hurtful satire. He was deeply humane and tender. At times he appeared as a comedian who even laughed at himself. On one occasion a friend said that Uztapide's ears were his only shortcoming because they were very large. The bertsolari replied that they were not a *shortcoming* but rather a *surplus*. His witty remarks contained the mischievousness of an inoffensive child.

Uztapide's art was highly regarded by his fellow bertsolariak. These men, along with critics and many enthusiasts, considered him to be the greatest un-educated classic bertsolari of his day. His friend Xalbador defined him as *bertso-laririk osona*, or the most complete bertsolari of our time.[76]

Uztapide was very skilled at choosing his topics and the appropriate words for each situation. He always knew just the right thing to say in each town. This careful backgrounding is the key to understanding how Uztapide made history as a bertsolari, both as an individual and with his partner, Basarri. He will be remembered as a legendary and mythic figure of bertsolaritza, compa-rable to Fernando Amezketarra and Xenpelar. During the postwar period he and Basarri became the resounding voice of a people who had been silenced.

Uztapide improvised verses with great ease. He regarded the activity as pleasure rather than work. He was confident and possessed extraordinary elo-quence. His reflexes were very quick in responding to questions. Once when asked "How many wheels does a good train have?" he answered, almost with-out thinking, with the following verse:

> Jakitia nai dunak
> azpira begitu;
> jarritako guziak
> or izango ditu:
> baldin norbaitek orain
> kendu ezpaditu.[77]

> He who wants to know
> should look underneath it;
> there it should have
> all that were put on it,
> if someone
> hasn't taken them off.

Uztapide possessed a great talent for beginning a topic and logically devel-oping it until the end. He always saved the best line for last, in order to get a big round of applause from his audience. In the section called ofizioak, in which two bertsolariak compete against each other, his favorite tactics were logical argumentation and subtle irony. He generally used eight-line verses composed of 7/6 and 10/8 syllables.

Among his many strengths it is noteworthy that, in addition to being a model bertsolari in the old tradition, he served as a bridge between the older bertsolariak and the new generation of young artists, who perceived him as a father and teacher. Many of his improvised verses are worthy of inclusion in an anthology. Those dedicated to his mother and the baptismal font of his village are good examples.[78]

Balendin Enbeita (1906-1986)

Balendin Enbeita's greatest contribution to bertsolaritza was his promotion of the art form in Bizkaia. He was responsible for founding the Basque Country's first school of bertsolaritza in his village tavern. It produced several great bertsolariak, including his son Jon Enbeita and Jon Lopategi. Twelve bertsolariak met every Saturday from 1958 to 1959 to receive his instruction. At each session they improvised verses and read the ones written the week before.[79] Enbeita honored his ancestors by carrying on this family tradition.

Balendin was born in a farmhouse called Usparitxa. His grandfather (Juan Antonio Enbeita, alias "Txotxojeuri"), his father (Urretxindor), and his two uncles (Imanol and Xanti) spent hours improvising verses. Balendin Enbeita was five years old when he sang his first verse, one that he had memorized. As a child he preferred improvising verses with his grandfather in the kitchen, because he was in awe of his father's talent. He had his first public performance as a bertsolari in Eibar when he was eighteen years old. When he was twenty-three he won a competition in Mungia and went on to win the next year in Getxo. He was married at the age of twenty-nine. Today three of his sons improvise verses in competitions and the other three compose bertso jarriak.

Between 1931 and 1935 Enbeita participated in political meetings with his father and the bertsolari Esteban Uriarte, as well as Basque politicians José Antonio Agirre (who became the first president of the Basque Country) and Manuel Irujo (who first served as minister in the Basque Country's government and later in the Spanish government), and poet Lauaxeta. In 1932 he went on a four-day tour of all the Basque provinces with Basarri, during which they improvised verses with political themes. When the civil war broke out he worked for the Basque government transporting the injured. He was wounded and taken to a hospital in Santander. He was later imprisoned in the infamous prison of El Dueso (Santoña), where fourteen Basque prisoners were executed. Balendin Enbeita was sentenced to twelve years and transferred to prisons in Gasteiz, Bilbo, and Puerto de Santa María. At the end of four years he was released and he returned to his home. From 1941 until 1954 he had to maintain absolute silence and could not perform publicly as a bertsolari.

He resumed his improvisations before an audience in 1955, and discovered he was out of practice. Despite this disadvantage, he went on to become champion of the Bizkaian txapelketak in 1958 and 1959. In these competitions he promoted young Bizkaian bertsolariak (such as Jon Azpillaga, Jon Mugartegi, and Jon Lopategi) and raised the level of enthusiasm for bertsolaritza in the community.

Another important contribution of Balendin Enbeita was his success in restoring the prestige and regard for bertsolaritza. If formerly bertsolariak were regarded as drunkards, dirty night owls, lazy clowns, garrulous and immoral individuals, Enbeita gave them a very different image. He was like his father, Urretxindor, in that he earned love and respect through his kindness and personal integrity.

Balendin Enbeita died in an accident while working on his new farm.[80] Present champion Sebastián Lizaso referred to him as "maisuen maisu" (the master of the masters) at his funeral ceremony. Xabier Amuriza described Enbeita in the following four verse lines:

> Larogei urte makurtu barik
> bertsolari ta gudari
> begi batean zeukan euskara
> bestean zeukan Euskadi.[81]

> Without reaching eighty years of age
> he was a bertsolari and a Basque soldier;
> he had Euskara in one eye
> and the Basque Country in the other.

Among his favorite topics were the family, work, peace, Euskara, independence for the Basque Country, and God. At times he seemed to be a preacher who spoke of the need for religion. On other occasions he condemned the lack of unity among the Basque people.

His style, however, never reached his father's artistic level. Although he chose good rhythms his rhymes were sometimes poor, and on certain occasions he did not demonstrate a mastery of syntax. Unfortunately, he did not have the opportunities that young bertsolariak have today. He was forced into silence for nineteen years and could not perform publicly. However, even in his old age, Enbeita maintained a young spirit with regard to bertsolaritza, Euskara, and Basque politics. Until his death he continued to learn new techniques, encouraged young artists, and looked forward to a bright future for the Basque Country.

Mattin Treku, Alias "Mattin" (1916–1981)

Mattin was the descendant of a family that had to flee the southern Basque Country to the other side of the Pyrenees as a result of the second Carlist War. He was born in Ahetze (Lapurdi). He began improvisational performances in Sara (Lapurdi) when he was seventeen and was an active bertsolari for the next forty-seven years. He died on July 22, 1981, as the result of an injury received in 1977 while working.[82]

The Basque press unanimously honored Mattin and his art. One newspaper called him the ambassador of laughter and the songbird of the Basque Country.[83] On stage he was the personification of humor. His presence alone inspired laughter. He was obsessed with making his audience happy; consequently he was well loved by enthusiasts of bertsolaritza. His humor matched his lyrical tenor voice and sincere amiability. Although he often portrayed himself as a buffoon, he was much more than that. For thirty years he was Xalbador's partner. They traveled throughout the Basque Country proclaiming their love for Euskal Herria and Euskara while singing the joys and woes of the Basque people. Xalbador's serious disposition complemented Mattin's constant smile and happy, simple nature. They formed an ideal partnership at festivals, where art should go hand in hand with enjoyment and entertainment. Xalbador considered Mattin to be an expert bertsolari:

> Zarelakotz pertsutan osoki jakina,
> lagun bila naiz egun zure ganat jina.[84]

> Because [I know that you have] such great knowledge
>   of versemaking,
> I have sought you out as a partner. [paraphrase]

It was Mattin's humor that Xalbador was seeking, his ability to make people laugh, along with his desire to make their joint performances enjoyable and entertaining:

> Jarrai ba beti poza ezartzen
> euskaldunen bihotzetan.[85]

> Always continue to fill
> the Basque people's hearts with joy.

Mattin's last wish was that his fellow bertsolariak carry the casket at his funeral with joy and spirit rather than sorrow.

As previously discussed, humor and the ability to use irony are essential in a bertsolari. All bertsolariak know how to ridicule and make fun of their opponents, but not all know how to respond to the verbal blows they receive. Mattin, however, had a special talent for this. He liked to be verbally attacked so that he could respond in kind and thereby make the performance more entertaining.

Basarri observed this rare quality in Mattin's humor. There is a saying in Euskara about this subject: "He who says whatever he wants to say, hears things he does not want to hear." Mattin never became flustered. He knew how to lead his opponent on to where he had the advantage:

Nik ondo dakit ortako danak
nola balio ez duten,
zuk bietara dakizu ondo:
esaten eta entzuten.[86]

I know very well that not everyone
is good at that,
You know how to do both things well:
speaking and listening.

Mattin was not an educated bertsolari. His humor, irony, mischievousness, wit, and consistency over forty-seven years of activity provided the tools of his success. He sang as naturally as a songbird. He could utter the same words that Martín Fierro put in the mouth of his protagonist:

Yo no soy cantor letrao,
mas si me pongo a cantar
no tengo cuándo acabar
y me envejezco cantando:
Las coplas me van brotando
como agua de manantial.[87]

I am not an educated singer,
but if I begin to sing
I cannot stop
and I grow old singing:
Couplets flow from me
like water from a spring.

Mattin had very quick reflexes. Eloquence was paired with swift improvisation. This ability in bertsolaritza has been the subject of much debate. Many believe that past bertsolariak composed similar verses in less time that their modern counterparts. Once, when Mattin was informed that he had spent forty-five seconds on a verse that the old bertsolariak would have sung in thirty seconds, he went on to improvise a similar one in just fifteen seconds.

Both Xalbador and Mattin, who were from the northern provinces of the Basque Country, knew how to foster linguistic as well cultural cohesiveness in their country, in spite of the political borders and at times difficult circumstances. The unified dialect of the Basque language was made possible to a great extent because of the efforts of these men, who were representatives of different Basque dialects.

Manuel Lasarte (1927-   )

Manuel Lasarte was born in a farmhouse called Franki in Leitza (Nafarroa). When he was twelve years old he moved to Eibar for employment. He later settled permanently in Aia (Gipuzkoa), where he lives today. Although Lasarte is Nafarroan by birth, he is Gipuzkoan by adoption. He, therefore, has the advantage of mastery over the two main dialects of the Basque Country. Because of this, he is able to reach a larger audience easily.

When he made his first public appearance in Zaldibar (Bizkaia), he was very nervous and uncomfortable. He later performed frequently with Basarri and Uztapide, and occasionally with Zepai and Txapel. For thirty years Lasarte has gone from town to town throughout the Basque Country improvising verses. He does not like competitions. Poor health prevents him from participating in txapelketak, which he finds too strenuous. However, he realizes that they are necessary because they provide young bertsolariak the opportunity to perform publicly. He also accepts these contests because they are popular with the Basque people, who love challenges.

Lasarte chooses his words very carefully. His language differs drastically from that used by nineteenth-century bertsolariak because he does not employ Spanish words. His vocabulary, sayings, idiomatic expressions, and refrains are in pure Euskara, which is indicative of an artist who completely masters his language. Both his expressions and his point of view are unique. He has a deep appreciation of literary beauty and is careful to use variation and to avoid repetition in his verses. This is a relatively easy task for him because he has an excellent memory. His work is characterized by profound ideas, variation of structure, linguistic richness, and technical perfection.

Lasarte is exceptional both as an improviser and as a composer of bertso jarriak. This is demonstrated in his book *Gordean neuzkanak* (Verses I have saved, 1975) and in three cassette tapes of his verses. The most remarkable quality of his work is his perfect use of rhythm and especially rhyme. According to Uztapide, Lasarte is a master of this formal, technical aspect of bertsolaritza: "Neurrian eta puntuetan ez du bere berdiñik" (In rhythm and rhyme no one can compare with him).[88] This opinion is shared by critics and other bertsolariak who have performed with him in recent years.

Lasarte's good ear is responsible for his success with rhythms and melodies. It is practically impossible to find any error in his verses.[89] He normally utilizes zortziko and hamarreko handiak eta txikiak (verses of eight and ten lines, respectively, with 10/8 and 7/6 syllables). Of these rhythms, the zortziko handia is his favorite. He does not rely on poetic license in his rhythms, and weak verses do not occur in his work. He uses many and diverse melodies. In his book we find fifty-four different melodies, some of which are Lasarte's own while others are traditional. His verses are an artistic treasure for young bertsolariak and for anyone wishing to study this literary expression. He is a true master in combining melody and lyrics.

Lasarte devotes a great deal of attention to his rhymes, which are usually complex and consonant. He demonstrates extraordinary confidence and precision in this area. He generally likes to begin rhymes from the antepenultimate syllables of words. However, on some occasions he rhymes two or three vowels, for example: *ekarri* (to bring), *egarri* (thirst), *elkarri* (mutually), and *ezarri* (to put).

Lasarte's themes are not particularly original. He generally prefers to use traditional ones such as God, love, the Basque language, death, and the world. He is one of the few bertsolariak who avoids politics as a theme. He is good at choosing and approaching a subject in order to develop it fully and demands a great deal of himself in this regard. His introverted spirit, poor health, and domestic problems have provided depth to his approach to this literary art form. Lasarte seems very sensitive and at times quite sad, seeking refuge in his Christian faith:

> Ni nazu luzaroan
> gaixo egondua . . .
> Supritzeko izan da
> neretzat mundua.[90]

> I have been ill
> for a long time . . .
> The world has been
> the source of suffering.

When he performs publicly, he seems absorbed in his thoughts, concentrating on his private world. His gaze becomes lost in the distance. He does not gesture or give visible indication of his thoughts or feelings. In this respect, he resembles his partner Xalbador. However, he produces verses with ease and gentleness, making his work seem effortless. For those who would like bertsolaritza to focus exclusively on political themes, Lasarte's art may seem trivial and of inferior quality. However, since bertsolaritza is mainly an art form, Lasarte will be noted in history as a great bertsolari.

José Miguel Iztueta, Alias "Lazkao Txiki" (1926–1993)

Lazkao Txiki demonstrates both humor and lyricism in his work. The latter is especially evident when he deals with sentimental themes. His humor resembles that of Fernando Amezketarra, Pello Errota, Txirrita, and Mattin. His short stature and sense of humor automatically provoke laughter among his listeners. He defines himself as follows:

> Txiki xamarra bañan
> ez oso illuna.[91]

> Pretty small
> but not too sad.

Others have commented on his humor and lyricism:

> Bertsozko lorez zuk jantzi dezu
> Gipuzkoa'ko Goierri . . .
> Miñik gabeko piper bizia.[92]

> You have dressed the Gipuzkoan
> zone of Goierri with flowering verses . . .
> You are hot pepper that doesn't burn.

Lazkao Txiki was born in Lazkao (Gipuzkoa) in a farmhouse called Abalin. His favorite books on bertsolaritza include those of Udarregi, Xenpelar, Gaztelu, Pello Mari Otaño, and especially the account of Saint Genevieve's life by Juan Cruz Zapirain (1867–1934).

Lazkao Txiki is from the old Gipuzkoan school of bertsolaritza. He is a man who is concerned about his culture, possessed of great natural talent, and a keen and clever observer. His audiences love his humor and simplicity.

He improvised his first verse in a neighborhood tavern when he was fourteen years old and began performing in public at this young age. Later, in 1944, he performed with Saiburu and Basarri in his town's square. In his youth he received a great deal of recognition in competitions and txapelketak. He won first place in several provincial contests in Gipuzkoa; but his finest moment was the 1965 txapelketa when he ranked second behind Uztapide. In the controversial 1967 txapelketa he took third place, tied with Jon Lopategi.

His favorite themes are sentimental, romantic, or lyric, and include nature and birds. He frequently uses humor and at times sees himself as a clown who must act happy and make the audience laugh, even when he is sad.

In recent years he has grown weary of traveling from town to town. He does not feel fulfilled as an artist and no longer enjoys competitions and txapelketak because they make him very nervous. He shares Basarri's pessimism concerning the future of the Basque language and bertsolaritza. The use of Spanish is on the rise in Basque villages because of the influx of Spanish immigrants, thus changing the cultural environment of the Basque Country. Some bertsolariak simply repeat well-known melodies and do not create new ones.

It is impossible to analyze closely all the talented bertsolariak of this period. However, the list that follows may serve as a reference. Most of these bertsolariak are still living and continue to compete. Some of them will be discussed later:

1. Gipuzkoan: Joxe Lizaso (1927–   ); Joaquín Mitxelena; Joxe Agirre (1929–   ); Jesús Alberdi, alias "Egileor" (1931–   ); Cosme Lizaso (1937–   ); Patxi Etxebarria; Txomin Garmendia; Imanol Lazkano (1936–   ); and Xabier Zeberio (1949–   ).
2. Nafarroan: Bautista Madariaga; Mikel Arozamena; Dominique Ezponda (1937–   ); Andrés Navarte (1927–1971); and Juan Perurena.
3. Bizkaian: Jon Mugartegi and Joseba Arregi (1934–   ).
4. Lapurdin: Emmanuel Sein, alias "Xanpun."

The modern period is sometimes referred to as the sociopolitical period of bertsolaritza. The last years of the 1960s saw the beginning of armed struggle against the Franco dictatorship. Assassinations, torture, and violence became commonplace.

These years were extremely hard for bertsolariak. Jon Lopategi and Jon Azpillaga became well known for their courage and political commitment. Performing as partners, they seized every opportunity to improvise verses of a sociopolitical nature; other themes were secondary. Bertsolaritza and Basque song in general became a means of defending Basque culture and liberty.[93]

After the 1967 txapelketa a dark cloud settled over bertsolaritza. For thirteen years there would be no national competitions. Bertsolariak became the defenders of a small nation that was struggling to survive against harsh odds. They were the voices that expressed the rage of an oppressed people.[94]

The most important social issue of this period is the decline of the Basque farmhouse. The vast majority of the population has been integrated into an urban lifestyle. The bertsolaritza of this period is influenced by technological advances, the new Basque leftist movement, the restoration of democracy, and a national trend toward radicalism.[95]

The pedagogical aspect of bertsolaritza has also drastically changed. It is now taught in ikastolak (schools) and *gau eskolak* (night schools for adults) rather than at taverns and during the celebrations of Saint Agate. The training methods of modern bertsolaritza schools vary because many of the students are *euskaldun berriak* (Basques who have learned Euskara as a second language) and young people from urban centers. There has also been an increase in publications about bertsolaritza. Xavier Amuriza's books have contributed to this movement. As a result of these changes, a new generation of bertsolariak has arisen that has not been educated with traditional methods. This period is the first in which bertsolaritza has been taught at the university level.

Jon Lopategi (1934–   )

Jon Lopategi was born on May 17, 1934, in a farmhouse known as Aldauri in Areatza, Muxika (Bizkaia). The proximity of his house to the Enbeitas' was one of the factors that influenced his decision to become a bertsolari. Whenever the Enbeitas had a family gathering they improvised verses. As a child, Lopategi was drawn to his neighbors' kitchen window where he listened to them.[96]

At the age of twelve he was enrolled in a Catholic school in Tolosa (Gipuzkoa) run by Sacramentine priests. This experience was very beneficial for Lopategi. There he learned and mastered the Gipuzkoan dialect in an ideal atmosphere where instructors favored and nurtured Basque culture. He left the seminary when he was twenty-two years old upon the completion of his studies in humanities, philosophy, and one year of theology. He then made his first attempt at bertsolaritza during a local celebration by improvising verses with a group of friends. He performed professionally for the first time at the age of twenty-six in the town square of Mungia (Bizkaia) and won third place, although he was extremely nervous. In 1961 he won first place in three different competitions (in Mungia, Gernika, and Bilbo). In the years that followed he was named champion of the Bizkaian txapelketak of 1962, 1964, and 1967. At the 1967 national txapelketa held in Donostia, he won third place along with Lazkao Txiki. He was awarded second place in the txapelketak of 1982 and 1986. In 1989 he became champion.

In the early 1960s Basarri and Uztapide were well known in Gipuzkoa, as was Balendin Enbeita in Bizkaia; however, their verses were not politically oriented. The first verses of a political nature that Lopategi heard were by Jon Azpillaga in 1960. These two bertsolariak later formed a politically involved team supporting their national minority in response to the Franco regime's oppression. Lopategi regards that era as the best period of his life. He was undaunted by the six incidents in which he was prohibited from performing in public, fined, and then imprisoned for not paying the fines.

The bertsolariak he admired most were Urretxindor and Xalbador. Urretxindor impressed him because he was in tune with his times. One of Lopategi's greatest desires is to be a bertsolari who addresses the concerns of the Basque people. He respects and admires Xalbador for a different reason. Lopategi has always regarded Xalbador as the greatest poet of all bertsolariak.[97] The Euskara he used still holds some mystery for Lopategi. It is unfortunate that Xalbador's verses were not fully appreciated because of his audience's difficulty in understanding the Behe-nafarrera dialect. It is even more unfortunate, however, that even when individual words were understood, his profound messages were often missed. Xalbador has exercised an important influence on Lopategi's poetic art.

Lopategi is also especially fond of his teacher, Balendin Enbeita. It was the Garriko school of bertsolaritza, founded by Enbeita in Areatza, that enabled young Lopategi to begin an artistic journey that has made him one of the best bertsolariak of the Basque Country. However, his beginnings were not especially promising. According to his teacher, Lopategi lacked a good ear and therefore could not be expected to have a bright future. However, Lopategi is living proof that not all bertsolariak are born with natural talent and that the necessary skills of bertsolaritza can be acquired.

Improvised verses dominate Lopategi's artistic production, even though as a young man he dedicated a lot of time to writing them. Today he rarely pens verses. He prefers improvisation and is one of the most confident bertsolariak of our time. He is completely at ease with the Bizkaian and Gipuzkoan dialects as well as Euskara Batua. Because of this he attracts a larger audience and is understood throughout the Basque Country. Lopategi learned the Bizkaian style of bertsolaritza from the Enbeitas, and in 1962 he shifted to the more classical Gipuzkoan tradition.

Lopategi's technique is excellent. His verses contain no major flaws. The education he received provided him with the confidence necessary for improvising in front of an audience. One of his most notable traits is his ability to attract the attention of his audience. Lopategi is an alert artist who is always concerned with the interests and problems of the Basque people. He feels that making an audience laugh is not a bertsolari's main responsibility. Although he recognizes that laughter and humor are important, he feels that bertsolaritza should be regarded as a testimony with a message set to music. Since bertsolariak are responsible for raising the consciousness of the Basque people, he also maintains that a bertsolari's worth is directly related to his ability to serve as a spokesperson for his people and to convey their worries, joys, and anguish.

His patriotism and involvement in the struggle for Basque liberty have been Lopategi's main motivations for being a bertsolari. He is a militant artist who defends causes. Lopategi sees Euskal Herria as a small nation that is struggling to survive. He longs for its independence, free from Spain and France, with all seven provinces unified and politically socialist. He aspires to combine Basque nationalism with humanitarian socialism in which social injustice created by the capitalist bourgeoisie would disappear. Many young bertsolariak of the modern period have followed in Lopategi's footsteps along this path of sociopolitical enlightenment.

One of Lopategi's missions as an artist is to introduce children and young people to Basque culture and to bertsolaritza. The rural Basque society that lacked a high level of culture has evolved into a learned and industrialized society. Today the majority of bertsolariak, especially in Gipuzkoa, come from industrial environments. A bertsolari must keep up with his times if he is to become a spokesperson for his people. According to Lopategi, a bertsolari should have broad cultural knowledge. He feels that this art form needs more educated and professional bertsolariak like Xabier Amuriza, Abel Muniategi (1943-), Jon Sarasua (1966-), Andoni Egaña (1961-), and Xabier Pérez, alias "Euskitze."

Lopategi has been so committed to his art that he quit his regular job in 1983 in order to dedicate his time completely to the promotion of bertsolaritza in Bizkaian schools. He also teaches bertsolaritza at the Basque university during the summer. The movement to establish bertsolaritza schools began in earnest in 1981. Xabier Amuriza's book *Hiztegi errimatua hitzaren kirol nazionala* (Rhyming dictionary: The national sport of words) was an essential tool in this undertaking. New schools opened in Bizkaia and Gipuzkoa where adults could learn bertsolaritza.

Lopategi established his own school in Gernika (Bizkaia), where he currently resides. His first task was to acquaint his students with other Basque dialects, with the goal of eventually teaching them Euskara Batua. At the present time Lopategi is the coordinator of a network of bertsolaritza schools in Bizkaia, a collective movement that has gained a great deal of force in just a few years.

The university-level summer courses are a direct outgrowth of these schools. These courses prepare students to improvise verses in a friendly and collaborative atmosphere. Thanks to the work of Lopategi and others, this type of experience is becoming increasingly important and is transforming traditional bertsolaritza.

Jon Azpillaga (1935-   )

Jon Azpillaga was born on November 26, 1935, in Pasaia (Gipuzkoa). When he was sixteen months old his mother took him to live in Berriatua (Bizkaia) where he remained until he was twenty-two. Although enthusiasts of bertsolaritza in the provinces of Bizkaia and Gipuzkoa debate his origin, he considers himself Bizkaian.[98] He speaks both dialects well, but demonstrates special mastery of Bizkaian. He had his debut as a bertsolari during the night festivals of Saint Agate where, protected by the darkness and friends, he sang and improvised verses. He performed publicly for the first time in 1950, when he was just fifteen years old.

He remembers the decade in which Basarri and Uztapide as partners dominated bertsolaritza (1945-1955). The people were always eager to hear them perform. Young Azpillaga repeatedly told himself he too could be a bertsolari. He soon began performing with two bertsolariak from his town, Jon Mugartegi and Joseba Arregi. Unfortunately, Mugartegi became ill so Azpillaga was unable to perform for four years. In 1959 he won first place in a contest in Markina (Bizkaia). He ranked second in the Bizkaian txapelketak of 1959 and 1960. Azpillaga's rite of passage as a bertsolari came during the 1960 national txapelketa in which he took third, behind Basarri and Uztapide. He was twenty-five years old at the time. In 1961 he won first place in the Bizkaian txapelketa.

The 1960s was a very important decade for Azpillaga. In 1962 he began to perform with Jon Lopategi. Together they were to leave their mark on modern bertsolaritza by reintroducing political themes. Azpillaga, who was less radical than his partner, got into trouble because of his views about Euskara and the national values of the Basque people.[99] On three occasions his fines were greater than his earnings in the plazas. Although public performances of bertsolaritza were permitted in Nafarroa, because of the people's loyalty to Franco during the Spanish Civil War, similar performances were prohibited in Bizkaia for six years by the governor's orders.[100] During this long period Azpillaga seized every opportunity to convey his message to the Basque people at events like weddings and certain religious ceremonies. This was not an easy task because, in most cases, he had to submit a written copy and a Spanish translation of what he planned to improvise to the local authorities.

Azpillaga has been in great demand as a bertsolari. The first year after Franco's death, in 1975, he performed 178 times. In 1985 he performed on 101 occasions. He was one of eight finalists in the national txapelketak in 1980 and 1982. However, he refrained from competing in the 1986 txapelketa so that younger bertsolariak would have an opportunity to do so. At the same time, he does not plan to retire as long as the people want him to perform and he is healthy. In June of 1987 he performed in Boise in response to an invitation by Idaho Basques. During that same year he was honored by many, including other bertsolariak and the Basque government. These honors serve as further proof of Azpillaga's talent as an outstanding bertsolari. Azpillaga is a great bertsolari who has always been highly regarded. He has never won a national competition, but was always a finalist. He is a mature bertsolari who has earned a reputation for being one of the best.

Azpillaga is considered an outstanding plaza gizona. He has a way of filling a plaza with his physical presence, his beautiful voice, and his special talent for improvisation. His verses flow naturally, as if he were conversing with another person. He enjoys his audience, which inspires him and gives him a sense of responsibility as an artist. He has the rare ability that Basarri had for performing with a partner. He never belabors a topic and always sets up his verse so that his partner can pick up the dialogue where he left off. Azpillaga is also suited for long festival sessions in which bertsolariak must perform for hours. His physical endurance is exceptional and his artistic resources are limitless. He greatly admires Pello Mari Otaño and Uztapide for the quality and depth of their verses as well as their proficiency in Euskara.

Modern bertsolaritza is manifesting new dynamics never before seen. Today there is such a great number of talented bertsolariak that it would be impossible to list them all. The following individuals serve as representatives of the modern period: José Luis Gorrotxategi; Jon Enbeita; Sebastián Lizaso (1958-   ); Angel Peñagarikano; Rufino Iraola (1945-   ); Gregorio Larrañaga, alias "Mañukorta" (1944-   ); Eusebio Igartzabal (1944-   ); Jean Pierre Mendiburu (1941-   ); Mixel Aire (1944-   ); Andoni Egaña (1961-   ); Iñaki Murua (1956-   ); Mikel Mendizabal (1956-   ); Jon Sarasua; José Luis Mugarza, alias "Elgetxu" (1954-   ); Xabier Pérez, alias "Euzkitze"; Ernest Alkat (1951-   ); Luis Otamendi; Jean Louis, alias "Laka" (1954-   ); Josu Arriola (1964-   ); and Millan Tellería (1957-   ).

CHAPTER SEVEN

Regard for

Bertsolaritza

Bertsolaritza, as we know it today, has been greatly influenced by the txapelketak. These competitions, which began in 1935, were crucial to bertsolaritza because they legitimized the art form by promoting it in the plazas. More important, however, these competitions changed its direction.

As we have seen, very little is actually known about the early development of bertsolaritza. This chapter examines the recorded criticism of it since the eighteenth century. Some of the commentary is very negative but some of it is quite positive. There are also comments concerning the formal aspects of bertsolaritza. Although a great deal of information is not available, what we have is sufficient and clear enough to demonstrate how Basques regarded this literary phenomenon over time.

During the second half of the nineteenth century the literature written in Lapurdin lost the dominion it had held in the Basque Country for two centuries and was replaced by that published in Gipuzkoan. Jesuit priest Manuel de Larramendi (1690-1766) was the proponent of the first literary renaissance in the southern Basque Country. Although he wrote very little in Euskara, he influenced and educated a group of fine Basque writers. During the second half of the eighteenth century and the beginning of the nineteenth, there were fifteen writers who were in one way or another influenced by Father Larra-

117

mendi.[1] Few imitated the neologisms and purism that their teacher had wished to instill in them, but all of them were affected by the prestige that Larramendi had bestowed on Basque literature.

At the end of his book *El Impossible Vencido* (The Impossible Conquered, 1729), Larramendi refers to bertsolaritza. The early publication date and the author's influence make this work especially important. In chapter 6 Larramendi makes a distinction between two types of Basque poetry, created through different processes, that people were quite familiar with.

In the first and older form, melody served poetry. As an example Larramendi cites Lapurdin writer Joannes Etcheberri (1668–1749) from Ziburu, who had a special talent for poetry and who said poets composed verses "with imagination, creativity, and noble thoughts . . . and in such a way [that] poetry came to be superior to the music."[2]

The second process was different. In Larramendi's time more attention was given to the music and melody than to the number of syllables in a given line of verse. The lyrics were secondary to the music. Bertsolariak created the music first, then added lyrics, and this was common practice throughout the Basque Country. In his opinion, this type of music was lively, but the verses were very dull.[3] Such an opinion from an authority on aesthetics of both learned and popular poetry indicates the lack of regard for bertsolaritza.

One of the most valuable testimonies about bertsolaritza comes to us from Juan Ignacio Iztueta who, as we have seen earlier, was the first historian of this artistic phenomenon. Iztueta was one year old when Father Larramendi died. The opinions of both of these men are very useful for an understanding of the attitudes held toward bertsolaritza in Gipuzkoa at the beginning of the nineteenth century.

In our earlier discussion of the Billabona challenge, it was clear that many Gipuzkoans demonstrated great interest in this type of competition. However, this should not lead us to believe that appreciation for bertsolaritza was widespread, or that the bertsolariak did not have problems with the authorities.

Juan Ignacio Iztueta bitterly complained about people who heckled the bertsolariak while they performed, making faces and taunting gestures. He referred to these people as pseudointellectuals. His opinions are reflected in *Guipuzkoako dantzak* (Dances of Gipuzkoa), which he wrote in 1822: "How many times have I been disgusted upon seeing, in the plaza, those tiresome rogues who make mocking gestures at their honorable, competent, and happy versemaking countrymen."[4]

Iztueta also criticized the mayors of many Gipuzkoan towns who prohibited bertsolariak from performing in the plazas or who stopped them as soon as they began to improvise in public. The performance adjective *cascabel* (foolish) that he used to describe these officials is especially significant: "Isn't it painful to see . . . how many foolish mayors order bertsolariak to be silent as soon as they begin to sing in the plazas?"[5]

Iztueta's work reflects only Gipuzkoan sentiments toward bertsolaritza. The lack of regard for this art form by some southern Basques was not limited to just one province, however. The northern Basque priest Jean Baptiste Camoussarry (1815–1842), from Lapurdi, also criticized bad bertsolariak.

Of the twenty-two poems that Camoussarry published in 1838, one entitled "Basa-koplariari" (To the pseudo-koplari) is especially interesting. This poem of sixteen verses provided a harsh and direct attack on bad koplariak from the northern provinces. (The koplariak were the equivalent of the bertsolariak in the southern provinces.) The title of the poem itself is self-explanatory. The word *basa* has a derogatory meaning in Basque when used to describe an artist. Etymologically its meaning has to do with the forest or woods, but in this case it is equivalent to phony, uncultured, and barbaric.

As an educated poet, Camoussarry criticized the art of popular poets, their voices, and their verses. In his opinion, the koplari's inspiration was influenced by the consumption of wine and, as a consequence, his verses bordered on absolute inanity. I have chosen the ten best verses in "Basa-koplariari," maintaining their original numbers, to demonstrate Camoussarry's sentiments. He maintains that each verse is worse than the previous one and asserts that this kind of bertsolari deserves to be committed for insanity and condemned to hell for the immoral ambiance he creates:

1. Hunat ene aintzinerat
   O, koplari eskalduna!

   Come before me
   Basque versemaker!

2. Boza makur txar batekin
   Bertsu txarragoko batzuk
   Aire lele batzuekin
   Kantatzen ohi dauzkiguk.

   With a bad voice, out-of-tune
   He sings for us
   with silly airs
   Each verse worse than the last.

4. Ez du kopla moldatzeko
   Hanitz entsegu eginen,
   Astokeria bai asko,
   Nahi baduzu erranen.

   He doesn't try too hard
   to create verses;
   but if you want,
   he will tell you a lot of
   foolishness.

6. Oi, sensu gabeko kopla!
   Egilleari didurik;

   Badakigu ez duela
   Koplariak ez sensurik.

   Oh, foolish verse,
   You remind me of your
   composer;
   We know the versemaker
   has no sense.

7. Adi zazue kantazen
   Boza morgan dardaratzen;
   Au ixilik koplaria!
   Hausten dautak beharria.

   Listen to him sing
   with his voice trembling;
   Silence yourself, versemaker!
   You are hurting my ears.

8. Zer erran nahi deraukun
   Ez dezakegu ez, adi:
   Xuxen, makur, ezker, eskun,
   Oi! Badarasa zer nahi.

   We cannot understand
   what he is trying to say:
   Straight, crooked, left, right,
   He says any silly thing.

10. Bazka ona ikustean, Nola astoak irrintzina, Hala arnoa dastatzean Koplariak umor ona.	Like a donkey that brays upon seeing good fodder, the versemaker rejoices at the sight of wine.
12. Zerratu behar badire Presondegian zoroak, Zerra beraz, zerra ere Basa koplari erhoak.	If the insane should be locked up in prison, lock up the crazy versemakers, too.
13. Ezin detzake arrima Lau bertsu txar elgarrekin, Ez baditu, o lastima! Lokarritzat lau hitz zikin.	He is not capable of composing four miserable verses. Without linking them with four dirty words. What a shame!
16. Ikara hadi, tristea! Laster bahoa tonbarat, Ikusak hire zortzea! Kantaz hoa ifernurat![6]	Tremble poor wretch! You will go to your grave soon, See what awaits you! You will go to hell singing!

In the southern Basque Country, we find one of the most objective and balanced opinions on bertsolaritza. It comes to us from Pablo de Gorosábel (1803-1868) in his book *Noticia de las cosas memorables de Guipúzcoa* (Update of memorable events in Gipuzkoa, 1899). Since the book was published thirty-one years after his death, we can situate his opinions about bertsolaritza in the historical context of the mid-nineteenth century.

Pablo de Gorosábel was born in Tolosa (Gipuzkoa) and died in Donostia. He came into the world at a critical moment when the traditional ideological foundations of society were disappearing and were being replaced by others that had arisen out of the French Revolution (1789). He was a historian and a jurist who wrote an outstanding account rich in information on the history of Gipuzkoa. The work provides a series of opinions about bertsolaritza, some of which are very positive. Gorosábel could not explicitly praise bertsolaritza because this art form did not follow the literary rules of the time. However, he is credited with being the first to call attention to the Gipuzkoans' negligence in not collecting and preserving their popular verses.

Gorosábel explained the essence of bertsolaritza, the challenges of the nineteenth century, the Gipuzkoan people's enthusiasm for improvised verse, and the literary value of the uneducated bards. He then rendered a favorable judgment on bertsolaritza:

> One can understand that such poetic compositions, which are completely improvised, can hardly claim much merit if considered as literature. Neither should one expect to find in them lofty concepts that only come about as products of instruction, study, and education when coupled with natural talent. However, it is unquestionable that many of these verses express

different emotions of the heart, including love, jealousy, envy, gratitude, hate, disdain, courage, friendship, etc., with naturalness, refinement, and expressiveness.[7]

In 1901, two years after Gorosábel's publication, Carmelo de Echegaray wrote an extensive appendix to the work.[8] According to bertsolaritza expert Antonio Zavala, this distinguished Basque journalist offered the most bitter and pessimistic opinion regarding bertsolaritza ever recorded.[9]

Carmelo de Echegaray was born in Azpeitia (Gipuzkoa) and lived in Zumaia (Gipuzkoa) for many years. In 1896 he was named chronicler of the Basque provinces. Later he moved to Gernika (Bizkaia) and died there. One of the least-known aspects of Echegaray's literary career was his talent as a Basque poet. He began his career by writing poetry in Euskara but later switched to prose. On November 22, 1924, the Academy of the Basque Language appointed him a member to replace Luis de Eleizalde (1878-1923).

Echegaray lived in the period during which the linguistic purism proposed by Sabino Arana began to take root. As we have seen, this linguistic change was accompanied by disregard for bertsolaritza. Echegaray considered bertsolaritza themes trivial subjects, prosaic accidents, hopelessly superficial creations, rural gossip, and ridiculous rivalries in spite of their musical accompaniment. He also felt that, on some occasions, bertsolariak offended not only aesthetically but morally as well:

> If one could gather all of the leaflets that, over the last three quarters of a century, have been spread throughout the Basque region under the name of Basque poetry, they would make up an enormous collection of nonsense and vulgarity, presented in an eminently prosaic manner, including incorrect language that is plagued with Spanish expressions.[10]

The use of Spanish expressions, so common among such bertsolariak as Udarregi, Pello Errota and Txirrita, was also condemned by novelist Domingo de Aguirre (1864-1920) from Ondarru. His literary purism did not reach the radical extremes of some of Sabino Arana's disciples. His prose was lively, popular, and elegant in spite of some neologisms.

In chapter 5 ("Azoka ta dema") of his novel *Garoa* (The fern, 1912),[11] Aguirre expresses his disapproval of the impure Euskara used by some rural folk who were improvising verses in taverns. He felt that they were inspired by wine and spirits. To demonstrate his point, in the space of two stanzas he identified the occurrence of the following unacceptable rhymes: *paratu* (to prepare), *pasatu* (to pass), *portatu* (to behave), *inportantzia* (importance), *sustantzia* (substance), *poltsia* (pocket), and *alegrantzia* (joy).[12]

Aguirre's novel was featured a chapter at a time in the magazine *Revue Internationale des Etudes Basques* beginning in 1907. The following year Basque writer Gregorio de Mújica (1882-1931), who published an article in the same magazine, described the art of bertsolaritza:

Who has not seen the bertsolariak singing one verse after another in a dark tavern, sitting at a greasy table, with festive red wine in front of them or in a cider shop, among barrels, holding a yellow-colored liquid in their hands, surrounded by friends, taking turns verbally mocking one another in jest? We will not praise them simply because they are our own; we will not say that their work is good enough to be published and read throughout the whole world, because it is not. Some [bertsolariak] are good, others are worse. They are constantly looking for ways to find fault with their opponent. One could say that they come from their homes with their answers already prepared in order to be very fast and witty.[13]

This criticism about bertsolaritza accurately reflects the generally accepted views of the time. Gregorio de Mújica does not attack bertsolaritza as blatantly as did Echegaray, but his critique does not contain the praise that we will see in later years.

Since the fourteenth century the clergy has fostered and promoted the culture of the Basque people. There have been a number of populist priests who were sympathetic to cultural and political issues. Some clergymen played a very important role in the nationalist movement created by Sabino Arana, although it was counter to the spirit of the fueros for priests to be affiliated with the Basque Nationalist Party. It is a fact that many Basque priests were the most fervent promoters of Basque culture.

The seminary at Gasteiz served as an important center for Basque culture during the twenty-five years prior to the Spanish Civil War. José Miguel Barandiarán, anthropology professor, and Manuel Lekuona, professor of language, literature, history, art, and ethnography, viewed the seminary as the focal point for cultural transmission and the seedbed of future teachers. Barandiarán's twenty-three-volume *Obras completas* (Complete works) and Lekuona's twelve-volume *Idaz-lan guztiak* (Complete works) attest to their important contributions.

Within the field of oral literature Manuel Lekuona greatly promoted bertsolaritza. His early conferences and articles, including "Métrica vasca" (Basque metrics, 1918), fostered a great deal of regard for this literary art. Lekuona *zaharra* (old Lekuona), as he was affectionately called, possessed great sensitivity for music, song, and verse. Gabriel Aresti praised Lekuona's artistic talent. Upon analyzing some of his poems he wrote: "They possess a great deal of musicality. I believe that from this point of view, there is no other work in Basque that is as fine. From a formal standpoint they are unsurpassable."[14]

Lekuona paved the way for the esteem that bertsolaritza was to receive. If today bertsolariak are considered artists instead of clowns, it is largely due to the efforts of this venerable clergyman.

Since that period, appreciation for bertsolaritza has grown steadily. Many Basque writers and artists have found bertsolaritza to be a genuine manifestation of the Basque spirit. Perhaps the most lavish praise comes from Basque sculptor Jorge de Oteiza (1908-   ). In his work this innovative artist tries to retrace the essence of the Basque spirit. For him, Basque linguistics, literature, and sculpture are complementary manifestations of a single reality. He feels that the language and its musicality, the spontaneity of the bertsolariak, verbal intensity and duration, style and expression, are distinct facets of the Basque being.

For Oteiza, the bertsolari represents it all. In general he feels that today's Basques do not understand the profound narration of the bertsolariak. In *Quousque tandem . . . !* (1963), he explains his view of the Basque bard:

> [What still remains of] our bertsolari is the purest style and
> most moving and inspiring clarity of our people. The intention
> of this essay is to achieve genuine understanding, because he
> has never been truly understood. And in the key to his style lies
> the explanation of all authentically Basque creations, and all
> creators of our history and those of the present. [It is] the expla-
> nation and even the hope [through aesthetic comprehension]
> of our regaining what belongs to all of us. I can say even more:
> The Basque who does not possess within him some notion of
> the essence of bertsolaritza is a poor soul.[15]

Orixe and Gabriel Aresti are among the learned poets who have taken an interest in this literary phenomenon. Orixe is one of the most admired and controversial poets of the twentieth century. Luis Michelena says that Orixe "is perhaps the most important writer in the history of Basque literature."[16] The canons of his cultivated poetry at times did not mesh with the norms of bertsolaritza. In Orixe's short summary of Basque literature, called "Euskal literatura'ren atze edo edesti laburra,"[17] he dedicates two pages to bertsolaritza —a significant fact in a world where most books on Basque literature have not dealt with its oral aspects.[18]

Orixe observed a lack of interest in reading and writing among Basques, yet great enthusiasm for improvising and listening to sung verse. He did not disapprove of bertsolaritza, but as an educated poet he was critical of some its stylistic aspects. His question: "Zer balio du literatura xarpil onek?" (What good is this common literature?) is revealing because his response addresses the difficulty of improvisation.[19] He asserts that not even educated men would be able to create so many profound ideas if they had to improvise. In fact, bertsolariak are capable of successfully carrying out the task of improvisation: "These uneducated versemakers of ours are intelligent and although [the verses] may not be in beautiful language with rich imagination, they often possess merit and essence."[20]

Years later, in the prologue to *Musika ixilla*, a book by Gaztelu, Orixe restated his reservations about the structure of bertsolaritza. Once again, his opinions demonstrate the great differences that exist between the literary art of learned poets and that of popular folk ones. While Orixe revealed his considerable regard for bertsolariak, he also confessed that the rhymes used and the monotony of rhythms, such as the zortziko handia (eight-lined verse), bored him. He tried to create these types of verses, but found them tiresome to read. As a remedy, he suggested breaking the wearisome chain of assonant rhyme. He concluded the prologue with an unfavorable assessment of bertsolaritza: "I wish that only 5 percent of the verses that are composed in our language were ever written! Thank goodness most of them disappear and are forgotten! Such vulgar ideas should not be considered—with or without rhyme." [21]

Gabriel Aresti was another educated poet who showed a great deal of interest in bertsolaritza and included some of its flavor in his own poetry. As mentioned earlier, he admired the bertsolariak, especially Txirrita. From time to time Aresti tried to write authentic bertsoak, but he did not succeed because he was not a bertsolari. His area of expertise was learned written poetry. He writes in one of his poems about the lack of quality in complex rhymes and rhythms in bertsolaritza:

> Bertsolariak
> puntu aberatsen
> eta
> neurri gaitzen
> etsai
> deklaratu dira.[22]

> The bertsolariak
> Have declared themselves
> enemies
> of complicated rhymes
> and
> difficult metrics.

Today work by critics and specialists in bertsolaritza is furthering the popularity of this improvisational literature and creating greater regard for the art than ever before. Santiago Onaindia, Antonio Zavala, and Juan Mari Lekuona are the greatest promoters and nurturers of bertsolaritza. Xabier Amuriza has also made very important and positive contributions in advancing the appreciation of this oral literature, as we shall consider in more detail later.

Santiago Onaindia was born in Amoroto (Bizkaia) on March 24, 1909. His most outstanding books after World War II are *Milla euskal olerki eder* (A thousand beautiful Basque poems, 1954); his translations of Virgil, Horace, and Dante; and his seven volumes of *Euskal literatura* (Basque literature). His noteworthy works on bertsolaritza are *Gure bertsolariak* (Our bertsolariak, 1964) and *Enbeita oleskaria* (Enbeita's versemaking, 1966).

Onaindia is a Carmelite friar who, in the solitude of the seminary, submerged in old papers and books, has contributed works of great importance to Basque literature. He considers poetry to be the best vehicle to awaken the Basque people and to raise their consciousness. His works have encompassed the areas of written and oral literature, learned and popular folk genres, great

Basque poets, and the modest bertsolariak. He has written many poems and is editor of the magazines *Olerti*, which is dedicated to Basque poetry, and *Karmel*, which deals with Basque literature in general. Onaindia holds the opinion that learned poetry and bertsolaritza are not incompatible, in spite of their differences. He and others feel that educated poets describe reality more beautifully, even though bertsolariak are sharper and more alive.[23] Onaindia's studies of bertsolaritza and individual artists have helped elevate this phenomenon to an artistic and dignified realm.

Another great promoter of bertsolaritza is Antonio Zavala, who was born in Tolosa (Gipuzkoa) on January 23, 1928. When he was seventeen he joined the Jesuit order and completed his studies in Loyola, Oña, and Javier. In 1964 he published a book entitled *Bosquejo de historia del bertsolarismo* (Outline of the history of bertsolaritza), which has become a classic. Zavala has compiled the most complete collections of modern bertsolaritza. He focuses exclusively on the oral folk poetry that has survived throughout the years on scattered sheets of paper or in the collective memory of community members. Zavala carries out his work by interviewing the families of bertsolariak and older people from rural areas. His personal library at the Colegio de Javier in Nafarroa was an extremely valuable source for my research. His collection *Auspoa* (Bellows) contains more than two hundred volumes, most of which are dedicated to bertsolaritza. *Auspoa* is the greatest tribute to bertsolaritza that has ever been written. Zavala collected and compiled thousands of verses that otherwise would have been lost forever. In this respect his work is comparable to that of Resurrección María de Azkue and Padre Donostia in the field of music.

Last, there is Juan Mari Lekuona, who was born in Oiartzun (Gipuzkoa). Lekuona acquired an interest in song and poetry from his family, especially from his uncle Manuel. Today he is a professor at the Estudios Universitarios Técnicos de Gipuzkoa (the Basque private university) in Donostia, where he teaches Basque literature with an emphasis on oral tradition and bertsolaritza. He began to show an interest in these literary expressions at an early age. His role as a panel judge at txapelketak has been almost compulsory. Because of his vast knowledge as well as his articles and books, today Lekuona is considered the leading authority on Basque oral literature and bertsolaritza.

Lekuona's knowledge and admiration of oral literature and bertsolaritza are evident in his works of poetry: *Muga beroak* (Hot borders, 1973), *Ilargiaren eskolan* (In the moon's classroom, 1979), and *Mimodramak eta ikonoak* (Gestures and icons, 1990). His greatest work on bertsolaritza is *Ahozko euskal literatura* (Basque oral literature, 1982), which has become an indispensable tool for any study of the phenomenon.

It is because of the quiet work of these specialists that bertsolaritza now enjoys the high regard it deserves. Euskaltzaindia has made many bertsolariak members of the academy, including Basarri, Uztapide, Xalbador, and Balendin Enbeita. Having a bertsolari in the family or for a friend is no longer regarded negatively. Bertsolariak now enjoy the same status as other artists. The old image of the bertsolari as a clown has vanished forever.

CHAPTER EIGHT

Phenomena Similar

to Bertsolaritza

The art of singing improvised verse is not a rare phenomenon, nor is it unique to the Basques. Although similar literary expressions exist, a complete comparative study of these oral folk expressions has never been undertaken. According to Samuel Armistead:

> Orally improvised poetry is (or was) widely cultivated in the Hispanic world. Its existence is known in the Basque provinces, in Galicia, Mexico, Louisiana, Cuba, Puerto Rico, Brazil, Argentina, and elsewhere, but relatively little has been written on it. A comparative monograph is an urgently needed desideratum.[1]

This work does not intend to carry out an extensive study on the phenomenon because there are insufficient data. Literary traditions similar to bertsolaritza do exist in other parts of the world, including Portugal, Sardinia, Turkey, Cyprus, Greece, Crete, Russia, and Japan. However, the available information is often very limited and quite vague. On the other hand, there is sufficient information on similar phenomena in Spain (Galicia and Cartagena), Cuba, Chile, Argentina, Brazil, the former Yugoslavia (now Bosnia, Montenegro, Serbia, and Croatia), Africa, and England. Brief descriptions of the characteristics of these oral traditions, beginning with Spain and followed by those of several Latin American countries and other nations, are provided in this chapter.

GALICIA (SPAIN)

According to a study by Carmelo Lisón Tolosana in 1964-1965, the Galicians maintain a tradition of improvising verse through song. Although Spanish (the official language of the state) prevails in Galicia, the natives maintain their own language and it is in Galician that they improvise their verses.[2] In rural areas, such as the province of Lugo, improvised verses are called *loias*, while in coastal villages and cities like La Coruña this type of improvisation is known as *regueifa*.

Loias, verses consisting of four lines and assonant rhyme, are improvised at Mardi Gras, festivals, weddings, pig slaughterings, and *carretos*. The carreto is a very old tradition that accompanies the construction of a house. The house owner provides dinner for all who lent a hand, and after the meal loias are improvised.

Loias are arguments between two people carried out in song format. They are characterized by an atmosphere of challenge, struggle, and competition. The second improviser must begin a verse with the last word of the opponent's verse. After each verse the audience applauds or expresses its dissatisfaction, thereby allowing the opponent a few seconds to prepare an answer. These pauses must be kept short or the audience will show displeasure, as they do when the improvisers use poor rhymes.

The regueifa consists of verse, song, and improvisation. It differs somewhat from the loias in that the second improviser is not required to begin a verse with the opponent's last word. The regueifa challenge is carried out by two pairs of improvisers. If one partner tires the other can take over. Either of them is allowed to change the theme at any time.

An atmosphere of challenge and aggressiveness permeates these literary competitions. This aggressive tone carries over into all of the oral folk poetry of Galicia.

Generally, the audience understands that the errors and defects attributed to the improvisers should be directed at the team, rather than at an individual artist. In spite of this, performers or their families are sometimes subjected to harsh verbal attacks. Although these performances are usually peaceful, sometimes they end in violent fights and, on at least one occasion, even death.[3] Drinking, rivalry between parties, and the late hours (sometimes lasting until dawn) contribute to these brawls:

> One group favors one of the poets, perhaps because he is a neighbor; another group favors another. The former applauds

and the latter protests, and they become involved in heavy discussions. Being partially drunk, some [members] of the audience come to blows.[4]

The audience plays an important role in these events. The improvisers, usually men, perform on a platform surrounded by spectators, who show their approval or disapproval with applause and shouting. The organizing committee is generally responsible for choosing the winner. This committee is sometimes influenced by the preferences of the spectators, who value mental quickness, quality of improvisation, wit, and humor.

With respect to style and structure, these poets use verses composed of four lines, with eight syllables per line. Generally, assonant rhyme is employed. No special attention is given to the music or variety of melodies used.

CARTAGENA (SPAIN)

Public performances of *troveros* (improvising poets) are the most popular forms of folk art in Cartagena. These artistic expressions reached a peak of popularity at the beginning of the twentieth century. Today, these performances are not held as frequently, but continue to draw large, fervent audiences. The crowd's enthusiasm is sometimes so great that *rutineros* (members of the audience) express their desire to compete with the poets. Modern troveros are characterized by their superior knowledge of the culture.

At the turn of the century, José María Marín was considered the best improviser even though he did not sing well. On some occasions he relied on others to sing the verses he improvised. José Castillo, another famous improviser, commented on Marín: "He always understood that the polemics of improvisation is a cockpit where the loser has to flee like a coward or lose his life in the fight."[5]

This popular poetry differs greatly from learned poetry in theme, audience, and the personality traits of the improvisers. Their quickness in improvising is especially noteworthy, as is their aggressiveness and sense of rivalry. Their themes are related to daily life: love, lies, nature, rural versus urban life, injustices committed against the working class, or special events such as the feat of the pilots in the airplane *Non Plus Ultra*.[6]

Two poets take part in these literary competitions. They usually use stanzas consisting of five rhyming lines with eight syllables each. They also make use of ten-lined stanzas. Each of these lines also contains eight syllables and the rhyme is *abbaaccddc*. One improviser sings a verse and the other must respond quickly, using the same verse form. The contestants set their verses to nati e melodies of Cartagena as well as to *malagueñas* and *guajiras*.

CUBA

The middle of the nineteenth century was a time of preparation for the Cuban rebellion against Spanish colonial power. Cuban folk poetry from this period is a manifestation of the latent conflict between native Cubans and peninsular Spaniards.[7] Long before learned poetry had developed on a national level, Cuban folk poetry was widespread. Improvised and sung guajira poetry was a folk tradition that originated in Cuban peasant culture.

These improvised or memorized verses were composed of ten lines each and, apart from their romantic themes, served as a means for peasants to voice their opposition to colonial rule. The improvisation of verses served as a form of entertainment and recreation and also provided a way to protest Spanish power while promoting a political avenue for the restoration of Cuban rights.

The *guajiros*, or Cuban folk poets, compose traditional verses consisting of . ten lines each. They are troubadours who have inherited the indigenous cultural traditions of their island. Nature is their only teacher and they find inspiration in Spanish folk melodies. These artists are blessed with a good ear and extraordinary memories that enable them to preserve the verses they have heard since childhood:

> Anyone who has not seen a guajiro, or heard the verses that he stores in his memory or composes with an ease that comes naturally to a tropical imagination, does not truly understand the traditions of the country and is not able to appreciate this poetry.[8]

The themes addressed by the guajiros are usually related to love, women, God, and patriotism. Poetic sessions usually take place in huts where the improvisers carry on a dialogue of verse and song. Their poems are printed and sold in the streets. Both urban and rural residents regard these verses as the most authentic form of native folk poetry in Cuba.

CHILE

The tradition of the ten-lined verse imported by the Spaniards at the beginning of the colonial period has been preserved in Chile, especially in rural areas. It was the pattern used by most of the nineteenth-century Chilean folk poets called *payadores*.[9] This tradition spread to urban areas where it was first preserved through oral transmission from parents to children, and later survived because the verses were published. They dealt with national events and were presented in a colloquial language that was peppered with indigenous expressions, images, and metaphors.

These written verses fall into two categories, divine and human. The divine category consists of topics of a biblical nature: the creation of the earth, Cain and Abel, the prophets, Samson, Noah, David, Solomon, Joseph and Potiphar's wife, the seven plagues of Egypt, Daniel and the lion's den, and so on; the most common theme from the New Testament is the passion of Christ.

The human category encompasses all themes that do not fall under the headings of religion or the Bible. Love is the most common, but social and political issues are also included, as are the earthquakes and natural disasters common to Chile. Historical events and the feats of Charlemagne and Napoleon also appear.

Under the general theme of love, there are many lyric poems in which a lady's beauty is described in a delicate manner. The majority of the verses describing love affairs, however, are picaresque and filled with erotic and burlesque satire.

Within this folk poetry tradition, a distinction is made between *hecho*, a nonimprovised verse that is passed down through oral tradition, and the *compuesto*, an originally improvised verse. The most important types of improvised verses are *pallas* and *contrapuntos*.

Pallas are verses consisting of four lines with an *abab* rhyme pattern improvised by two poets in public competitions. In "pallas a dos razones" two poets (referred to elliptically as "dos razones," or two reasons) improvise two of the four lines. Various themes are used and are presented in a question-and-answer format. The same idea of competition and challenge is present in the *contrapuntos*, verses usually consisting of ten lines improvised on a specific theme.

Although the payadores use a narrow range of melodies, mostly two or three, their capacity for improvisation and their memories are extraordinary: "It is common for them to be able to sing for two or three nights in a row without repeating a verse." [10]

Not all folk poets are considered payadores, only those who improvise with guitar accompaniment in public competition. These competitions, however, have greatly declined in recent years. Literary contests in which payadores present verse after verse for hours, or even an entire day, are steadily losing importance and cultivated written poetry is gaining popularity.

ARGENTINA

The harsh and deserted geography of Argentina contributed to the creation of the gaucho, whose world revolved around his horse and guitar. The guitar was his inseparable companion and shared his loneliness and misfortune and witnessed his feats.

The largely erroneous, old-fashioned image of the gaucho as a dirty troublemaker, murderer, and drunkard is changing because gaucho artists, after drinking a few beers, are able to improvise and sing verses for two days and two nights. The hero of *Martín Fierro* was a gaucho who improvised verses and "was born to sing."[11] He had such great talent for improvisation that verses flowed from him like water from a spring:

> When I open my mouth,
> you can be sure that as soon
> as one verse comes out,
> another one pokes its nose around the door.[12]

José Santos Vega and Juan Poca Ropa are known as two of the best payadores of the Río de la Plata region. José Santos Vega was especially admired for his voice, his charm, and his style. He did not know how to play the guitar, but his beautiful voice made up for it as he improvised verses. His charm and good nature were coupled with simplicity and kindness, attributes that won him the love and respect of other payadores. He is believed to have died sometime around 1871.[13] His favorite themes were his country and its glories, traditions, and legends.

Juan Poca Ropa played the guitar in addition to improvising and singing. Many of his melodies have been preserved, but most of the lyrics have been lost. In his day verses were passed on orally rather than through writing; as a consequence the melodies were retained, although the lyrics were changed according to the circumstances of the performance.

Generally, each payador seeks to present his opponent with a theme he feels comfortable with, so that he can excel and dominate the performance. The object is to defeat the opponent and win the applause of the audience. When a theme has been exhausted the payadores go on to another until the audience is satisfied.

Some lyrics from past payadores have survived, although most have suffered substantial changes because of the oral nature of the literature. The great majority of lyrics have been lost forever, like the memories of the artists who created them. The little information we do possess comes to us from current research on oral literature by specialists on Argentina, such as Alfredo De La Fuente.[14]

It is difficult to give an exact definition of the earlier payador, but he could be described as independent, self-taught, individualistic, and illiterate like the majority of the Argentine population of that time. These payadores participated in rebellions and struggled together to defend their country and the interests of the people. The payador was essentially a folk artist who stood up for the working class and fought against injustice.

The payador was, and continues to be, much more than an ordinary singer, because he improvises. *Payada* literally means improvisation, and performances of this art form vary according to the number of participating payadores (one, two, or more).

The payador rarely sings the refined songs or traditional ballads that are transmitted by parents to their children. Instead, he improvises and plays the guitar. The beginning of a public performance, however, is usually not improvised. The payador prepares the first few verses in advance as an introduction. After this short prelude, improvisation is required, and the payadores must interpret and develop themes in a competitive setting. The contenders take part in a game of point-counterpoint, presenting questions and themes before a demanding audience that is familiar with the possible pitfalls.

In the past, payadores came from rural areas. They were not educated, but they knew how to improvise. From what De La Fuente tells us in "El Lazarillo de ciegos caminantes," we know that in the eighteenth century these payadores used "a guitar, which they learn to play poorly, and ruin several couplets, singing them off-key. Often they make up verses in their heads, which usually have to do with love. They stroll around the countryside . . . to the satisfaction of those semibarbarous colonists."[15]

At the beginning of the twentieth century it seemed that this form of Argentine folk literature was on the verge of disappearing. However, a few years later it regained new life not only in Argentina but in Uruguay as well, where the activity of the payadores became known as the gaucho crusades. As a result of this revival, the modern payador has attracted the attention of large audiences with a better understanding of this complicated form of oral literature.

Payadores have adapted to the demands of modern times. They have abandoned the rural way of life for urban surroundings where the news and communication media often echo their literary art. A good representative of this is Gabino Ezeiza, who preceded modern urban payadores. Ezeiza demonstrated one of the differences between modern payadores and their older rural counterparts by always performing in a suit, tie, and dress shirt.[16] He did not use trite sayings, memorized verses, or improvised versions of popular songs in his performances.

BRAZIL

The improvisation of sung verses in Brazil is known as *desafío* (a poetic duel). In western and southern Brazil, desafíos are no different from those found in Galicia and Portugal. However, in the northeastern state of Pernambuco there is a different tradition with unique characteristics.

Improvised poetry is extremely popular in this part of the country. Improvisers captivate audiences with their timely sayings, their way with words, and their mental agility. A special characteristic of this tradition is that musical instruments are not used to accompany the improviser. Like Basque bards, the Brazilian improvisers depend solely on their voices. Instruments are used only between couplets and between question-and-answer periods.

Common themes cover subjects from the Bible, history (Greek heroes, Charlemagne, the twelve noblemen from France), literature (Luis de Camões, Juan de Encina, Lope de Vega), politics, geography, and Brazilian history.

Competitions follow a fixed scheme. The improvisers make their presentation in front of an audience, exchanging pleasant words or insults, then move on to a section consisting of questions and answers.

The *sestina*, the *mourão*, and ten-lined verses are the structural forms used. The sestina is a lyrical fixed form made up of six lines, each containing seven syllables, with a rhyme scheme of *abcbdb*.[17] The mourão is a six-lined verse in dialogue form. One artist improvises two lines, the other sings the next two, and then the first artist finishes by singing the last two lines. The ten-lined verse employed by these artists contains seven syllables per line with an *abbaaccddc* rhyme.

BOSNIA, MONTENEGRO, SERBIA, AND CROATIA

As mentioned in Part I, in 1928 Milman Parry published a work dealing with the *Iliad* and the *Odyssey* in which he defended the hypothesis that the renowned Greek author had borrowed from the oral collective poetry of many anonymous bards.[18] His colleague, Albert B. Lord, applied these theories to the *guslari*, the illiterate bards from Slavic-speaking, Serbo-Croatian Moslem villages in Bosnia, Montenegro, Serbia, and Croatia. He reported his observations in *The Singer of Tales*, which has since become an indispensable handbook on oral literature throughout the world.

One of the most outstanding characteristics of the bards is their extraordinary memory. They are accompanied by a musical instrument and they sing epic poems with more than ten thousand lines. Lord insists that this is attributable to their talent for improvisation rather than memory.[19]

Parry sought out the best bards from among Moslem, Orthodox, and Catholic populations in the Bijelo Polje region. This Slavic Serbo-Croatian tradition shares roots with Russian oral epic poetry. In his comparative studies of Homeric poetry, he observed that songs performed by Moslem Serbo-Croatian bards were more interesting than those of their Christian counterparts. These bards are the last representatives of an ancient and disappearing oral tradition.

For his study Parry did not choose the best singers or the most skilled artists of gusla, a type of rustic guitar that is used to accompany the song. Neither did he include educated men of the region who did not possess the talent to sing long epic poems. Instead, he focused his attention on Avdo Međedović, a man who had a memory that allowed him to sing poetic compositions of twelve thousand lines. Međedović was born, lived, and died in Obrov near Bijelo Polje, a region situated east of Montenegro that belonged to Novi Pazar in the Turkish Empire until World War I. He was illiterate and a butcher by trade. His father was not able to send him to a Turkish school as a young boy, but he learned to speak Turkish during his three years of military service even though he did not learn to read or write. He was married when he was twenty-nine, two years after completing his military service. As a Moslem, he witnessed the atrocities committed against other Moslems during World War I. He died at age eighty-five in 1955. He was probably the last great bard of the Slavic tradition in the former Yugoslav Balkans.

Međedović was part of a long tradition of bards who passed on their art to other generations. His first teacher was his father, who was a disciple of the great bard Cor Huso Husein of Kolašin. It was necessary for Međedović to undergo three levels of instruction, all essential to becoming a good guslar: a passive stage of listening in which the young apprentice begins to develop an interest and to learn the narrations of stories sung by the experts; a second level in which the young artist creates his own essays and practices his skills; and a third level in which he sings a complete poem for the first time. Had it not been for this special training he would have lacked the necessary elements to carry out his art.

Although he did not have a good voice or play the gusla exceptionally well (he suffered an injury to his right arm during the Balkan wars), his songs and story narrations were excellent. He was able to sing poems as long as the *Iliad* and the *Odyssey*. Međedović was very proud of his ancestry and his favorite theme was the glory of the Turkish empire in the age of Suleiman, in spite of the corruption of the powerful men who surrounded the sultan.

He had an exceptional memory and an extraordinary ability for composing thousands of verses. He could sing ten to twenty lines of ten syllables each in just one minute. When Milman Parry arrived in Montenegro in 1933, Međedović was nearly sixty years old. He confessed that mentally he reached his peak for oral poetry at the age of forty. In 1935 Parry put Međedović's mental ability to the test. After another great bard, Munin Vlahovljak, had finished a song containing 2,294 lines, Parry asked Međedović if he could repeat it. Although he had never heard the song before, he was not only able to repeat it in its entirety, but he added another 4,019 lines of his own creation.[20] Five years before his death, between 1950 and 1951, in spite of the fact that he was ill and weak, he sang two long compositions that contained a total of 14,000 lines in just in one week.

Međedović, like other Serbo-Croatian bards, did not repeat another bard's verses word for word. Instead, he preferred to wait a day or two so that the essence of the composition could settle in his mind. He then embellished it with complementary themes and, upon mastering the technique, applied certain formulas. In addition to these abilities, Međedović also possessed an extensive repertoire of words, phrases, and ten-syllable lines.

The Slavic Balkan bard phenomenon is a very interesting aspect of oral folk literature, and Parry and Lord's studies have generated a great deal of admiration for this type of literature.

AFRICAN BEDOUIN WOMEN

The phenomenon of singing improvised verses is found in the southern Sahara, where Tuareg, a language belonging to the Berber language family, is spoken by approximately four million Bedouins. The majority of improvisers are women who sing without the accompaniment of any musical instrument and perform only for small groups of female friends. These female improvisers sing of their daily joys and pains.

This oral-lyric folk poetry provides women with a way of intensely sharing the experience of being a part of Bedouin society. Bedouins respond to issues about important events with poetry, and the regular get-togethers of these women are often punctuated with sung short poems about daily life. These poems usually deal with family problems, husbands, children, economic needs, separations and divorces, the death of loved ones, and so on.

These nomadic women share a sensitivity that allows a special kind of communication among them. When a woman is having problems with her husband, her greatest confidante is her mother-in-law. The older woman listens as her daughter-in-law confides in her through improvisation. She shares her troubles, her abandonment, the birth of a child, or the death of a respected husband. These women take care that their husbands do not find out what is said in these improvisation sessions. In general, the family unit is viewed as a means of procreation, not as a source for love or sexual pleasure. Consequently, the relationship between husband and wife is based on distant respect. This situation leads wives to seek the friendships of other women. This women's poetry is called *ghinnaawa* and is characterized by short verses and lack of rhyme. Long verses and rhyming are generally reserved for men.[21]

GREAT BRITAIN

In Wales there is a phenomenon similar to bertsolaritza that is worth mentioning. In the region of Snowdonia, located across from the traditionally Celtic Isle of Anglesey, there were bards who sang improvised verses. The available data date back to 1896. During popular festivities these poets were purported to "improvise simple poetic compositions for the audience that surrounds them."[22]

SIMILARITIES AND DIFFERENCES
ACROSS CULTURES

Although each culture expresses itself according to its distinct personality, all of the manifestations of oral literature share characteristics. In general, improvisation, song, and the presence of an audience are constant factors, while variety of rhythms, rhyme, and instruments for musical accompaniment vary from culture to culture. In some cases improvisation is mixed with memorization and repetition of ancient traditional poems. With the exception of Bedouin women, men are the improvisers of sung verse, usually in competition, challenges, or dialogues between two individuals or groups. In cultures where two languages coexist (a native language and a language imposed by a conquering culture), improvised oral literature occurs in the native language by choice.

Through the examples presented in this chapter, certain differences between bertsolaritza and similar literary phenomena become evident. In general, ten-lined verses, consonant rhyme, and guitar accompaniment are common in countries with Hispanic influences. However, this is not the case of bertsolaritza. Nor is the high level of competition and the offensive tone that exists among Galician improvisers present in bertsolaritza. It is also important to point out that, compared with the limited number of melodies and rhythms used by other troubadours, the bertsolari has a rich variety of eighty melodies and twenty rhymes at his disposal. Last, the degree of improvisation in bertsolaritza is very high when compared with that of the Serbo-Croatian bards, who rely on preestablished formulas. The bertsolari uses no formulas.

PART III

Analysis of

Representative Bertsolariak

Etxahun, Pello Mari Otaño, Xalbador, and Xabier Amuriza are examined more closely in this part because they represent the geographical, historical, and dialectal unity and diversity of the Basque Country. In selecting them, it is not my intention to put other great bertsolariak in a lesser position. Others, including Bilintx, Xenpelar, Txirrita, Kepa Enbeita, Uztapide, Basarri, Manuel Lasarte, and Jon Lopategi, could easily have been studied in depth. However, I have chosen these four because they represent both the northern and the southern parts of the Basque Country and the four provinces noted for bertsolaritza: Gipuzkoa, Bizkaia, Nafarroa Beherea, and Zuberoa. These four bertsolariak also span a considerable time period because they lived during the nineteenth and twentieth centuries, and they differed considerably with regard to versemaking techniques and themes.

Etxahun is especially notable because he was Zuberoa's first prominent bertsolari. Zuberoa is rich in tradition and has a very distinctive dialect and music. Etxahun lived during the eighteenth and nineteenth centuries and created verses in the Zuberoan dialect, considered most difficult by Basques from other provinces. His tragic and dramatic life lent depth to his art, and the pain he experienced contributed uniquely personal qualities to his art form. Etxahun's voice represented the romantic Basque *me* of the nineteenth century. He was a shepherd and a bertsolari with little education. Although he was an improviser, he is especially known for his written verses.

Pello Mari Otaño represents the province of Gipuzkoa, the seat of bertsolaritza. He lived during the nineteenth and twentieth centuries and is particularly interesting because of his bertso jarriak, which were previously discussed. He was a good improviser, but because of his poor voice he did not obtain the kind of success he might have hoped for in public performances. His themes reflected a new political world characterized by fervent patriotism and the birth of Basque nationalism at the beginning of the twentieth century. Otaño also echoed the voices of Basque emigrants. From the Argentine pampas, he exuded nostalgia for his faraway homeland, Euskal Herria, especially Gipuzkoa. Although he was a shepherd, he achieved a certain cultural level uncommon to herders. He used the vernacular Euskara in his verses and was careful with his verse constructions. His technique was pure. He influenced the works of many bertsolariak, including Basarri, Lazkao Txiki, and Jon Azpillaga.

Xalbador was Nafarroa Beherea's greatest bertsolari and brought the eighteenth-century tradition of Basque lyrical poetry to modern bertsolaritza. He was a bertsolari who represented the Basques of the twentieth century living separated by a border that divided their nation into two states, Spain and France. The quality of his art form was exceptional in both improvised and written verses. He was known as the best poet among all bertsolariak. Although he did not establish a school, his lyric style has become a model to emulate in poetic bertsolaritza. He was known for the depth and novelty of his ideas, even with such traditional themes as religion, family, and love. He was self-educated and cultured (he spoke three languages) in spite of the fact that he was a shepherd and had dropped out of school at the age of eleven.

Xabier Amuriza is characterized by his renewing spirit in all of his endeavors. Although a native speaker of the Bizkaian dialect, he has also mastered unified Euskara. He is a very educated man, a bertsolari, novelist, poet, and musician, as well as creator of new melodies and new schools of bertsolaritza that ensure the future of this art form. Amuriza is dedicated to the culture and politics of his country, which he would like to see independent, reunited, and socialist. His bertsolaritza technique is traditional yet modernized and pure. His art is also characterized by the dramatic flair with which he infuses his verses.

CHAPTER NINE

Pierre Topet,

Alias "Etxahun"

"Etxahun, to a great extent, owes his being the most original, personal, and moving poet of all our Basque literature to his misery and his own defects."[1] This description from Pierre Lhande (1877-1957) prompted me to study in depth the life and works of Pierre Topet, alias "Etxahun" (1786-1862). The uniqueness and artistic contributions of this great bertsolari and folk poet are also recognized by other artists, including Xabier Amuriza. When I interviewed Amuriza he stated that if he had to save the best works of Basque literature from a fire, he would choose *Odolaren mintzoa* (The Language of the blood) by Xalbador and the poetry of Etxahun.[2] Basque writers who have carefully studied Etxahun's work have been surprised by its artistic value. Jon Etxaide (1920-   ) states: "Etxahun was not only a bertsolari, but also a poet, and a great one at that."[3]

Who was this man so admired by twentieth-century critics, yet so ignored by his contemporaries and even disdained by his own family? The answer is not an easy one because many details of his life are missing. The disappearance of nearly all parish records in Barcus, his hometown, makes piecing his biography together a difficult task. Writer Jean Haritschelhar (1923–   ) has studied Etxahun in great detail.[4] He says that there was a silent conspiracy against Etxahun and his works.[5] Since concrete data were lacking, he began to reconstruct Etxahun's life by weaving a sort of legend that started at the end of the eighteenth century. Haritschelhar's lack of accuracy is largely due to the fact that Etxahun did not circulate his verses in written form as did Xenpelar and other Gipuzkoan bertsolariak later on. It is not true, however, that Etxahun did not write verses; we know that he kept a notebook of them. Unfortunately, his relatives burned the records shortly before his death, as if his work carried the plague. Pierre Lhande confirms it: "I am sure his heirs burned his manuscripts because they were convinced that they would bring a curse upon their home."[6]

Intellectuals from the north of the Basque Country were largely responsible for Etxahun's banishment into oblivion. Many of these men chose to ignore him completely because he came across as impetuous. As time passed the general public forgot about his aggressive behavior. Basques resist putting things in writing and are not avid readers, but collectively they possess a good memory about Etxahun and his work.

At the end of the nineteenth century bertsolari Jean Baptiste Otxalde entered a literary competition in Mauleon with a poem entitled "Etchahun eta Otxalde." In this poem he expressed his admiration for the bertsolari from Barcus, referring to him with the northern term *koblakari*:

Halaco coplaririk ez omen da nehon.[7]

It is said that nowhere can you find a bertsolari like him.

Attitudes toward Etxahun changed within intellectual circles during the twentieth century. As early as 1922 Pierre Lhande became interested in the life and works of this Zuberoan poet. In 1941 Basque scholar Pierre Lafitte dedicated part of a conference held at the Basque museum in Baiona to Etxahun.[8] Etxahun also became the topic of literature in a novel and a play.[9] Poets, including Jean Diharce, alias "Iratzeder" (1920–   ), have dedicated poems to Etxahun.[10]

Since the bicentennial in 1986 of Etxahun's birth, attention to his art has steadily increased. What was so special about this bertsolari who possessed so little education and wandered aimlessly throughout most of his life with only a loyal dog for company? As the myths about Etxahun give way to more precise historical data, interest in this bertsolari grows. In addition, his work is crucial for understanding the dialect and folk poetry of eighteenth-century Zuberoa.

I have chosen Etxahun for this study because I consider him to be a good representative of the combined roles of improviser and folk poet. As early as 1870 Jean Dominique Julien Sallaberry referred to him as "barde ou improvisateur basque" (Basque bard or improviser).[11] In 1941 Pierre Lafitte defined him as "le bertsolari le plus extraordinaire dont on ait gardé le souvenir et les vers en Pays Basque" (the greatest bertsolari whose memory and verses have been preserved in the Basque Country).[12] My analysis of Etxahun is presented in two parts. In the first, I examine his life by focusing on his personality and his existence as a sorrowful traveler on the journey of life, elements that lend depth to his literary art. In the second part, I analyze his poetry and focus on his themes and style.

THE LIFE OF ETXAHUN

Etxahun's exact date of birth is not known because the parish records were destroyed and no other official document exists. It is possible that he was born on September 27, 1786.[13]

The only information we have about his childhood comes to us from a poem he composed in 1834 entitled "Etxahunen bizitzaren khantoria" (The song of the life of Etxahun). In this poem, he portrays himself as small in stature and as a weakling. He is persecuted and scorned by nearly all members of his family. We do know several details about his family. His father, Jean Topet, heir to the farmhouse Topetia, married Engrâce Etxahun, heir to the farmhouse Etxahun. Etxahun was the second of seven children.

His uncle and godfather, also named Pierre Topet, was a wealthy man. Since he and his wife, Marie Belchun, had no children, one would have thought Etxahun, their godson, would be the sole heir to their wealth. However, that is not what happened. That disillusionment, along with many other factors, contributed to the wretched life that Etxahun would lead. The primary reason for his misery, however, was the disdain his father showed him throughout his life. He always considered him a bastard child born out of adultery because they did not look alike:

Haren egiteik gabe ni amak sorthü ükhen.[14]

My mother gave birth to me without the collaboration of my father.

To make matters even worse, his mother showed him no affection either. In his poetry, Etxahun has no kind words for her. He describes her as cold and callous, both physically and emotionally:

Amac idor bihotça, bai eta thitia.[15]

My mother's heart was dry, as was her breast.

The only person in his family who showed him any affection was his maternal grandmother, who defended him from the scorn of other family members. His classmates also treated him badly:

Çortzi guerren ourthia nian escolaco
nic hanere çorthia, etchen beçalaco.[16]

When I was eight I went to school.
My predicament there was just like the one at home.

He stayed in school just long enough to learn rudimentary reading, writing, catechism, and mathematics. The many errors present in his written French bear witness to his lack of education. When he was just ten years old he had to assume responsibility under the orders of a servant, for a flock of sheep.

When he was seventeen he fell in love with Marie Arrospide, who was employed as a servant in his family's home. A few months later she became pregnant. The child, whom they named Jean, was born on September 27, 1805. Etxahun's parents would not accept the baby as their grandchild or the servant girl as their daughter-in-law. Etxahun found himself in a very difficult situation. His choices were either to marry Marie Arrospide and lose his inheritance, or to leave her forever. He opted for the latter because his family exerted pressure in the form of blackmail.

It took Etxahun thirteen months to make a decision. During this time his uncle voided his first will and in 1806 designated Joseph, the third son, as heir to the estate. Etxahun would not inherit anything from his godfather, not even indirectly through his father. It was the uncle's way of punishing his godson and nephew.

Etxahun wrote a poem, "Urxaphal bat" (A turtledove), about his relationship with Marie Arrospide, and his shirking of responsibility toward her. His love for her was genuine and his decision to enter into a relationship with her was one of the few independent ones he made during his youth. Monetary concerns, however, overruled his feelings and gave rise to a series of problems that were to plague him the rest of his life. His parents and uncle had gotten their way. They later introduced him to a young woman named Engrâce Pelento, who was three years his senior. Although he did not love her, he married her two years later. Etxahun saw his marriage as a way of ending family tension and ensuring his inheritance of Etxaunia (the farmhouse) as well as other benefits from his wealthy uncle.

Etxhaun and Pelento were married on July 26, 1808, when Etxahun was only twenty-two years old. The religious ceremony took place on September 27 of the same year. His bride, in lieu of love, contributed a considerable dowry. A year later Etxahun's godfather died and all of his assets became the property of Etxahun's brother Joseph. In 1813, when Joseph had to fulfill his military service, he drafted a will in which he left all his assets to his other brother Pierre. This will, intended to favor Pierre, actually never benefitted him at all. Although Joseph never returned from the Napoleonic wars, his death was never proven. In 1817 disputes over Joseph's will divided the family. Etxahun's parents and siblings left Etxaunia and moved into Topetia to live with the godfather's widow.

Etxahun's mother died in 1818. Her assets were divided and Etxahun inherited a little over half of the property. This did not go far in providing a remedy for his economic situation. In 1819 the court in Saint Palais nullified his godfather's will over formal technicalities. This in turn voided Joseph's will and Etxahun lost his inheritance of Topetia. This was just the beginning of his troubles. Etxahun began to hate his brother Jean, who began to buy from his relatives the land that formed part of Topetia, so that one day he would own that property. Etxahun became progressively more aggressive and anxious.

Between 1808 and 1821 Etxahun and his wife had six children in Etxaunia, but that was not enough to save the loveless marriage. It was not long before insults and quarrels began.

Envy, suspicion, and jealousy ate away at Etxahun, who already believed that the world was against him. From the beginning of his marriage, he experienced jealousy because his wife had a lover, Jean Héguiaphal, their closest neighbor. The year 1821 was a trying one for Etxahun. His marriage was quickly deteriorating. A confrontation with another neighbor, Benoît Goyhenex, on October 21, 1821, ended tragically and Etxahun was incarcerated. A simple argument about monetary problems escalated into a physical confrontation in which Etxahun mortally wounded Goyhenex with an axe. He was charged with attempted murder, robbery, and trying to pass a counterfeit gold coin. He was sentenced to two years in prison and two years on parole.

While he was serving his sentence in Saint Palais the family arranged to redistribute their mother's inheritance. Her brother Joseph was designated as sole heir and Etxahun was left empty-handed. He became vengeful and his heart filled with hate. His self-respect suffered. Etxahun found himself alone and powerless against an accusatory society. He escaped from prison in 1822. (The exact length of his incarceration is not known.) He felt himself the victim of constant persecution. He hid in the mountains of Sainte-Engrâce (Zuberoa) but was captured by the police who considered him dangerous. On December 30, 1823, he was sentenced to two additional years in prison and another two under house arrest. In 1824 he was transferred to the central prison of Eysses in Pau. There he was visited by André Chaho, the father of romantic writer Augustin Chaho.

His loneliness and misery could not have been more intense. His wife was having an affair, he was deprived of his children's affection, and his siblings did not want to come to his aid. His well-known poem "Mundian malerusik" (Miserable in this world) is an imaginary dialogue between himself and his unfaithful wife—a reflection of his state of mind during that time. Etxahun accuses Engrâce Pelento of having an illegitimate child, although in reality she did not bear any children during his imprisonment. He wrote:

Aguri da frutia ecin dirot ukha.[17]

The child is evident and cannot be denied.

Etxahun was released from the central prison of Eysses in 1826, where he had served five years even though he was sentenced to only two. His freedom did not last for long. He was incarcerated once again in Pau, and later in Saint Palais. He was finally released in 1827 when the robbery and counterfeiting charges could not be proved. He returned to his village, but no one acknowledged his homecoming. His home was empty. Pelento had taken two of their children and gone to live with her sister. Etxahun stayed at Etxaunia with two of his other children. His heart was overflowing with hate, resentment, and plans for revenge, which had been building up over the five years in prison. He blamed his neighbor, Jean Héguiaphal, for all his misfortunes and on one occasion threatened him with a knife.[18]

He did not stop at threats, however. On May 1, 1827, the infamous crime of Barcus was committed. Two friends, Dominique Etchegoyhen and Pierre Hegoburu, were on their way back from the market in Oloron in the middle of the night when a shot rang out. Young Etchegoyhen fell dead to the ground. Etxahun was immediately suspected of committing the crime. Years later he himself said:

> Bestec eraman derik hic behar colpia.[19]
>
> Someone else received the bullet you deserved.

Although Etxahun was not arrested, the police had well-founded suspicions that he had been the perpetrator, and they began a search. Etxahun was forced into hiding once more in the mountains of Sainte-Engrâce as if he were one of

> desertuco ihicic genten beldurrez.[20]
>
> the beasts of the desert in fear of humans.

When the police gave up their search because of insufficient evidence, Etxahun was able to return to Barcus. His respite was short-lived, though, because the village was soon struck by yet another misfortune. On October 23, 1827, Jean Héguiaphal's farmhouse burned down. Once again, suspicious eyes turned to Etxahun. This time he fled to the mountain of Larrau. In his loneliness his only consolation was romantic poetry, in which he related his misfortunes and spoke of his own sad and solitary existence. He also later criticized his parents, his wife, her lover, Jean Héguiaphal, and his wife's uncle, Father Dominique Haritchabalet, Sainte-Engrâce's parish priest.

When he returned home in February of 1828, the Mauleon police arrested him. He was imprisoned in Saint Palais for another six months. His trial was held on August 18 and 19. He was charged with arson and the murder of Etchegoyhen. Etxahun was belligerent during his trial. He wrote his own defense in Euskara because it was the only language in which he could display his talents for improvisation, irony, and satire. He admitted his guilt in shooting the innocent friend he had mistaken for his archenemy Héguiaphal. The trial attracted many people from Pau. Etxahun, faced with the possibility of a death sentence or life in prison, put his talents to good use. He unnerved the judges and witnesses with his jokes, questions, and indignant outbursts. He claimed to be the victim of a conspiracy. The verdict was "not guilty" and Etxahun was released. His trial also attracted attention from outside the Basque Country. Upon hearing of Etxahun's situation, German poet Adelbert von Chamisso (1781–1838) dedicated a romantic poem to him.[21]

His homecoming did not put an end to his problems. Even though he was to inherit five houses, he found himself penniless and in debt because of legal fees:

Bost lekhutaco primu, ican cena sorthu.[22]

He who had been born to inherit five houses.

The people of Barcus abandoned Etxahun. Many of them were disappointed with the result of his trial. Everyone regarded him as a bad son, father, husband, and neighbor. To escape this climate of opinion, Etxahun devised a plan to go on a pilgrimage to Rome where he would fulfill a promise he had made in prison three years earlier:

Promes bat egin neion sendo nahiz Jinkuari.[23]

I made a pact with God that he would give me strength.

On this pilgrimage Etxahun wrote one of his best poems, "Bi berset dolorusik" (A few painful verses).[24] In it, he assumes the role of a pilgrim. He seems to be truly sorry for his past errors and very sincere about his effort to repent. He forgives his wife and asks his rival, Héguiaphal, to leave her. He laments his weaknesses, gives advice, and forgives everyone.

He left Barcus with the intention of visiting Santiago de Compostela, Rome, and the sanctuary of the Virgin in Loretto, Italy:

Izan nüzü Jundane Jakan, Loretan ta Erruman.[25]

I have gone to Santiago de Compostela, Loretto, and Rome.

This trip, which proved to be less than pleasant, lasted six months. We do not have many details about it. It appears that when his father died on September 28, 1831, Etxahun left for Rome. After visiting Rome he planned to continue his pilgrimage by going to Jerusalem, but he lost his passport in Ancona (Tuscany). He was imprisoned and later deported to France. When he was picked up for vagrancy in Nîmes, he was chronically ill. The six months of pilgrimage evidently did not benefit him in any way.

Upon his return to Barcus he took legal action against his brother Jean in an effort to reclaim Etxaunia, the farmhouse that should rightfully have been his upon the death of his father. The desire for property was deeply rooted in Etxahun's heart. He finally managed to become the owner of Etxaunia and some of the land that surrounded it. In 1832 he was reunited with his wife and children in his parents' house. In a little less than a decade he regained all the property that he wanted except Topetia, which remained under Jean's ownership.

Etxahun, however, was not to be satisfied until he had control of Topetia as well. As heir to all five houses, he was determined to claim all that was rightfully his. He even resorted to forgery. Posing as Jean on July 20, 1841, he appeared with a friend before the notary of Nabarrenx. He committed a grave error in impersonating his brother and forging a public document. This document had Jean agreeing to turn over 13/16 of Topetia to Etxahun. The document was denounced before the law, however, by the real Jean. In 1843 Etxahun was sentenced to ten years of forced labor in Pau. He wrote: "Hamar urtheren galeretan nahi ükhen naie sarthü" (They wanted to send me to the galleys for ten years).[26] He escaped prison and spent two years in Spain as a pilgrim, probably traveling the road to Santiago. In his poem "Ahaide delezius huntan" (About this delicious melody), we find echoes of this experience:

> Bi urthe igaran ditiat Españan pelegri gisa.[27]
>
> I spent two years as a pilgrim in Spain.

When he returned once again to Barcus in 1845, his son Joseph did not allow him to enter the house. (Etxahun's property had been confiscated, and Joseph had purchased it.) During this same visit, however, his wife gave him a new shirt, something he would later thank her for in his verses. Having nowhere to sleep, he wandered from farm to farm looking for a straw loft in which to pass the cold nights of winter:

> Bi hilabete igaran tiat sabaietan hotzez ikhara.[28]
>
> I've spent two months in lofts shivering from the cold.

He was finally arrested and, on August 11, 1845, at the age of sixty, he was imprisoned again in Pau. He played his role of bertsolari, improviser, and actor well before the judges. He resorted to old tricks. He passed himself off as a deeply religious man, frequenter of sanctuaries, an elderly pilgrim whose mind had been affected by age and constant journeys. He appeared in court dressed in pilgrim's garb with all the accoutrements (a staff, a gourd, a scallop shell, and a rosary). Throughout the trial he told tales of his misfortune and played the part of a half-wit. The judge took pity on him and reduced his sentence to three years in prison. On February 24, 1846, he was transferred to the prison in Eysses from which he had escaped twenty years earlier.[29] A year later his wife, who had not lived with him in many years, was granted a legal separation.

He finished his sentence in 1847 and returned to Barcus. Once again he was shunned. He was sixty-two and a broken man. Although one of his brothers, Jean Pierre, took him into his home in Garindein, the arrangement did not last. Jean Pierre's family, especially one of his sons, loathed Etxahun, and he was once again homeless. He found a place to sleep in the hayloft of a farmhouse. From that time on his hatred toward his brother's family became apparent. In 1850, in the middle of the night, Etxahun was brutally attacked, and lost an eye in the ordeal. According to him, his nephew, Pierre, was the perpetrator. Many people did not believe this allegation. On February 28, 1851, the nephew was declared innocent at a hearing in Pau. This made Etxahun's reputation worse. He abandoned Barcus and went begging throughout the villages of the province.

His wife died in 1855 as a result of a cholera epidemic that swept the Basque Country. Etxahun bade her a biblical farewell:

> Josafatera artino.[30]
>
> Until the Valley of Jehoshaphat.

In 1856, at age seventy, he went to live in Saint-Engrâce. While adults disparaged and avoided him, children gathered around him to hear the tales of his miserable life. Etxahun found in these children the audience that he had needed. It was through these oral lessons that his poetry has been preserved.

His youngest son, Pierre, was married in 1856. Etxahun left Saint-Engrâce to live with him in Eskiula. He spent the last six years of his life in relative peace there. On many occasions he complained about the meager amounts of money he received from his children, but he also had moments of consolation and happiness:

> In his last years Etxahun enjoyed his greatest popularity. He was invited to every festivity and the poet gave his all to the people he was beginning to love. Without respite, he improvised and composed songs about the most varied themes.[31]

Etxahun knew how to read and write. Sitting on a bench in the kitchen, he remembered verses he had sung on his journeys and recorded them in a notebook. Unfortunately, his family burned his notebook after his death to avoid any curse they thought might befall Etxaunia. In 1861, after the death of his son, Pierre, he went back to Etxaunia where he lived with another son, Joseph.

Etxahun died on January 17, 1862, from complications caused by asthma. The priest who administered his last rites gave testimony to the fact that Etxahun professed his Catholic faith before dying. Besides family members, there were no more than ten men at his funeral. His mortal remains rest in the cemetery in Barcus. In spite of the burning of his notebook, the beauty of the Basque language in his verses was not lost. Through the memory of villagers and shepherds from the area of Barcus and Igelu his poems were passed down for generations. The solitude of the mountains, the shepherds' idle moments, and the autumn farm chores (like shucking corn) provided the setting for the transmission of Etxahun's most popular verses in song.[32]

THEMES AND STYLE

In order to study the themes and style of Etxahun's work, it is necessary to examine some of his best poems. These are, without a doubt, his autobiographical compositions: "Urxaphal bat," "Mundian malerusik," "Bi berset dolorusik," "Etxahunen bizitzaren khantoria," and "Ahaide delezius huntan." The following poems are also pertinent to this study: "Ofizialenak," "Barkoxeko Eliza," "Musde Tiraz," "Bi berseten eguitez," "Musde Chaho," and "Amodio gati." In these works we find bursts of anger, thirst for revenge, and bitter humor.

"Urxaphal bat" (A turtledove, 1805–1808)

As previously discussed, "Urxaphal bat" describes the forced separation between Etxahun and his love, Marie Arrospide. Every line except the first is in dialogue form. The image of the young, weeping, abandoned mother is present throughout. She is represented by the turtledove, a traditional Basque symbol of innocence and loyalty. There is dual sorrow because Etxahun is forced to leave his love and then she is left abandoned. Etxahun favors Marie Arrospide, condemning his family's posture as well as his own. The abandoned young woman in his poem accuses him of lack of love and courage.

"Mundian malerusik" (Great misfortune, 1827)

After revealing his pain in several lines, Etxahun sets forth his complaint in "Mundian malerusik." He brutally expresses his indignation. Although he does not mention his rival's name, his attacks are intended for Héguiaphal, his archenemy. Threats and bitter irony are his preferred weapons, and he uses them on his family as well. He sarcastically describes his father as loyal, "ene aita fidela" (my loyal father). In essence this poem is a bitter criticism of his wife and her lover. Toward the end, in line seventeen, he acknowledges that he has spoken a great deal about his enemies. The poem exudes profound sorrow and melancholy. The purity of the Zuberoan dialect and the conciseness of his style stand out particularly in this composition.

"Bi berset dolorusik" (A few painful verses, 1831)

"Bi berset dolorusik" is chronologically his third autobiographical poem. In it he remembers the saddest periods and moments of his life: his childhood (verse 3), his marriage (verse 4), his imprisonment (verses 5–6), the crime of Barcus in 1827 (verse 7), his second imprisonment in 1828 (verse 8) and the trial of that same year (verse 9). He moves on to describe his life as a wandering pilgrim. It is interesting that this poem was written before his pilgrimage. He bids farewell to his wife and family as well as the people of Barcus. This is one of the few poems in which Etxahun indicates a sincere desire to repent and change his ways as well as to pardon his enemies. In twenty-one five-lined verses, Etxahun recounts his sad life.

"Etxahunen bizitzaren khantoria" (Song of the life of Etxahun, 1834)

"Etxahunen bizitzaren khantoria" describes the story of Etxahun's life in detail, emphasizing the most important events. He was approaching fifty when he wrote it. From the perspective of a mature man, full of pain and hate, he reproaches all those he considers his enemies: his parents, wife, siblings, and family members. In the end, in an unusual gesture, he shows his gratitude to several people outside the family. His attacks are frontal and his style is direct and clear throughout. The poem seems to be a harsh judgment of his family. Beginning with the second verse, he attacks his parents by evoking images of childhood years during which he suffered so greatly. His mother is depicted as a cruel stepmother devoid of any human sentiments. According to Etxahun, he tried to please her, but she showed only indifference.

He treats his father no better. He is depicted as demonic, largely responsible for the misery that Etxahun suffered during his life. Etxahun was considered a bastard by his father for not bearing a physical resemblance to him, and that was the root of all the misfortunes in his life.

His wife is treated equally harshly. There is not even the slightest indication of affection for her in the entire poem. Their marriage was a total failure in which there was not one happy moment. When Etxahun escaped from prison, it was she who turned him in. She wanted to see him imprisoned for life. It is in this poem that he also accuses her of having given birth to an illegitimate child while he was in prison.

Even though there is a generally negative tone in the poem, Etxahun ends the last two verses with gratitude for several authorities who took an interest in him during his imprisonment. He specifically mentions M. Maitie, M. Etchats, and Mousde Deffis. He refers to these individuals with great respect and affection. To Etxahun the world was divided into good guys and bad guys. The good guys included himself and the few who protected him. The bad guys were all those who opposed him.

"Ahaide delezius huntan" (In this delicious melody, 1840)

"Ahaide delezius huntan" is a passionate poem that was to be Etxahun's last autobiographical composition. The events he describes took place between 1841 and 1848. He focuses principally on his brother, Jean Pierre, and on one of his sons. Etxahun blames Jean Pierre for his imprisonment. He labels his own son as a traitor and speaks of his daughter-in-law with contempt. In this poem he takes pity on his other children, some of whom would be disinherited, and his wife, condemned to a life of domestic slavery. He also shows gratitude to his wife for giving him a shirt when he desperately needed it. Many critics consider this poem Etxahun's masterpiece.[33] For this work, Etxahun selected his rhymes carefully and used very expressive language. The slow rhythm of the verses complements the sad melody in which they are sung.

The poems examined thus far provide many details that aid in the reconstruction of Etxahun's biography. These poems also serve to illustrate Etxahun's passion, his capacity to criticize, and his satirical tone. Some of Etxahun's other poems help us understand his choice of topics and his style.

"Ofizialenak" (Verses about occupations, date unknown)

In "Ofizialenak" Etxahun systematically evaluates seventeen occupations. Although this work is not his best (because of weak rhymes), nor his most well known, it is significant. Here Etxahun demonstrates a rare gift for observation. He captures the psychological and picturesque elements in people. Each one of the occupations he describes is characterized by some limitation. When depicting a peasant he loses his aggressive tone and takes on a compassionate attitude, undoubtedly because he belonged to the same class. Generally, he uses humor and subtle satire to exaggerate the weaknesses of particular occupations. Etxahun chose verses of four lines: two eight-syllable lines followed by two long lines of seventeen syllables. These long lines contain a caesura after the ninth syllable.

"Barkoxeko eliza" (The church of Barcus, 1850)

"Barkoxeko eliza" is an ardent attack against the parish priest of Barcus, M. Schmarsow. He was of German ancestry and, although Basque, he was not a native of Zuberoa.[34] Etxahun spares no details in his criticism of the priest who kicked him out of the church of Barcus for sitting in a special pew reserved for wealthy parishioners.

Etxahun also denounces the priest for denying him alms and hiding in the garden to avoid having to visit with him. He compares him with a kinder priest who attended to the parish before, visiting the sick and carrying out works of charity. Etxahun also holds the priest's German ancestry against him. He attacks him harshly, saying that the Germans and the Spanish are a proud and vengeful people. He also tries to turn members of the parish against the priest, whom he refers to as a *manech*—a Basque who is not from Zuberoa. The priest's dictatorial nature revealed itself when he suspended the Corpus Christi procession against the wishes of the parish youth. Etxahun had intended to present some of his works in that procession. As a result, he came to the harsh conclusion that Christ was not of the same race (German) as the priest.

"Musde Tiraz" (1860)

Etxahun was not a supporter of priests. He is known to have ridiculed his wife's uncle and Barcus's parish priests, among others. In "Musde Tiraz" he berates the parish priest of Eskiula for denying him absolution because he had earlier criticized the priests in Barcus. He depicts Father Musde Tiraz as a man given to drinking, laziness, and a high lifestyle.

"Bi berseten eguitez" (Composing two verses, 1853)

On another occasion Etxahun dared to dispute the decision of a panel of literary judges made up mostly of priests. He presented a poem at the first poetry contest organized by Antoine d'Abbadie in 1853. The assigned theme was a Basque who had to emigrate to Montevideo. Father Maurice Harriet (1814-1904) from Baiona served as a judge along with other priests. The winners were two priests: Landarretche, archpriest of Mauleon, and Celhabe from Bardos. Etxahun perceived their decision as a personal offense and fiercely criticized the judges for giving the prize to the wrong men. He also criticized the winners for being unworthy of it.

"Bi berseten eguitez" is a vigorous satire against the clerical winners. Etxahun labels one of them as incompetent and the other as a renegade:

> Espeitu poeta denez eracousten . . .
> Celhabe Bardoceko apphez arnegata . . .
> Harriet çu cirade seminarin jabe,
> Bena etcirade houn coblarien juge.[35]

> He does not show the signs of a good poet . . .
> Celhabe, renegade priest from Bardos . . .
> Harriet, you are the director of the seminary,
> but you are not honest when it comes to judging poets.

"Musde Chaho" (1849)

Etxahun actively participated in the electoral campaign as the representative of the humble folk, *jente xehiak*. In "Musde Chaho" he makes specific demands that give us insight into the concerns of the Basques during that period of universal suffrage: the freedom to sell tobacco and wine, and the free movement of cattle on communal lands. He clearly supports Augustin Chaho, who fought for the rights of the common people before the French government in Paris.

"Amodio gati" (In the name of love, 1854)

In "Amodio gati" Etxahun criticizes the wealthy and the society they had established. It was his intent to demonstrate that justice served only those with money, that it condemned the poor and liberated the rich.

In expressing his opinion about an assassination that took place in Garindein, Etxahun once again turned to irony and verbal abuse. The assassin turned out to be Jean Aroix-Etchandy, the lieutenant mayor who years before had taken a stand against Etxahun. Here the poet expresses his hatred for a society that relies on a justice system that serves the wealthy exclusively. Etxahun saw the world in terms of a dichotomy of good and bad, influenced by the Manichean mentality of Zuberoan pastorales and their representations of angels and demons. He classified himself and most common people as good. The bad included the wealthy, the clergy, and the powerful:

Orai jüztizietan, krima handik
Kreditak dütienek pharkatürik
Eta praube jüstuak aldiz pünitürik.[36]

Nowadays
courts pardon powerful men
and punish the poor people who are honest.

Etxahun wrote in a very personal style. Within the scope of Basque literature, he was unique and exceptional in many ways. His suffering and the hate he harbored in his heart provided depth to his poetry. There is a total relationship between the poet and his work. His style is characterized by violent satire—a natural product of his passionate temperament. Although he used humor, it was of a bitter nature. The undertone of his work was sarcastic. His caustic and poignant verses were filled with profound sadness and bitter disappointment. His work often conveyed a sense of despair.

Etxahun was a man of extraordinary natural talent. His lack of formal schooling was compensated by his contact with nature. He was a rare satirical poet, a keen observer, and proficient in creating perfect caricatures of the people and the things he detested.

Etxahun also had an extraordinary command of Euskara. He had a special talent for choosing words and images to ironically describe people and situations. He generally used simple assonant rhymes. In this respect, he followed the tradition established for bertsolaritza. He compensated for any possible weakness through his expression of profound emotions and the beauty of his images, especially in his satirical and elegiac compositions. His style is unique and cannot be reproduced. His language is difficult to understand for anyone who is not a native of Zuberoa.[37] His Euskara is also too difficult to translate to other languages.[38] Etxahun avoided enjambment, a common feature of bertsolaritza style, and marked all his caesuras with a comma. He intended his verses to be sung and not read. This is what differentiates the folk poet and the kobla-kari (or bertsolari) from the olerkari, the composer of learned poetry who sets the work to paper after it has passed through a screening process. Etxahun generally utilized seventeenth-century Basque folk melodies. The musicality of the Zuberoan dialect lent a sweet archaic air to his literary art. His verses were not particularly original with regard to melodies or rhyme, if we compare them to the works of Basque writers of the seventeenth and eighteenth centuries such as Arnauld Oihenart (1592-1667) and Joannes Etxeberri (1668-1794).

With the passing of time, the image of Etxahun as an accursed poet is giving way to one of an exceptional koblakari. He is worthy of the reputation he acquired as the most important figure of Basque literature of the nineteenth century. Some, including Orixe, refer to him as "the Basque Verlaine."[39] Others, such as Pierre Lhande and Jokin Zaitegi (1906-1979), compare him to the great French poet François Villon (1431- ?).[40] Etxahun's verses will continue to attract attention from those interested in Basque folk poetry. His village, Barcus, recognized this fact and commemorated July 27, 1986, the poet's bicentennial. Pierre Bordazarre's pastorale, "Etxahun koblakari" (1953), was performed as part of the event.[41] Several thousand Basques flocked to Barcus to honor the memory of Etxahun as a great folk poet and bertsolari. The few examples of his work that remain are of tremendous value to Basque folk literature.

CHAPTER TEN

Pello Mari Otaño,

Alias "Katarro"

Two forces exist among the Basque people, one centripetal and the other centrifugal.[1] The former encourages them to maintain their ties with their native land, but the latter has made the Basque Country one of the nations of Western Europe whose people have the greatest tendency to emigrate, especially to America. Basques have long been characterized by this tendency. Along with their great attachment to their native land, there exists a great desire to explore, to better their situation in as yet unknown places, and to seek out fortune at the same time as they test fate. It was not a coincidence that the first man to sail around the world was Basque.[2]

At times the Basque diaspora was generated by internal conflicts, persecution, and wars. For example, the ominous aftermath of the French Revolution forced many Basques from the northern part of the Basque Country to flee to the Americas. The same thing happened in the south of Euskal Herria after the two Carlist wars. Many Basques, especially the young ones, were obliged to cross the Atlantic and seek refuge in Latin America and the United States.

The diaspora is reflected in different expressions of Basque art. Thus, for example, within Basque music we have a series of songs that have emigration as their theme. Along with sentimentality and sadness, we occasionally find humor and the desire to make one's fortune, as in the following popular song:

154

Ameriketara joan nintzan
xentimorik gabe.
Andik etorri nintzan maitea
bost milloien jabe.
Txin, txin (bis) diruaren otsa
Aretxek ematen dit
maitea biotzean poza.[3]

I went to America
without a cent,
and I returned
with five million.
Clink, clink.
The sound of clinking money
warms my heart.

Another popular song expresses the search for something better, the desire for a better life and for change:

Amerikara noa
nere borondatez
emen baño obeto
bizitzeko ustez.[4]

I'm going to America
of my own free will,
with the hope of living
better than here.

In the nineteenth and early twentieth centuries emigration to the Americas was massive. The assigned theme in the poetry competition organized by Antoine d'Abbadie in 1853 was the suffering a Basque experienced when forced to emigrate to Montevideo. Basques embarked at Baiona, Bordeaux, and Pasaia in ships that were not very big and contained at least three hundred people. Food was scarce and hygiene and lodging left much to be desired. Pello Mari Otaño made at least two trips, and perhaps three, to Argentina. Very few details are known about his life, although he left behind many poetic compositions of great merit.[5]

Pello Mari Otaño (known as Pedro María Otaño in Spanish) was born on October 26, 1857, on the Errekalde farm of Zizurquil (Gipuzkoa), in a family with a long tradition of bertsolariak. Although it was not a frequent occurrence in bertsolaritza, the Otaños constituted a dynasty of bertsolariak.[6] Otaño's grandfather, also named Pedro María Otaño, alias "Errekalde Zarra," was a bertsolari, but unfortunately very few of his verses have been preserved. Otaño's uncle, Joxe Bernardo, was one of the best bertsolariak of his time and several of his verses have survived.[7] He took part in contests in the town squares and participated in the famous Azpeitia competition organized by Antoine d'Abbadie, where he performed opposite Pello Errota and Udarregi.

Pello Mari Otaño was famous for his bertsoak on Basque emigration. No one sang like he did about the emigrant's homesickness. While still very young he sailed from the port of Pasaia (Gipuzkoa) and went off to be a sheepherder in Argentina. Fortune must not have smiled on him for he returned to Donostia where he married and had three children. Later, he returned to the pampas to seek his fortune and settled in Rosario (Santa Fe). There, another three children were born. He worked hard at sheepherding and occasionally taught Euskara at the Laurak Bat Basque center of Buenos Aires. He also wrote the lyrics of an opera entitled "Artzai mutila" (The shepherd), set in 1900 in the capital of Argentina.[8] Otaño died as the result of a freak accident (he slipped on the stairs of his house) in 1910, at the age of fifty-three. He never achieved his greatest dream, to have his bones rest in the shade of the walnut tree on the family farm in the Basque Country:

> Bañan joan nai det ostera,
> Euskal-lurreko zuaizpe artan
> Nere ezurrak uztera.[9]

> But I want to return once more
> to lay my bones
> beneath that tree in the Basque Country.

Before sailing from Pasaia, Otaño composed his famous verses "Aitasemeak" (Father and son) using the hamarreko txikia meter. He dedicated these verses to, and sang them for, a teacher at the Misericordia School of Donostia. In six verses he relates the departure of a son leaving for America. His Christian father gives him last-minute advice at the foot of a cross. These verses are famous for their depth of feeling and are still sung today in the Basque Country. Here are three of those six verses:

> Lagundurikan denoi
> gugatik il zanak . . .
> Orain gurutze onen
> oñean esanak
> ondo goguan artu
> biaituzu danak.

> Seme izan goguan
> zeure gurasuak
> eta uzten dituzun
> senide gozuak;
> Jayo ziñan tokiko
> mendi ta basuak,
> euskerazko otoitzak

edo errezuak,
erakutsiak zure
Amatxo gaxuak.

Iritxi da ordua
joan bear dezuna
Badakizu ait'amak
emen dauzkatzuna;
ez dezazula aztu
gaur neri entzuna.
Itz baterako au da
eskatzen zaizuna:
izan zaitez nonnai ta
beti euskalduna.[10]

Counting on the help
of He who died for us . . .
Remember well
what I am about to tell you
now at the foot of this cross.

Son, remember
your parents
and the beloved relatives
you leave behind,
remember the place where you were born,
its mountains and forests,
and the prayers in Basque
that your beloved mother
taught you.

The time has come
for you to leave,
you know your parents
will be here;
do not forget
what you heard from me today.
In a word,
this is what I am asking you:
always be Basque no matter where you are.

Otaño had a great desire to see new lands, but when he arrived in Argentina he had to settle for a little corner of the New World as a sheepherder on a ranch. Next to his shepherd's hut there was a solitary ombu tree, the sight of which reminded him of the walnut tree on his family farm and the woods where he spent his youth. That ombu tree was his oasis. In his verses, the tree was personified—treated as his best friend. He promised always to remember it, although he wanted to return to the Basque Country to rest eternally under the shade of the tree on his family farm. From the remote and treeless pampas, he expressed his homesickness with the following verse:

Euskal-Erriko lur maite artan
jayo nintzan baserrian,
itzal aundiko intxaur arbol bat
dago gure atarian . . .

Denak utzi ta etorri nintzan
lur au ikusi nai nuan! . . .
Oraiñ artzantzan Ameriketan
Arrantxo baten onduan,
eguna igaro larrian eta
jiratzen naizen orduan,
nere begiak gozatzen dira
aldameneko ombu'an.

Txabol ondoko ombu laztana
maitatzen zaitut gogotik
eta biotza erdibitzen zait
nere burura ekartzen dezun
oroimen gozuagatik.
Zure itxura nai det ikusi
ez dizut eskatzen frutik
ni emen bizi naizen artean
Arren! Egon zaite zutik!

Nere lagunik maitatuena
ombu laztana, zu zera,
argatik nator zure kolkora,
ni malkuak isurtzera
iduriturik naramazula
atariko intxaurpera . . .
Beti izango zaitut goguan.[11]

In that beloved land the Basque Country
on the farm where I was born
there is a walnut tree
that stands next to the door of the house and gives
    wonderful shade . . .

I came here, leaving everything behind,
because I wanted to see this land! . . .
Now I find myself in America
working as a shepherd on a ranch.
When I return home
after a hard day at work,

I rest my eyes
on the ombu tree that grows nearby.

Beloved tree near my hut,
I love you with all my heart,
and that heart is torn
by the sweet memories
that you evoke in me.
I want to keep looking at you.
I will ask no fruit of you
while I live here.
Please, remain standing!

You, my beloved ombu,
are my best friend,
that is why I come to you
to shed my tears,
thinking that you will carry me back
to the tree by the door of my farmhouse . . .
I will always remember you. [paraphrase]

In 1889, at the age of thirty-two, Otaño was living in Rosario. The years he spent in Argentina did not cause him to forget his beloved Basque Country. He corresponded with his relatives, especially with his uncle Joxe Bernardo. Since they were both bertsolariak, their letters were written in verse. Nothing remains of that correspondence except a letter, one of the best poetic examples of written bertsolaritza. The title of the verses from it is "Ameriketatik osaba José Bernardori bialduak" (Verses sent to uncle Joe from America). In them Otaño sings about the beauty of Donostia while expressing the nostalgia he experiences living far from his homeland:

Milla zortzireun larogei eta
bederatzi da aurten
orra ogeita amabi urtek
nola arrapatu nauten . . .
Errosario Santa Fen . . .

Gu geienian gabiltza emen
esna ere ametsetan
beti pentzatzen berongan eta
Euskalerriko gauzetan
askok dionez bizi gerade
txit toki aberatsetan
bañan ez dago Donostiarik
gure lurrian bestetan.

Ameriketan ikusten ditut
zenbat euskaldun "andare"

bizi diranak beren lurrari
aitormenik eman gabe
bañan ez dute ezagutzen
oiek barkatuak daude
Nik Donostia eskatuko det
paraisora joan ta ere.[12]

The year is 1889 and
look at how the thirty-two years
have taken hold of [me] . . .
in the city of Rosario, Santa Fe . . . [paraphrase]

Often we walk around here
as if in a dream, even though we are awake,
thinking always about you and
matters of the Basque Country; according to many,
we live in a precious place
but a city like Donostia
is found only in our country.

In America I live
with many "pretend" Basques
who go through life without giving their homeland
a second thought,
but they are excused
because they do not know her.
I will choose Donostia,
even when headed for paradise.

Otaño left the Basque Country after witnessing the tragic outcome of the second Carlist War. He experienced firsthand the frustration caused by the loss of the fueros and the old liberties. He was saddened both by the oppression of his country and by the retrogression of the Basque language. One of his favorite verse themes involves the possible loss of the Basque language and the hope that it will not happen. For that reason he tried to urge native speakers living in the Basque Country to preserve the old traditions. Using simple similes like the bandanna, scissors, and the tree and its branches, Otaño describes in emotional verses the reality of a nation divided by a river and a border:

Oyaltzat artu zagun Euskera
goraizitzat Bidasoa,
Ibai koskor bat besterik
ez da utsa balitz itxasoa:
Elkarren urbil daude Zazpiak
muga deitzen da "pausoa"
Zergaitik izan bear ez dugu
famili bakar osoa?

Arbola baten zañetatikan
sortzen diran landariak
bezela gera, Bidaso'aren
bi aldetako jendiak:
Berdiñak dira gure jatorri
oiturak eta legiak

Ama Euskerak magal berian
asitako senidiak.
Ama Euskera! bere semeak
gu Ameriketan zenbat
arkitzen geran! ta urrutitik
maitiago degu, an bat:
Emen ez dago Bidaso'arik
ta beste trabik an ainbat;
Ama maitia indartu dedin,
Bizi bedi "Zazpiak Bat."[13]

Let us take Euskara for a bandanna
and the Bidasoa River for a pair of scissors;
it would be no more than a stream
if the sea were empty;
the seven provinces lie next to each other,
the pass is called a border,
can we not form
a single united family.

All of us on both sides
of the Bidasoa are
like new shoots born
on the branches of the same tree.
We have the same origin,
the same customs and laws,
we are siblings that our mother Euskara
has nursed from the same breast.

Mother Euskara, some of your sons
are here in America,
even though we are far away
we love the one we are far from even more.
Here there is no Bidasoa
to divide us, nor so many difficulties;
may the seven provinces live on
so that our dear mother will regain her health.

Unamuno was a controversial figure during this time period and served as a riveting subject for Otaño's work. Although Unamuno considered himself "Basque through all . . . blood lines," his aversion to the language of his ancestors is all too well known. Unamuno was a philosopher from Bilbo who held the opinion that nothing differentiates the spirit of a race more than its language. But when it came time to support Euskara, this so-called universal Basque attacked the language like no one else had. This contradictory attitude toward the Basque language was an obsession that plagued him for half a century. Unamuno felt that Euskara was dying in accordance with the laws of nature and that there was no need to mourn the death of its body because the best of its soul would survive. He maintained that the Basque language was inferior to Castilian because it was an elemental language that was barely useful for naming material objects.

Unamuno thought he could foretell the future of Euskara but failed for the most part. He predicted its death, although the current reality appears to indicate the opposite is happening. In his day he was rejected by such famous people as Sabino Arana, the poet Lizardi, and Florencio Basaldua (1853– ?). Otaño, rejected as a defender of the Basque language and a fervent Basque nationalist, also spurned Unamuno. Patriotism was one of Otaño's favorite themes because he belonged to the growing Basque nationalist movement:

> Esaera zarra da
> inoiz jakintsubak
> egin oi dituztela
> txit gauza txatxubak,
> zailak dira bildutzen
> ondra ta protxubak,
> nola ez du pentsatu
> au gure maixubak!

> Guk nai diyogulako
> euskarari fidel,
> ipintzen diguzu
> bekoskua goibel?
> asko dakizularik
> gaizki zaude, Migel,
> ezin biurtu leike
> amorrayik igel.

> Ezagun da erritik
> urruti zaudena . . .
> Ez da gaitza euskaldunak
> eskatzen dutena
> baizik izan dedila
> ongi mundu dena
> ta utzi deigutela
> ostu zigutena.

> Bilbao'tik irten da
> Salamanka'raño

Noraño joan zerade
zu, Migel, noraño?
Gu etorriyagatik
beste mundurano,
uste det alderago
gaudela zu baño.[14]

There is an old refrain
that says that at times
wise men
do absurd things,
it is very difficult to combine
honor and profit,
how can it be that our teacher
has not thought of that?

Because we are
loyal to Euskara,
you frown at us.
You think you know a lot,
but you are mistaken, Miguel,
the trout cannot turn into a frog.

It is well known that you
live far from your country.
The Basques are not asking
for anything bad.
They want the whole world
to be well,
and they want what was taken from them
returned.

You left Bilbo
and you went to Salamanca.
How far have you gone,
Miguel, how far?
Even though we have come
to another continent,
I believe that we are closer
[to the Basque Country] than you are. [paraphrase]

Although he composed his best verses in Argentina, during his stay in the Basque Country he enjoyed (and still enjoys) great fame as a bertsolari. Koldo Mitxelena (known as Luis Michelena in Spanish) says of him: "If there is a name well known among the Gipuzkoan bertsolariak, it is naturally that of Pello Mari Otaño."[15]

There are no memories of Otaño improvising verses in cider shops or taverns while he lived in the Basque Country. Neither was he able to do so very often in the town squares because of a chronic cough that kept him from singing. But on the occasions when he performed in public he aroused admiration in both the educated and the uneducated. Emeterio Arrese, a poet from Tolosa (Gipuzkoa), narrates his impressions after having heard Otaño improvise verses for the first time:

> I was nineteen when I met Pello Mari. Fortunately I had the chance to hear his verses in a corner of the old part of Donostia. In fact, each one of Pello Mari's verses carried with it the scent of mountain chamomile, springs that never run dry, and all the other beautiful things. . . . Pello Mari was the best versifier and poet of his time; he was also the greatest teacher of all the young lovers of Euskara . . . his verses are the most special treasures that our language possesses.[16]

Otaño was very good with improvised verses and he wrote the best jarriak (written verses) of his time. In 1897 he won first prize at the Basque festivals of Oiartzun (Gipuzkoa) with the long poem entitled "Anaitasuna" (Brotherhood).[17]

His preoccupation with Basque was not a feeling engendered by the homesickness he suffered during his stay in Argentina. Many years earlier he wrote the poem "Aitona gizagaixoa" (Poor grandfather) in which he relates a dialogue between a grandfather (aitona) and his grandson (iloba). The bertsolari played the role of the grandson. His hopeful attitude contrasts strongly with the old man's pessimism:

Aitona:	Nere euskera gaxua . . . !
Iloba:	Erantzun nion: Jauna, Euskera ez dago ain aldegina . . .
Aitona:	Ez da biziko, laster ilko da gure Euskera gaxua . . .
Iloba:	Gaur Donostian ez dakiyenik
	ez du aitortu nai inork.
Aitona:	Bañan erderak betiak dauzka
	erriya eta basua . . .
Iloba:	Jauna, alaitzen asi gintezke
	Euskera maite degunak;
	badatoz, ustez iya betiko
	galdutzat zeuden egunak . . .
	Miru gaiztoak menderatutzen
	duten bezela usua.
	etzazutela iltzera utzi
	gure Euskera gaxua.[18]

Grandfather:	My poor Basque language . . . !
Grandson:	I replied, sir, Basque is not so lost . . .
Grandfather:	It will not survive, it will die soon, our poor Basque language . . .

Grandson:	Today in Donostia those who do not know the language do not want to admit it.
Grandfather:	But Spanish has filled the villages and forests . . .
Grandson:	Sir, those of us who love Euskara have begun to grow happy again; days that we thought were lost forever are returning . . . Like the goshawk overcomes the dove, do not let our poor Euskara die.

Otaño also sang about nature. He was born in a little village where contact with farm animals and birds awoke in him feelings for beauty and a love of nature. His poem dedicated to "Txepetxa" (Kinglet) is legendary in bertsolaritza because of the expert manner in which he shaped his allegories around the tiny bird. Otaño demonstrated in this poem his refined sense of observation, his appreciation of beauty, his mastery of the language, and his gift for narration. I have transcribed here two of the five verses:

> Euskal lurreko txoriyetan dan
> txikitxuena da bera:
> gaztañ kolore bakarrekua,
> nai bada ez da ederra;
> begi argiyak, buru xanpala,
> moko ttentia aurrera;
> Gorputza motxa, anka laburrak,
> xaltoka ibillera;
> xapalartako egalariya
> eta kantari ergela.

> Txotx batek aisa jasoko luke
> nola karga gutxi duan
> bañan gustazen zayo jartzia
> adar sendoxiaguan;
> amildu arren ez leike galdu
> dakiyelako eguan;
> bañan arkitzen baldin bada ere
> burnizko aldamiyuan,
> iru-lau aldiz xanpatutzen du
> seguro ote daguan.[19]

> It is the smallest bird
> in the Basque Country;
> all chestnut-colored,
> perhaps it is not beautiful,
> with lively eyes, a flat head,
> a beak pointed upward;
> a short body, stubby legs,
> it walks in little jumps;

a noisy flier
and a clumsy singer.

Since it weighs so little,
a twig will easily support it
but it prefers to perch
on a stronger branch;
even if it falls, it will not be lost
because it knows how to fly;
but if it perches
on a metal scaffold
it stamps around three or four times
to make sure it is secure.

Otaño's stylistic technique was very good and he was quite careful about the form of his lines. One of his greatest virtues was that he was both a learned and a popular bertsolari. Illiterate peasants understood him, as did intellectuals. He was one of the very few old bertsolariak who managed to cross over the line that separated popular and learned poetry. Occasionally, he used verses of several lines, a practice begun by Bilintx but that was not generally emulated.

José de Aristimuño, alias "Aitzol," arbiter of aesthetics during the literary renaissance prior to the Spanish Civil War, asserted that Otaño was both a bertsolari and a poet:

> I must confess that only a few bertsolariak are poets. . . . I fear to state openly that Otaño was a simple bertsolari. . . . Neither can it be said that he was a poet of the highest category . . . but having read the poems "Aitona gizagaizoa" and "Amerikako panpetan" you find yourself obliged to declare that Otaño was a poet.[20]

Although his language was poetic, he never strayed far from the common vocabulary used by the people. Everyone could understand his verses. That is why it is no mystery that several bertsolariak considered him to be their master. I must confess that no other recordings of bertsolari poetic compositions produced the reaction I felt when I listened to the one dedicated to this Gipuzkoan bertsolari.[21]

Unfortunately, Otaño died in his prime. During his last years in Argentina, he transcribed some of the verses he had previously improvised in the Basque Country. In 1904 the collection of his bertsoak were published in Buenos Aires and in 1930 *Otaño'tar Pedro M'ren olerki onenak* (The best poetry of Pedro Mari Otaño) was republished in Donostia. With his death Euskara lost the bertsolari of Basque emigration, a defender of the Basque language and patriotism, and a singer of nature. Thanks to his compositions Otaño will always remain in the memories of the Basques as a great learned bertsolari.

CHAPTER ELEVEN

Fernando Aire,

Alias "Xalbador"

In the last decade there have been an abundance of books about bertsolariak, some written by the versifiers themselves. *Odolaren mintzoa* (1976) by Fernando Aire, alias "Xalbador," is notable because of the prose in his introduction and because of the extraordinary quality of the part written in verse.[1] The first part is basically autobiographical. The second is divided into seven smaller units that deal with Xalbador's farmhouse, the people of Urepel and neighboring towns, the provinces of Nafarroa and Gipuzkoa, the Basque Country, the family, Euskara, religion, friends, love, and death. This work is the primary source of my study of Xalbador's life, work, and verse style. I also studied two of his other books, *Ezin bertzean* (To force, 1969) and *Herria gogoan* (With an eye on the people, 1981) as well as many of his verses, the majority of which are found in Antonio Zavala's collection *Auspoa*.

I do not presume to analyze the entire contents of these works fully; rather, I limit myself to the aspects mentioned above. Neither will I attempt to elucidate the much-debated question of whether Xalbador was a poet or a bertsolari. I think that he was the best poet of all the bertsolariak of his time.[2] His improvised verses were very good, and his written ones were incomparable. His lyricism, his capacity to identify himself with the person he was representing, and the depth of his thoughts set him apart from other bertsolariak. It is therefore not just the external form that makes Xalbador's art so attractive. His thinking, his ideas, and the messages he conveys also make him a unique individual.

XALBADOR'S LIFE

Xalbador was born in 1920 in Urepel, a little village situated at the bottom of a narrow pass surrounded by high mountains, and died there in 1976. The Errobi River cuts through the green valley. It is located in the province of Nafarroa Beherea on the border that separates Spain and France. For political reasons, the Basque nation remains divided between the two large states of France and Spain, as was the ancient kingdom of Nafarroa.[3] Xalbador never accepted the separation of the two Nafarroas. He always thought of them as one entity as they were in the old days. Unlike many Basques who use the slogan "zazpiak bat" (the seven united provinces), which recognizes the two Nafarroas, he always spoke of "seiak bat" (the six united provinces). The bard from Urepel considered the Basques on both sides of the border to be united by origin, language, and culture.

In spite of the fact that Nafarroa Beherea belongs to France, Xalbador never accepted being a Frenchman, and he felt it was the greatest insult to be considered so. His personal values caused him to oppose the spirit of the French Revolution, which, in the name of "liberté, égalité, fraternité," destroyed the ancient liberties of the three Basque provinces in the north of Euskal Herria.[4] Xalbador shifted his focus from the unity of Nafarroa to that of a unified Euskadi. For him there was only one Basque Country and it was dying. The country's suffering ("Ene penak, ene penak") stemmed from the many Basques forced to flee for political reasons, from the loss of Euskara, and from the internal divisions among the Basque people.

At the age of eleven Xalbador stopped attending school of his own volition. This fact is of capital importance and would mark the rest of his life. He began school as a small child and passed two grades. In the second grade he had a teacher who was an anti-Basque Frenchman, but he received his religious instruction in Euskara from a parish priest. In spite of the priest's stern personality, Xalbador appreciated him a great deal because of their common tie—the Basque language.

As a child Xalbador suffered the same trauma many other Basque children experienced—numerous punishments for speaking in their native language. School alienated him and he decided to quit, to the great displeasure of his parents. He preferred being an unlearned man while preserving his maternal tongue than to be a learned Frenchman without Euskara.[5]

Euskara was the element that set the Basque nation apart, according to Xalbador. The title of his book, *Odolaren mintzoa*, is very significant because it literally means the language of the blood as the expression of the Basque race. Xalbador repeatedly emphasizes the importance of the language:

> Euskalduna naiz eta maite dut herria,
> oroz gainetik gure hizkuntza garbia.[6]

> I am Basque and I love my country;
> above all, our clean Basque language.

Apart from his broader concerns for Nafarroa and Euskal Herria, there were two dwellings that were very important in the life of this bertsolari: the *sortetxe*, or family farmhouse, and the *etxola*, or shepherd's hut. The sortetxe was Xalbador's best friend and his refuge where he took shelter at difficult times:

> Zu zaitut lagun lehena,
> ihes leku hoberena.[7]

> You are my first friend,
> my greatest refuge.

Xalbador began herding sheep at age eleven when he left school. While his formal education was not extensive, he had at least learned to read and write. In the absence of adequate schooling, the adolescent Xalbador began the process of becoming a bertsolari through his contact with nature. Long hours spent watching the flock and the eloquent silence of the mountains gave depth to this bard's poetic art. There in the mountains he learned to be a contemplative shepherd and to meditate intensely. His sense of drama and his deeply felt thoughts originated in the young shepherd's solitude.

His life was intimately linked to the etxola. He dedicated one of his best poems to it. "Etxola" is a lyrical work in which he converses with the hut as if it were his beloved. His deep-seated sensitivity is reflected in its verses, in which thoughts and images spring more from the heart than from the mind. Xalbador had stopped sheepherding by the time he wrote them. He relates his memories of a youth spent in the solitude of the mountains:

> Aita zenak ninduela goiz argi batez ereman.
> Orroit zirea, ahapetik, zer botu egin nuen han?
> Beti maiteko zintudala nik nola nerautzun hitzeman![8]

> My dead father called me to his side one clear morning.
> Do you remember what I whispered to you there?
> I promised you I would always love you!

These lines were written a few years before Xalbador died. The memory of his beloved hut was still vivid. Those were happy years for him. During the winter, in spite of the snowy blanket that covered the hut, he went to visit his beloved on the mountain. In the spring, after the thaw, he promised to visit again with his flock:

Negu batez pentsatu dut elurrez elur joaitea,
ikusi behar nuela mendiko ene maitea;
gure etxola elur hotzak azpian zaukan ordea,
gizon bat zuen hila iduri, mihise xuriz gordea.

Gaur elurrak hurtu ditu, zabaldu da primadera;
artaldea ere berriz igan da mendi gainera;
ahal bezain maiz sartuko naiz, etxola, zure barnera,
nehoiz ukatu ez derautazun bake hortaz gozatzera.[9]

One winter I thought about going to visit
my beloved of the mountain along the snowy road.
But the cold snow covered our cabin
like a white sheet covers the dead man.

Today the snow has melted; spring has arrived.
Even the flock has gone up the mountain again.
As soon as I can I will go to visit you, my cabin,
to enjoy the peace you have never denied me.

Xalbador's early public appearances are interesting examples of his capacity for self-instruction. By the age of fourteen he had taken charge of an entire flock. With friends, he prepared a small Basque vocabulary list that would be useful to him in his artistic performances.[10]

Occasionally, on the weekends, he would descend to the village for a visit with his companions. He describes his first public appearance at the age of sixteen. In a tavern in Urepel he heard some men improvising verses; among them was a shepherd from Zaldibia (Gipuzkoa) named José Tolosa. Tolosa must have been a mediocre bertsolari because Xalbador later wrote in *Odolaren mintzoa*: "Batere etzuen molderik" (He possessed no quality).[11] Nevertheless it was Tolosa who spread Gipuzkoa's fondness for bertsolaritza to Urepel. It was because of Tolosa that Xalbador was able to perform before a group for the first time, and he was always grateful to him for that. Once when performing in Zaldibia, he dedicated a verse to Tolosa:

Artzain bat jun zen gure herrira
hemen jaio ta hazia,
ni bertsolari azaldu banaiz
hari zor diot guzia.[12]

A shepherd born and reared here
went to our village,
if I appear to be a bertsolari
I owe it all to him.

Tolosa and his friends were improvising verses one day when the adolescent Xalbador did not dare enter the bar. From the outside, near the window, he followed the progress of their exchanges. The quality of the verses must not have been very high because, in spite of his timidity, Xalbador improvised a bertso, to the amazement of the group. Afterward he took off running toward the mountains, embarrassed as if he had done something wrong.[13]

Between the ages of sixteen and nineteen Xalbador refined his improvisational skills, sometimes while alone on the mountain and at other times with friends in the bar. He had realized his lifelong dream—to become a professional bertsolari. Four or five friends would gather at a bar with a pitcher of wine. As was traditional with many wagers in the Basque Country, the one who lost would pay the bill. In this case, the one who could not finish a verse paid the tab. This was the school of bertsolaritza in which the young Xalbador passed his first tests. His verses could not have been bad because he says: "Eni etzaut behin ere gertatu pagatu behar izaitea" (I never had to pay).[14]

When Xalbador was nineteen, there were two important events that would affect the rest of his life: the death of his father and the onset of World War II. The war years did a great deal of harm to the bard's artistic vocation because he could not improvise any verses in public. After the war, in 1946, Xalbador took part in his first public competition at Saint-Jean-de-Luz. The event was organized by Teodoro Ernandorena, who helped him a great deal in his early years. Xalbador was twenty-six at that time, and during this competition he met Mattin, who would later be his inseparable companion. Sixteen bertsolariak from the north of the Basque Country gathered for this event. Among them were the well-known Joanes Harriet, alias "Permundo," and Felix Hiriarte. Xalbador ranked seventh in this contest. In 1948 he won first prize in Sara (Lapurdi).

When his father died, Xalbador's chores around the farm increased greatly. Furthermore, his family obligations kept him closer to home, and thus limited his public performances. Nevertheless, his art form continued to improve and he soon began his numerous public appearances. The invitations to perform came from many places in Gipuzkoa and Bizkaia. He began crossing the border, usually accompanied by Mattin. There were times when, in the north as well as in the south of the Basque Country, there appeared two inseparable teams of bertsolariak: Xalbador/Mattin and Uztapide/Basarri.

Xalbador's wife, Leonie, played a very important role in this artistic endeavor. Marriage brought a serious dimension to the life of this young bard, who would occasionally arrive home late after his bertsolaritza performances. He dedicated the most romantic verses of his *Odolaren mintzoa* to her. The harshness and brusqueness of the Xalbador who created "Aurpegi iluna" (Dark face) was transformed into the delicate tenderness of an adolescent in love.[15]

During a medical examination necessitated by an accident, doctors diagnosed Xalbador with mitral insufficiency, a medical condition that results in heart failure. On July 20, 1976, five months before his death, the city of Saint-Jean-de-Luz paid tribute to him and awarded him a gold medal as the city's favorite son. At the time of the tribute Xalbador promised the audience that he would continue to work on behalf of the Basque Country in spite of his illness. He intended to return to improvising verses before an audience after taking a few months off to rest:

Ez otoi enegatik naigabez sumindu,
ez ere nitaz pentsa: Horrenak egin du!
Gogo hunek oraino kantuz atsegin du,
ez da zuen Xalbador betiko ezindu,
zuendako sendotzen nai naiz alegindu.

. . . Hitz emaiten dautzuet, Jainkoa lekuko,
hemendik hilabete batzuen buruko
berriz hor nauzuela zuen zerbitzuko.[16]

Please don't be sad for me,
or think that I am finished!
This wish is fulfilled, still singing,
your Xalbador is not incapacitated forever,
I want to get better for you.

. . . I promise that with God as my witness
within a few months
I will be at your service again.

Death took him on November 7, 1976, on the day of Urepel's tribute to him. His happiness was twice as great because the tribute coincided with the release of *Odolaren mintzoa*. Several thousand people came from all over the Basque Country to gather at Urepel. At five o'clock in the afternoon, with the weather threatening snow, Xalbador excused himself for a few minutes from the proceedings. He had a heart attack a few meters from the square where the tribute was being held. He died at six o'clock. He barely had time to speak to his wife; they had only a quarter of an hour together. He knew he was dying and he spread his arms, saying: "I am afraid." He was distraught because he had not finished expressing his gratitude to the people. Among his last words were, "Gure herria ez dut behar bezala eskertzen ahal" (I could not thank the people the way I should).[17]

At the age of fifty-six, Xalbador passed away, to live on only in his verses. With his death a void was felt throughout the Basque Country. But his work remained, especially *Odolaren mintzoa*.[18] As long as the Basque language lives, this book will survive. As he would have wished, it will continue to be read in the corners of Basque kitchens. Xalbador's life was a legacy, a chapter in the history of Basque oral literature. The bard from Urepel did not belong to his family alone. He was the heritage of the entire Basque people. As they sang "Gernika'ko arbola," during the line "Eman da zabal zazu munduan frutua" (Spread your fruit throughout the world), he died. He gave his life for his beloved Basque Country, as he himself said in one of his improvised verses: "Orai bertzerik ezin dut eta eskaintzen dautzut bizia" (Now I can do no more and I offer you my life).[19]

MAJOR THEMES

Xalbador needed profound themes in order to compose verses of quality. He said on various occasions that his favorite topics were the serious ones. For that reason, the gai-jartzaile, the person in charge of assigning themes to the bertsolariak, usually offered him poignant and difficult ones. For example, Juan Mari Lekuona once assigned him "grandmother's hands," with the following comment: "Oneri gaia, beti bezala, sakona jartzen diogu" (As always, we give this fellow a substantial theme).[20]

If I had to choose the most outstanding aspect of *Odolaren mintzoa*, it would be without a doubt the author's presentation of combined thematic pairs, where one is never discussed without the other, for example, God and man, faith and country, religion and humanism, and sorrow and hope.

Religion

Religion is one of the most important themes in *Odolaren mintzoa*. The work is impregnated with the biblical instruction that Xalbador received as a child during his study of the catechism. He found the source of his poetic inspiration and his images, metaphors, comparisons, and similes in both nature and sacred books.

The reader can detect a notable change in Xalbador's religious life. From a childhood religion inspired by fear, he progressed to a spirituality based on a love of God as loving father. The religious atmosphere in which he was reared and the change that took place in his spirituality are reflected in his poem "Jainkoa eta ni" (God and I). It is quite likely that the sermons of the new priest in Urepel, Jean Baptiste Bascans (1924-   ), influenced this change. Xalbador admired him for eight years:

> Fede haundiko burrason ganik sortu bainintzan mundura,
> Jainko legean hezi ninduten jitean adimendura;
> hain zen beroa denbor'hartako eliz gizonen kar hura,
> ziotelarik gaizki eginak zeramala ifernura,
> muinetaraino sartu zitzautan Jaungoikoaren beldurra.
>
> Orai ez dakit, Jauna, Zu edo ni aldatu ote naizen,
> etzira egun ene gogoan lengo itxuraz agertzen;
> gertatzen denaz, o Nagusia, kartsuki zaitut eskertzen,
> gure arteko hoztasun hartaz hasia nintzan aspertzen,
> Jainko maitea, ordu zen noizbait lagunak egin gintezen.
>
> . . . Ez gaztigua urrun dezazun, ez eta sari eskerik;
> gaurkotz ez dautzut deusik eskatzen, amodioaz besterik.[21]

I was born to very religious parents.
When I reached the age of reason, they educated me in the law

of God. The fervor of the priests of that time was so great that they instilled a belief that if we did wrong we would go to hell.

I was filled to the marrow with a fear of God.

Now I don't know who has changed, You, Lord, or me, for You are no longer represented in my spirit as You were before.

I give You infinite thanks, oh Lord, for this change, for I was beginning to tire of the cold relationship between us. My God! It's about time we became friends.

. . . I do not ask that You reward me, or that You spare me from punishment .

For today, I ask only for Your love. [paraphrase]

Xalbador was a man of solid faith and trust in God. Without being the classic believer who practiced his religion daily, he internalized Christian principles that were deeply rooted in his soul. His faith was solid, but his works occasionally did not follow its light. He expressed the lust of which Saint Paul spoke. In his poem "Ortzirale saindu batetako gogoetak eta otoitza" (Thoughts and prayers of a Friday saint), we find a verse closely related to Pauline thought:

Aitortzen dut nor zaitudan bainan aitormen xoila bakarrik,
zure aski maitatzeko ez du ene bihotzak indarrik;
bekatuari estekatua naukate hainbat lotgarrik.[22]

I confess that now I know who you are for me, but my confession is merely words.
My heart has no strength to love you sufficiently.
Many ties bind me to sin.

Love and Humanism

One might think that this "little racist," as he defined himself in his youth, could love only his own people. Furthermore, although one might have thought that behind a visage as serious and somber as Xalbador's, there could not be a heart, nothing was further from the truth. This is demonstrated in his perception of himself as reflected in the following lines:

Sekulan ene kantu lan hontan, hitzetan ta idatzitan,
ez det ordea inon agertu amodioa baizikan.[23]

I have shown nothing but love in my artistic performances, whether singing or writing my verses.

One of the tenderest poems in *Odolaren mintzoa* is entitled "Haur batek bere amari" (A child to his mother), in which the feelings of a child who offers a flower to his mother are described. In the midst of the sweetness produced by the relationship between a mother and her little son, Xalbador's sensitive heart does not forget the orphans who are deprived of such maternal love:

Hotzak badago edo badago goseak,
gauaz dolamen egiten badu haizeak,
nortan goxatzen ote ditu oinazeak,
bere amarik ez duen dohakabeak?[24]

When he is cold or hungry,
when he shivers from the night wind,
who can alleviate the suffering
of the unhappy motherless orphan?

The best example of his treatment of love and humanism in verse is evident in his poem "Esperantzarik gabeko amodioa" (Hopeless love). Few Basque poets have sung about hopeless love like this bard from Urepel. Xalbador resembled Bilintx in this regard. The following verse expresses the pain felt by one who finds himself in this situation:

Aitortzen dautzut, ene maitea, goiz aski banakiela
etzintaizkela enea izan, bertze batentzat zinela;
bainan halere maitatu zaitut, ez bainezaken bertzela;
ene bihotza, bizi naizeno, izanen zaizu fidela,
zuretzat bizi ez banitzaike, zuretzat hil nadiela!
. . . Gizonarentzat hau baino malur handiagorik badea?
Ikusten eta ezin eskura maitatzen duen lorea! . . .
Hunela bizi baino aunitzez hobe litaike hiltzea![25]

I confess, my love, that I quickly realized
that you were not for me but for another.
In spite of this, I have loved you and it was impossible for me to
do otherwise.
As long as I live, my heart will continue to be faithful.
If I cannot live for you, I will die for you!
. . . Could there be a greater misfortune for a man than this?
To see the flower one loves and not be able to hold it! . . .
It would be better to die than to live like this!

Friendship

Xalbador was a family man but the boundaries of his family were not limited to the walls of his farmhouse. He knew how to combine love with friendship. For him it was important not to discard this aspect of his life. Few bertsolariak have been so admired and loved by other bards and the Basque public.[26] His appearance was harsh and austere, and his reactions were sometimes similar to those of a man awakening from a deep sleep. Xalbador lived in a deep, mysterious inner world.[27] He describes this double facet of his personality in the following lines:

> Ene aurpegi iluna,
> gorputza latza badaukat ere,
> bihotza daukat biguna.[28]

> Even if my face is somber,
> and my body also looks rough,
> my heart is compassionate.

In the Basque Country bertsolaritza has always joined the different poets and their audience and made them one big family. However, since this artistic expression normally transpires in a competition, it is not unusual for differences to arise between them. Not all of them love each other with the same level of affection. The deep love that tied Xalbador to his companions is expressed in the following line that Azpillaga dedicated to him on the occasion of the first anniversary of his death: "Zu bezelako gizonik ezta sekulan hilko" (A man like you will never die).[29]

One wonders how Xalbador was able to attract so many friends, given his somber external appearance. While the bard from Urepel lacked the light humor and wit of his companion, Mattin, he still penetrated the hearts of his friends. He never spoke without thinking, especially when he had to perform before the public.[30] He was not habitually jovial, and yet he was loved and appreciated by his friends because of his capacity for friendship.

Death

Death plays an important role in Xalbador's poetic work. He was a bertsolari who liked serious themes, and none was more serious than death:

> Munduko gauza segurrena da denek hil behar duguna,
> gizonak hori pentsatu gabe ez beza pasa eguna.[31]

> The most certain thing in this world is death,
> let no one go a whole day without thinking about it.

The theme of death occurred throughout his work. Sometimes death was present in his family (when his parents died), at other times it was among his friends, and on still other occasions it was prompted by political events, such as the deaths of John Fitzgerald Kennedy and Georges Pompidou. Xalbador felt that death ties us to the earth and, rather than forgetting about it, we should never lose sight of it. Xalbador is an intimate, elegiac poet, an artist through whom death is transformed into a sorrowful song. For him life was short and ephemeral. Xalbador knew that as the years passed he, too, was approaching that final goal. "Mundu huntako denbora dugu guk ere laster betea" (Our time also in this world will soon be over).[32]

Those who knew Xalbador closely regarded him, among other things, as a humble man. He impressed people with his simplicity. This contemplative shepherd was constantly introspective, even when he was singing before an audience. He was considered a lyric poet who perceived external reality according to the reflection it created within himself. He was also poetry and humanity personified.

On many occasions he defined himself as a somber-spirited man, but as we have seen, the reality was very different when he was among friends. His humility did not prevent him from defining himself with the Basque word *gizonki*, a word with a profound connotation (humanly, bravely, virilely): "Beti gizonki bizi izan naiz" (I have always lived like a human being).

We know that Xalbador was not a model of virtue. In his youth he occasionally had fun, and during the first years of his marriage he had his share of problems. He himself was perfectly aware of all this. Once he was given as an obligatory theme the task of defining himself: "Ni naiz" (I am). Xalbador defined himself negatively in a line containing his favorite simile, one that includes a star: "Ez naiz izar bat, hori badakit, ezta ere iguzkia" (I know that I am not a star, nor am I the sun).[33]

He will be remembered in the Basque Country as the man who gave everything for Euskadi. He suffered because he belonged to a small nation trying to recover its identity. By 1960 he was becoming increasingly involved in Basque nationalism. He fought against the unjust situation created by the attempted cultural genocide of his people. His words were his weapon. He was denied a passport on several occasions because he had signed a document in favor of Basque refugees, but he was not intimidated. He confronted the French authorities and Franco, to whom he dedicated several verses:

> Lege zorrotza duzu ordea
> muga hortan ezarria,
> anaiak berexten gaituena,
> hori da nigargarria.
> Zuk deraukuzun herra gaixtoa
> ez dautzut nik ezarria,
> nik ez deraukat bertze hobenik,
> bai, maite Euskal-Herria.[34]

> In exchange you have placed a harsh law
> on that border;
> it separates us brothers from each other,
> This is deplorable.
> I did not impose upon you
> the cruel hatred you have for us.
> Yes, my only sin is loving,
> my Basque Country.

Xalbador never accepted the separation created by this political border nor the division caused by the Bidasoa River. In the following lines, he asks heaven to dry up the river so that Euskadi may be united:

Zutik jarrita otoizka nago,
ene lagunak, zerura . . .
eskatzen dautzut izan zazula
herri ttipien ardura,
eta txukatu mendien negar
den Bidasoa'ko ura.[35]

My friends! I stand up and ask heaven to take pity on minority
    nations
and dry the mountain tears
that formed the Bidasoa River.

I have said that as long as Euskara persists, Xalbador's works will be read. I must add that as long as the Basque Country has bards like this bertsolari from Urepel, it will endure as a nation.

Style

We have discussed what Xalbador thought of himself, but we have yet to explore what others thought of him, especially from the artistic standpoint of the quality of his melodies and stylistic techniques.

Xalbador was an exceptional bertsolari whose talent went beyond his melodies and the quality of his improvised verses because he also wrote verses. He had a very individualistic style and was atypical in his lyricism and the intimate feelings he expressed. He is one of the few bertsolariak who managed to transcend the stage of oral poetry and attain what Urretxindor had attempted before him—to move from bertsolari to poet. As an improviser, he was exceptional, although he never won a national txapelketa. I believe that if those contests had taken place in the northern part of the Basque Country, without dialectal barriers, he would have won. At any rate, some of his improvised verses have become legendary. Among them we should highlight "Emazte il zanaren soñekoari" (To the dress of the dead wife),[36] "Bazkaria serbitu dizun neskatxari" (To the waitress who served your dinner), and "Ohea" (The bed). Basarri expressed the opinion that the first of these was the greatest verse he had ever heard. The second earned a special prize in the 1967 txapelketa,[37] and the third is an example of how Xalbador personified things and created dialogues with them.

His improvised verses were better when he performed alone than when he worked with a partner and were better when the themes were profound. Jon Lopategi's opinion is very clear in this respect:

Gauza sakonak asmatu eta
gauzak sakon adierazten
Urepeleko maixuagana
ez gera inor irixten.[38]

None of us reach the level
of the master of Urepel
in the creation of profound ideas
and his intimate style of expressing them.

This opinion is shared not only by many other bertsolariak and fans, but also by many Basque poets. Xalbador was a philosopher on the subject of loneliness. He was an artist who thought very deeply and expressed the most common trivial themes with originality. As a shepherd he enjoyed solitude in one of the most remote, bucolic corners of the Basque Country. Seated at the kitchen table of his farmhouse, he would often become completely lost in thought.[39] Although Xalbador was a man who enjoyed the company of friends and acquaintances, by nature he was introverted and pensive. He is noted not only for the beautiful way in which he expressed himself, but also for the beauty of the ideas he employed in his verses. Iratzeder, one of Euskadi's best modern poets, echoes the opinion that the bertsolari from Urepel had artistic depth:

Hain pertxulari sarkorrik ez zen nehonez nehor.[40]

Nowhere was there ever a bertsolari as penetrating as he.

When working with his preferred themes—the Basque Country, Euskara, God, love, and peace—his inspiration was inexhaustible and his reflections profound. When he expressed his feelings, he employed poetic lyricism and emotional dramatics uncommon among the bertsolariak. Perhaps because of these very personal qualities, Xalbador was unparalleled. Even though he did not form a literary school, or even attempt to, his influence can be clearly seen in such modern bertsolariak as Jon Lopategi and Xabier Amuriza. A description of Xalbador provided by one of his young admirers, the Nafarroa Beherean bertsolari Ernest Alkat, extols the high quality of his art, as well as his favorite themes:

Eskuara eman duzu
mailik gorenean
Aberria altxatuz
denen aintzinean
Izpiritua duzu
mundu zabalean
batean amodio,
Jainkoa bertzean
Ezin erranik ez da
zure mingañean.[41]

You have lifted Euskara
to its highest level,
praising your country
before the whole world;
you spread the spirit
throughout the whole world;
sometimes it is love,
other times God.
Nothing is impossible
from your lips.

In the first part of *Odolaren mintzoa* Xalbador analyzes the bertsolaritza style. This prose section of the book is a kind of *ars poetica* on the literary principles held by the artist from Urepel. The quality of his verses may make us think that Xalbador acquired his technique with no effort. There have been occasions when it has been stated that in order to be proficient, a bertsolari must be born an artist and that no amount of preparation will substitute for natural gifts. Xalbador is proof that it is not enough to be born with the qualities that make a good bertsolari. Hard work and practice formed the anvil on which his literary style was forged. He learned, among other things, to identify fully with the characters he was presenting:

Zonbaitek uste dute, sortuz geroz behin,
bihia segur dela hazi onarekin.
Ez badugu laguntzen handita ont dadin,
landare hoberena galduko da berdin:
uzta nahi duenak behar du lan egin.[42]

Some people think that every good seed
should surely give fruit once it has sprouted.
If we do not help it grow and mature
the best plant will be lost:
he who wants a good harvest must work for it.

Xalbador was born with some of the exceptional attributes needed for his art, but he was not born a bertsolari. He would not have reached such a high level of excellence if he had not labored intensively to perfect those qualities. His mind was constantly working like a tireless mill to crush and grind the Euskara he carried within. He chose a difficult path and he demanded much of himself:

Gutitan betetzen nau nihaurek egindako lanak.[43]

I am seldom satisfied with the work I do.

In spite of his capabilities, it sometimes cost him dearly to create verses. Some errors that seemed insignificant to others, or were accepted as local variations or poetic license, were grave mistakes to Xalbador, mistakes that he had to avoid. For example, it was more embarrassing to him to pronounce "hilt*zea*" (the act of dying) as "hilt*zia*" than to commit the error of poto egin. The latter is considered a flagrant error, while the former would go unnoticed by most bertsolariak.[44]

Music played a very important role in Xalbador's singular technique. His melodies were very different from those traditionally heard in performances by bertsolariak. As a Nafarroa Beherean singer, the old melodies of his province influenced him. Nafarroa Beherea and Zuberoa are probably the two Basque provinces with the greatest wealth of popular music. Conversely, the other five provinces have produced more composers of polyphonic and symphonic music, such as Maurice Ravel (Lapurdi), José María Usandizaga (Gipuzkoa), Pablo Sarasate (Nafarroa), Juan Crisóstomo Arriaga (Bizkaia), and Jesús Guridi (Araba). Xalbador knew the old ballads and love songs that were handed down through tradition. He inherited a great repertoire of folk music that he was able to cultivate and transmit to the younger generations. The melodies that appear in his books and records serve as examples.[45] He was not a creator of new melodies, as is Xabier Amuriza currently. He admitted that fact: "It is often very difficult for me to join a melody with the words I want to use. If only I had known how to compose my own music."[46]

In spite of this confession, he was no doubt a master at choosing traditional melodies appropriate to the message that he wanted to transmit. Melody is very important in Xalbador's bertsolaritza art because it precedes the words. His fondness for verses was born of his love of music: "I began to be something [of a bertsolari] when I was a shepherd, because I sang the old melodies a lot."[47]

As a child he sang in his village church. Later he thought that all music was composed by bertsolariak. In his melodies we can see the influence of Jean Baptiste Elizanburu (1828-1891).[48] As a shepherd, he needed music first in order to compose his verses. His voice, a bit wild and rough, did not possess the tonal quality of a Xabier Amuriza or a Jon Azpillaga. Nevertheless it was a perfect match for the verses of a shepherd who sang with great sincerity and wanted to convey a message drawn from nature. He used sad melodies in a minor key for melancholy themes. However, his suffering was always contained. Xalbador was not a whining poet like Felipe Arrese y Beitia (1841-1906). His verses did not drip with tears; rather, they bled from the heart.

Xalbador's artistic contribution was not limited to the musical aspect of his verses. He also contributed innovative rhythms. Although Xenpelar's and Txirrita's traditional techniques and poetic structures heavily influenced his work, Xalbador went beyond them. He possessed a precise technique characterized by lengthy rhythms seldom used in traditional bertsolaritza. His contributions provided a breath of fresh air, a literary gust different from the bertsolaritza art of the southern Basque Country. A good example is the first verse of "Esperantzarik gabeko amodioa" (Hopeless love). It is a long verse of thirteen lines. Each line has three caesuras containing five plus five plus eight syllables, respectively. In *Odolaren mintzoa* he uses this rhythm in twenty-six of his poems:

Amodioa / gauza tristea / bihotzen higatzailea,
guziz enea / bezala bada / esperantzarik gabea.
Gizonarentzat / hau baino malur / handiagorik badea?
Ikusten eta / ezin eskura / maitatzen duen lorea! . . .
Hunela bizi / baino aunitzez / hobe litaike hiltzea![49]

Love is a sad thing, it wears us all away.
If it were completely like mine, [it would be] without hope.
Is there a greater misfortune for man?
To see the flower he loves and not be able to have her! . . .
It would be better to die than to live like this. [paraphrase]

Another long rhythm employed by Xalbador has fallen into disuse in the southern part of the Basque Country. We see an example of it in the poem "Aitona gaztea" (The young grandfather). In the following four lines, the first two have sixteen syllables and the last two have eighteen:

Beti ez gaitezen higa tristeak diren gauzetan!
Zorion-tokia ere bada gure bihotzetan!
Alabak esan zeraukunean, aidatu nintzan pozetan,
zorionean aurkitzen zela haur baten esperantzetan.[50]

Let us not always be thinking of sad things,
for there is also room in our hearts for happiness!
When my daughter told us that she was pregnant,
I was filled with great happiness.

The use of images and similes drawn from nature also plays a part in Xalbador's personal style. He never ceased being a shepherd, and even in this he was unique. I do not know if any other shepherd has ever been accepted into any academy in the world, but the one from Urepel was named a member of the Academy of the Basque Language. On the day of this tribute, shortly before his death, his wife shared the good news. Xalbador loved culture. This was reflected in the small library he had in his house—a library that is still preserved—and by his fondness for radio and television.[51] But nature remained his greatest teacher and his source of inspiration.

Among his favorite similes was that of the star, izarra. He sometimes used it because the timing of the event required it, as in the verses he improvised on the Epiphany.[52] Sometimes he was assigned the theme of stars during a competition, as in Usurbil (Gipuzkoa) in 1970.[53] At still other times he used the image because of his fondness for it, as in the poem "Neskatoa, haur beharretan" (Young pregnant girl).[54] Xalbador took advantage of every opportunity to use this simile. He even called Etxahun the star of Zuberoa.

His long years as a shepherd taught him to observe and converse with animals. In this respect, he had a Franciscan soul. He knew the 150 sheep and 8 cows of his stable by name. Birds, flowers, and trees were also often used in similes that appeared in his poems. This was a tradition in the northern Basque

Country, as has been described by Dominique Peillen.[55] Xalbador's marvelous description of a pair of birds preparing their nest in a poem dedicated to spring is an example.

Not everything about his style was perfect. Incorrect contractions occasionally appear in his rhythms. He was somewhat flexible in this regard, but it was clear that he was using a style from the northern Basque Country. It was hardly noticeable in his improvised verses and he was very careful about it in his written ones.

The same can be said of his rhymes. In spite of their beauty, we do not discern in Xalbador's poetry the preoccupation with consonant rhyme of a Manuel Lasarte. In some of his best verses, such as "Emazte il zanaren soñekoari," he rhymes "jan*tzirik*" with "ema*zterik*." Xalbador used technique as a vehicle for conveying his message and not as an end in itself. The precise excellence of his technique was an important means for achieving his poetic art.

Xalbador exemplified artistic excellence and literary elegance, and he was known as the singer of profound suffering. He was the mournful, intimate poet through whom the suffering of the Basque people was converted into songs and sorrowful ballads.

Xalbador's death left a void that is hard to fill. The Basque Country lost one of the best bertsolariak in the history of the phenomenon. Many bertsolari fans share the opinion that he was the best poet among the bertsolariak of his time, and perhaps of all time.

CHAPTER TWELVE

Xabier Amuriza

There have been several qualitative changes throughout the history of bertsolaritza. In the middle of the nineteenth century the figure of Xenpelar brought about some of these noteworthy changes through his innovative rhythms and rhymes. The appearance of the bertso-paperak during his time also produced many changes. Basarri and the 1935 txapelketa brought about another essential change by taking bertsolaritza out of the cider shops and positioning it in the town square, while introducing it to modern means of communication. Another very important development in the history of this artistic phenomenon occurred with the appearance of Xabier Amuriza in the 1980 txapelketa.

Xabier Amuriza has been accused of breaking with tradition. Contrary to what some people say, however, I believe that the changes he made did not represent a break but rather a continuity of the art form but with the addition of profound innovations. Amuriza has defended himself repeatedly against these attacks:

> To certain reactions that have occurred I would say, Take care!
> Here history moves forward and there were changes before and
> there are now also. . . . They say the traditional style is being de-
> stroyed now . . . nothing is being destroyed here.[1]

The innovations Amuriza introduced affected three very important aspects of the bertso. The first change entailed his use of Euskara Batua. As a loyal Bizkaian, Amuriza is very fond of his native dialect; at the same time he recognizes the need for a language that is accessible to all Basques. In the tradition of Urretxindor, he is also very fond of the kopla zaharrak and combines the Gipuzkoan and Bizkaian schools of bertsolaritza in his performances. He was the only bertsolari to use Euskara Batua in the 1980 competition: "I wanted to demonstrate that Euskara Batua was not a dry and artificial language."[2]

The second area of innovation is Amuriza's selection of music. Some of the melodies he uses are his own. In the 1980 txapelketa he won not only the first prize, but also a special award intended for the bertsolari who used the most original melodies. Amuriza won both prizes again in the 1982 txapelketa.

Finally, Amuriza challenges the statement commonly accepted until now as axiomatic: A bertsolari is born, not made. According to this traditional view, bertsolaritza would be reserved for a few privileged individuals who were born with a special capacity for this difficult art form. One of the most notable proponents of this traditional position is Basarri, who asserts that a bertsolari is not made in school. For him it is not enough to learn the techniques required by the art form (rhythms, rhymes, and music). He feels that it is absolutely necessary to possess the gift, those certain qualities that are supplied only by nature. In order to support his position, Basarri cited the fact that he belonged to a family of ten siblings and only he managed to become a professional bertsolari. Nobody has dared to dispute openly this axiom. Both poets and bertsolariak have defended it as an unquestionable truth. For example, the poet Jules Moulier, alias "Oxobi" (1888-1958), stated:

> Odolean dute; sortzetikako dohain bat dute hor. Beraz, Jainkoari zor diote eta bakharrik Jainkoari.[3]
>
> It's in their blood; they were born with the gift. Therefore they owe it to God and only to God.

Amuriza demonstrates the opposite. He acknowledges that there are minimal qualities that all future bertsolariak must possess by birth. However, he also maintains that the rest are learned with practice, as in any other artistic and professional field. The title of one of his books, *Zu ere bertsolari* (You too are a bertsolari), is very significant in this respect. Amuriza has written extensive pedagogical materials and is the promoter of several schools of bertsolaritza. Many fine aficionados of bertsolaritza are emerging from them, and young bertsolariak are being promoted.

Perhaps the most balanced position in the controversy comes from the great bertsolari Xalbador. The bard from Urepel stressed the importance of inborn qualities without excluding personal work and schooling:

> I used to believe that God had given some people a gift to be bertsolariak the same way He had given the Apostles the gift of the Holy Spirit so that they could preach the Gospel. There are still people who believe this, but it is not true. It is clear that

God plants a seed within us . . . but it is up to us to germinate the seed and care for the plant.[4]

AMURIZA'S LIFE

Xabier Amuriza was born on May 3, 1941, on the Torreburu farm in the Etxano district of the village of Amorebieta (Bizkaia). Until the age of eleven he lived in that remote, solitary house, in intimate contact with nature—his great teacher and the principal inspiration for his art. Even today, Amuriza is considered a learned bertsolari although he reads very little. In spite of the fact that Amuriza has a multifaceted life and is a bertsolari, a writer of poetry and novels, a translator of books, a musician, and a singer, he also spends long periods of time without reading or writing, to renew himself in the silence of nature.

As a small child he attended the remote Etxano school. In the afternoons, when he returned from school, he took care of the cows with his faithful friend, the farm dog. It was in this environment that the child Amuriza began to observe life in the countryside: the songs of birds, the trees, and the seasons. He thus stored up a great warehouse of inspiration for his artistic future.

The family atmosphere of the farm also awoke in him a great fondness for songs and the old verses. From his father, a man who appreciated the bertsoak of the old Basque bards, he learned the first verses that he sang as a small child:

Bost urte egin nituen egunean kantatu nuen taberna batean.[5]

On my fifth birthday I sang in a tavern.

At the age of eleven he entered the school of the Carmelite fathers of Amorebieta, and the following year he entered the seminary of Derio (Bizkaia). During the first seven years of his ecclesiastical career, Amuriza had to give up his Basque roots completely. The atmosphere of the seminary was not conducive to awakening a fondness for Euskara or for bertsolaritza.[6] Amuriza's nickname, "Virgilio," dates from that period when his companions in his Latin courses baptized him with it.

At the age of twenty, Amuriza began to recover the love he felt as a boy for bertsolaritza because of the contacts with the people of his village during his summer vacation. Two years later, he began to improvise verses at popular festivals in some villages in Bizkaia. In 1965, at the age of twenty-four, he was ordained as a priest and assigned to the Bizkaian village of Gizaburuaga. The following year he took charge of the parish church of Amoroto as well. The young priest combined his pastoral work with cultural promotion and bertsolaritza performances. The years 1965 to 1968 constituted one of the most active and enjoyable periods of Amuriza's life: "I'm not sorry I was a priest. It would be difficult to find another period of my life as full as that period when I was a priest."[7]

In the late 1960s political tension flared up in the Basque Country. The

Basque guerrilla organization Euskadi Ta Askatasuna (ETA) switched from defensive to offensive acts. The assassinations of the first ETA militant, Txabi Etxebarrieta (1944-1968), and a police officer, Melitón Manzanas, exacerbated the tension. A group of some seventy Basque priests began to demonstrate publicly against Franco's dictatorship. In 1968 the group held a silent protest in Bilbo. The tension increased when masses were celebrated in behalf of the assassinated Basque militant. The police pressed charges against those who attended the ceremonies, and the civil governor of Bizkaia imposed fines of twenty-five thousand pesetas on some of them—fines that included a month in prison. Amuriza was falsely accused of attending one of the masses in Durango. He was fined and incarcerated in the prison at Basauri (Bizkaia). He was later transferred to the notorious concordat prison at Zamora.[8]

In November 1968 another group of seventy priests and religious people voluntarily locked themselves in the seminary of Derio as a protest. This group is known by the title of their musical recording, "Gogor."[9] The subtitle of the record reveals the reason for their actions: "Gogorkeriaren aurka gogortasuna" (Tenacity against violence). As the author of the verses and the soloist, Amuriza played a very active role in the creation of the recording. The group of priests wanted to attract the attention of both the public and the Vatican to the oppression in the Basque Country.[10]

In May 1969 Amuriza and four other Basque priests went on a hunger strike in the offices of the bishop of Bilbo.[11] They wrote a letter in which they denounced the political oppression of the Spanish government against the Basque Country and the injustices suffered by the working class. Their protest lasted only three days because the police entered the offices without the bishop's permission and arrested the five priests for inciting a military rebellion.[12] They were immediately tried by a military tribunal and condemned to ten to twelve years in prison.

After three days in the police station in Bilbo and the prison at Basauri, these priests were transferred to the concordat prison at Zamora. It was Amuriza's second time there, but this time he would spend six years and three months, from May 1969 to August 1975. He narrates these events in a book of verses he wrote in prison, *Menditik mundura* (From the mountain to the world):

> Maiatzeko egun batez
> hogeitamar hain suertez
> gose greba bat hasi genduan
> gure borondatez . . .
>
> Paper bat geunkan egina
> laburra baina gordina
> bertan azaltzen genduan Euskal
> Herriko samina.
>
> Heldu ginen Zamorara
> infernu zulo hontara.[13]

One day in May
the thirtieth by chance
we began a hunger strike
of our own free will . . .

We wrote a letter
short but raw
in it we explained the Basque
Country's suffering.

We arrived at Zamora
to this hell hole.

In another poetic composition of seventeen verses entitled "Bertso berriak horma zaharrei jarriak" (New verses dedicated to old walls), Amuriza recounts the internal conditions of the prison, the sordid atmosphere in which he lived, and the physical suffering of the winter cold and summer heat of the Castilian plateau. They did not see the sun for six months at a time. But the moral suffering was even greater. They were isolated, forbidden to speak Euskara with family members during visits, and held incommunicado in solitary cells when they protested. Neither could they communicate with other prisoners. When the Basque priests requested transfers to other prisons so that they could live with other prisoners, their request was denied by Franco's government. During the first years, the loneliness was not so harsh thanks to the news shared by new prisoners—other Basque priests who were Amuriza's companions. But as the years passed and the group of five was left alone, the loneliness became unbearable. The atmosphere was dehumanizing. They were under the constant vigilance of guards, without doors on the toilets, and they suffered despicable searches:

Espainian behera
han dago Zamora
basamortu hoberik
nonbait izango da . . .

Etxe zar bat hemen da . . .
gizonak piztitzeko
apropos egina
hobe zen infernura
erori bagina.

Ilunpe hontan bizi
gara erdi hilak
ondo itxirik daude
ate ta zerrailak . . .

Zerbait gorderik edo
neukan atxakian
batek eskua sartu

galtzontzilopian
sekula inork ukitu
ez didan tokian.

. . . Oraindikan burutik
sano gaude baina
badira motiboak
zoratzeko haina.

Lotsagarri da baina
sinestu hau jaunak
ate gabe ditugu
hemengo komunak . . .

Deskoiduz inork ezer
egitera oker
kalabozo batean
sartzen dute laster . . .
ez ohe ta ez aulki
ez mahai ta ez ezer
arratoiak hobeto
daude mila bider.[14]

Zamora is found
toward the south of Spain;
there is no greater desert
anywhere . . .

There is an old house here . . .
intentionally built
for brutalizing men;
we would have been better off
in hell.

We live half dead
in this darkness,
doors and cells
are locked tight.

With the excuse
that I was hiding something,
one of them put his hand
in my underpants
where no one had ever
touched me before.

. . . So far we are
sound of mind but
there are reasons
enough to go crazy.

It is shameful but
believe me, gentlemen,
our toilets
have no doors.

If by chance someone
does something wrong
they immediately
put him in a cell . . .
with no bed, no chair,
no table, nothing;
rats are
a thousand times better off. [paraphrase]

With the passing of time conditions in the prison deteriorated. While Amuriza was imprisoned, his father died. The authorities did not grant him leave to attend the funeral. He was only allowed to view the body for a few minutes.[15] He was transported in a patrol wagon under an armed escort. The bertsolari relived those sad memories:

Aita izena kanta bearrak
jarri dit biotza bero,
aukera eder au izango zenik
ez nuen emen espero;
preso nengoen Zamora'n eta
an gelditu ia ero,
joan nintzen ta bertan nengola
aita il zitzaidan gero,
naiago nuke edozer baño
emen bizirik balego.[16]

The need to sing about my father
warms my heart,
I did not expect
to have that chance here;
I was imprisoned in Zamora
and nearly went crazy there,
I went and while I was there,
my father died,
more than anything else I wish
that he were here and alive.

All these painful circumstances influenced the spirit of Amuriza and his companions. One reason for their imprisonment was their denouncement of the concordat between the church and the Spanish state. The group felt that the church was controlled by Franco's regime. Amuriza condemned the church's silence on the state's interference in ecclesiastical matters, the money that it received from the state for the priests' payroll, the economic aid it received for the construction of seminaries and repair of churches, the selection of bishops on the basis of input from the civil authorities, and many other matters. The tension between this group of priests and the Spanish hierarchy escalated and resulted in the Basque priests' refusal to accept both their bishops (José María Cirarda and Antonio Añoveros) and the papal nuncio in Madrid.[17] Amuriza wrote the following verses about this:

> Obispoak gurekin
> ondo egon nahiez
> noizbehin etortzen dira
> baina gu joan ez.
> Ia nazka gaituzte
> hainbeste folklorez . . .
>
> Konkordatu zikin bat
> hartuz atxakitzat
> militarren eskuan
> elizako giltzak.
> Obispo jaunok horri
> eusten gauza handitzat
> gaiztoak ez badira
> tontoak bai behintzat
> edo biak batera
> hobeto deritzat.[18]
>
> Wanting to be
> on good terms with us,
> the bishops come every now and then,
> but we do not go [to see them].
> They repulse us
> with so much folklore . . .
>
> Using the dirty concordat
> as an excuse, they leave the keys to the church
> in the hands of the military.
> The bishops maintain that
> this is a great thing;
> if they are not evil,
> they are at least fools,
> or it seems more likely
> that they are both.

Amuriza took advantage of his long years in prison to study and to dedicate himself to bertsolaritza. Generally his works were theoretical and in written form because the inhuman atmosphere of the prison was not conducive for improvising verses. He also composed melodies that he would later use in competitions. He busied himself with translations, writing poems and novels, and conducting research on bertsolaritza. As a result of his intensive labors we have the translation of Aldous Huxley's book *Brave New World, Bai mundu berria*. Amuriza also wrote a great many of the verses that would be included in *Menditik mundura*. In the area of research, two dictionary works on Basque rhymes are noteworthy and have been very useful for students in the schools of bertsolaritza.[19]

As a good Basque, Amuriza did not accept his unjust treatment and did what he could to attain freedom. Among other things this bertsolari was a singer who loved liberty:

> Euskaldunok libre bizi
> nahi dugu txoriak lez
> kantatzea maite dugu
> baina kaiolarik ez.[20]

> We Basques love to live free
> like the birds;
> we want to sing,
> but not in a cage.

Their love of freedom prompted Amuriza and his companions to try to dig their way out of prison. In 1971 they finished a tunnel seventeen meters in length, a task that took them a year and a half. But there was no happy ending because the police discovered the tunnel after it was finished, and as punishment they were all sent to isolation cells where they spent several days incommunicado.[21]

This last disaster dealt a harsh blow to Amuriza's morale. But somehow he found the strength to continue protesting against the church and the state for maintaining the priests' unjust situation. There was a room in the prison that was designated as a chapel for the priests to celebrate mass. However, they never used it for that; instead they gathered together the vestments and other liturgical paraphernalia, the altar, and the doors and set them ablaze. They spared only the crucifix on the wall to show that their protest was not against Christ. As they hoped, the ultra-Catholic Spanish press called their action a sacrilege, perpetrated by Communist separatist priests. Their protest was underscored by a hunger strike that lasted a month. Amuriza narrates these events in the following bertsoak:

> Ai gartzela Zamorako
> nola geratu haiz hi
> eskerrak sei apaizi
> ez zaik ezer sano utzi
> egik sutan garraisi.

> Lotegia gar eta ke
> eliza ere ondoren
> barka Jauna zer hoben . . .

Hemen nago hemen gaude
orain bigarren guda
gose greba heldu da
ez dugu ezer jan edango
horma hauetaz barrura.[22]

Oh, prison of Zamora,
what a state you are in
thanks to six priests;
nothing has been left untouched,
shout out in the fire.

The dormitory in smoke and flames,
later the chapel,
forgive us, Lord, what a sin . . .

I am here, we are here,
now the second war,
time for the hunger strike,
we will not eat or drink anything
within these walls.

After thirteen days of the hunger strike, the six priests were transferred to the Carabanchel Prison in Madrid. They were happy because they thought they had finally been freed from the shadow of the concordat prison at Zamora. Intended as a privilege, a special prison for priests, the concordat prison had become a double punishment for them because they could not see or talk with other prisoners. Their happiness did not last long. After a session of the council of ministers presided over by Franco, the priests were returned to Zamora. Once there they continued their hunger strike for another seventeen days.

Their situation became intolerable. Their lack of physical strength, their solitude, and their isolation undermined their resolve. But Amuriza described their unbearable situation with a certain amount of black humor in verses written in the form of a dialogue with his mirror:

Aizak ispilu esak egia
gure irudi al haiz hi? . . .
Gizonak ala mamu hondarrak
zer garen ezin berezi . . .
Gorpu da gure gorputza.[23]

Listen, mirror, tell the truth,
are you the image of us? . . .
Men or traces of phantoms,
impossible to determine which we are . . .
Our bodies are corpses.

Amuriza was finally set free in August 1975. In November of the same year Franco died.

Amuriza's departure from prison was gratifying but not free from problems. Many rumors had spread throughout the Basque Country that the priests were Marxist and *españolistas* (pro-Spaniards). Some friends who had lent their aid unconditionally before their imprisonment now refused to help them: "When I got out I perceived everyone as wanting to rip me with their claws . . . this left me with a very bad impression. . . . For that reason I did rather poorly for a couple of months."[24]

To escape from this social and psychological pressure, Amuriza took refuge in nature. He worked for several months as a tree cutter in the mountains, an activity that left him both physically and morally robust. At the end of a year he left the priesthood, leaving behind his religious vocation and a church that he believed had betrayed the Basque people and the spirit of the Gospel. His secularization brought an end to a long period of denouncing the Catholic Church. While he was still in prison he had demonstrated his break from the Church and his disenchantment with a religion that was used to oppress his people:

> Filosofoek teologoek
> zer hitz zer ipuin jario
> jakintsu ustez denen artean
> putz bat ez dute balio.
> Zer erlijio zer misterio
> zer eliza eta arraio.[25]

> Philosophers, theologians,
> what words, what a stream of stories.
> Of all of those who think they are so wise,
> none of them are worth a puff of air;
> what a religion, what a mystery,
> what a church, what a demon.

On April 27, 1976, on the anniversary of the bombing of Gernika, Amuriza took part for the first time in an official bertsolaritza performance. A large audience attended the event in the hopes of seeing him. He performed that summer in many villages throughout the Basque Country with other Basque bards.

In 1977 he began to write as a journalist for the "Semaforo Gorria" (Red Traffic Light) and "Arrano Beltza" (Black Eagle) sections of the daily newspaper *Egin* as well as for the "Haizelarreko Berrimetroa" and "Bertsolandia" sections of the magazine *Punto y Hora*.[26] The articles he wrote for "Bertsolandia" are very interesting from the point of view of bertsolaritza. They reflect the critical opinions of a professional bertsolari's own literary movement. All his literary work was written in Euskara.

In addition to the literary aspect of Amuriza's life, there is a political side. I would say that Amuriza is more than a politician. He is a man of commitment with a large following of Basques who want to see him enter the political arena. Basque radicals saw Amuriza as a fighter who lived the principles that he sang about. They regarded him as an incorruptible defender of the culture and of freedom for the Basque Country. He was a council member for four years and was later elected to the Basque parliament by the Herri Batasuna (HB) Party.

Amuriza saw in HB a way to fight for the ideals that he had always defended: a reunified Basque Country with seven provinces; the *Euskaldun* prevailing, where a Basque person would use Euskara as the first official language; and a socialist country with its means of production in the hands of the working people and not under the control of a few capitalist impresarios. The HB proposed to break democratically with the Spanish monarchy and refused to accept the Spanish constitution, which, by the way, was rejected by more than 70 percent of Basque voters.

On February 4, 1981, when the king and queen of Spain were visiting Gernika, Amuriza and eighteen companions from his party held a protest demonstration in the Casa de Juntas. As King Juan Carlos addressed his audience, Amuriza's group stood up and with raised arms sang "Eusko gudariak gara," the hymn of the Basque soldier, in which the singer offers his own life in exchange for the liberation of Euskadi. After ten minutes of surprise, noise, and shouting, Amuriza's group was removed by the Basque police. In a press conference held in Bilbo that same afternoon, the proindependence party HB justified their action as a means of "defend[ing] the interests of the majority of the Basque people before a monarchy that condones repression in Euskadi." [27]

In November 1983 these protesters were tried in Madrid. When it was Amuriza's turn to speak, he attempted to do what the bard Etxahun had done in a previous time: speak in Euskara and answer the judge's questions with improvised verses. As was expected, Amuriza was censured by the president of the tribunal. The protestors were convicted and fined fifty thousand pesetas. When they refused to pay, they were imprisoned. Once more Amuriza went to prison, in Basauri. During his monthlong stay something unexpected happened. The Euskadiko Ezkerra (EE) Party, whose ideology differed from HB's on certain points, paid the fines without the prisoners' permission. Amuriza and his companions returned to their homes and expressed their disagreement with EE's action at a press conference. There were some bertsolariak who defended EE's position. The Gipuzkoan Rufino Iraola, an EE sympathizer, criticized Amuriza and his group's condemnation of the party.[28] Amuriza responded by ridiculing Iraola with sarcastic humor, using bederatzi puntuko bertsoa. The tenth verse says:

> Muturra sartzen bada
> ipurdian berdin
> gero zikindu gabe
> atera ezin.
> Kolpe horrek ez zidak
> eman hainbeste min
> ni ez nauk haserretzen
> txorroskiloekin.
> Gernikan zer egin

ongi bagenekin
Errege-erregin
ta beste arlekin
ezkerra zein den hemen
haiei galdegin.[29]

If you put your snout
up your anus
you cannot retrieve it
without dirtying it.
Your attack did not
bother me much
because I do not get angry
with nitwits.
We knew very well
what had to be done in Gernika;
ask the king and queen
and the other buffoons
who represent the Left here,
ask them.

THEMES AND STYLE

I have used Amuriza's improvised verses, especially those created during the txapelketak of 1980 and 1982, and the jarriak that appear in his books *Menditik mundura* and *Laurehun herri. Mila bertso berri* (Four hundred villages: A thousand improvised verses) to analyze his work and literary style.

The 1980 txapelketa was the first major test for Amuriza as a bertsolari. His written verses were already known, especially those dedicated to the prison at Zamora. His research on bertsolaritza was also well known because of his study of suffixation and rhyme. But it was still not known how he would perform as an improviser of verses before a large audience. Some had even suggested that Amuriza was not an accomplished bertsolari. His political party affiliation contributed to many prejudices that impeded an objective evaluation of the true value of his improvisational poetry. Furthermore, the fact that there had not been a national competition for thirteen years meant the 1980 txapelketa was the object of great expectation.

Amuriza's contribution was like a breath of fresh air, a profound reflection on the art, the beginning of new era that would rejuvenate the old tradition of bertsolaritza. His mission was

bertsolaritzaren adar erdi ihartua berritzea eta freskatzea.[30]

to renew and refresh the almost dry branch of bertsolaritza.

Amuriza's description of the bertsolari helps us understand better his sensitivity and his favorite themes. He is the singer of everyday life in the Basque Country:

> Batzutan bare bestetan bizi
> gaur leuna bihar zorrotza
> Hala da edo hala behar du
> bertsolarien abotsa
> parean zer den hura kantatzen
> bizitza nahiz heriotza . . .
>
> Behin ariko da humore onez
> behin amorruzko indarrez
> negargileak barrez jarririk
> barregileak negarrez.[31]

> Sometimes calm, sometimes lively,
> soft today, sharp tomorrow,
> that's how the voice of the bertsolari
> is, or should be,
> singing about what goes on before his eyes,
> about life and death . . .
>
> Sometimes with good humor,
> sometimes with rage,
> he makes those who weep happy
> and makes those who laugh weep.

All around him he saw a minority people whose native values had been suppressed. He sang about the lack of freedom of his own nation, Euskadi. With a characteristic firmness and a radical outlook, he sang in dramatic tones about the most incendiary themes of modern times—the problems of society, politics, religion, and sex. Amuriza always stood tall in the defiant stance of a prophet caring for his people, in spite of the occasional gales and hurricanes of opposition:

> Zuek ezetz esan arren
> nik esango dut baietz.[32]

> Although you say no,
> I will say yes.

Amuriza continues to sow the seeds of his social and political bertsolaritza, a committed and precarious bertsolaritza that has had a great impact on young poets. As a shepherd of his people Amuriza sometimes attacks his own flock, condemning the lack of unity among the Basques. But in the majority of cases he confronts the rich and those in authority who oppress the working Basque public both socially and nationally:

Sentimentua sartu zitzaidan
biotzeraño umetan
geroztik ainbat gauza mingarri
ikusi mundu onetan;
Euskalerriaz batera nago
biotz barneko penetan;
anaiak alkar artu ezinik,
etsaiak su eta ketan,
esan dudana gezurra bada
urka nazazue bertan.

. . . Zoriontsuak izan gintezke
erri libre bat bagina,
baña au ezta orrela eta
orrek sortzen dit sumina.[33]

The feeling entered
my heart as a child,
I have seen so many painful things
in this world since;
I am tied to the Basque Country
through heartache:
brothers who do not get along well,
enemies [destroying us] with smoke and fire,
if what I am saying is a lie,
hang me here and now.

. . . We could be happy
if we were a free people,
but that's not the way it is,
and that infuriates me.

Among Amuriza's favorite themes we also find the description of the different villages of Euskal Herria, with their past and present problems. He is a chronicler, as were Xenpelar and Txirrita before him, detailing historical events with great precision. *Laurehun herri. Mila bertso berri* describes more than forty Basque villages. This work is the product of a historian who had taken an interest in and informed himself about the problems of those villages so that he could sing their stories in their own town squares. Whoever wishes to write a history of those villages in the twenty-first century will encounter in Amuriza's verses an echo of the effect of various events of our own time.

His verses dedicated to the bombing of Gernika are a good example of this. The events are narrated with details about time, place, people, and the magnitude of the destruction. Amuriza did not merely provide a cerebral chronicle of the events as a detached historian. Instead he shared the pain of his people and described the incident with dramatic details, as is his habit:

Hogeita hamazazpi
apirila zena
eguna hogeitasei
eta astelena.
Feria famatua
Bizkaiko gailena
han zen herria eta
inguru geiena
jakin gabe bidean
zetorren krimena.

Abioiak Gasteiztik
Bizkaira zetozen
Urkiola, Durango
han ditugu Oizen,
Munitibarren zehar
norantza doazen
Muruetan jiratuz
errekatik zuzen
Gernikako azkena
Berlindik heldu zen.

Gernika zer zen eta
nola zuten utzi
hauspean gelditu zen
hamarretik zortzi.
Tente zegoen dena
erre eta hautsi
hiru ordutan suak
herria irentsi
ikusi ezik ezin
ziteken sinetsi.[34]

It was Monday,
April 26,
1937.
The famous fair,
the most renowned in Bizkaia;
the people were there and
most of them
had no idea
of the crime that was coming.

The planes came from Gasteiz
to Bizkaia, Urkiola, Durango,
we have them in Oiz,
through Munitibar,

where are they going?
They turn in Murueta,
go straight along the river,
they arrived from Berlin
to their destruction in Gernika.

What a town Gernika was,
and how they left it,
eight-tenths of it was in ashes.
Everything standing was burned and in ashes,
in three hours the fire swallowed the town,
impossible to believe if you did not see it.

I have said that one important qualification of any bertsolari is a mastery of Euskara. Not all bertsolariak have been able to create a poetic language. A few, like Xalbador, Pello Mari Otaño, and Xabier Amuriza, have reached that level. Language—Euskara that has been labored over—is one of Amuriza's obsessions.

Euskara garbia eta freskoa nahi dut.[35]

I want a clean and fresh Euskara.

To do this, Amuriza often uses wordplay, idiomatic expressions, the occasional rare verb form, metaphors, similes, and comparisons that give a learned flavor to his bertsolaritza art. Among the seldom-used verb forms, he employs many synthetic and defective verbs, such as *ihardun* (to persist) and *etzan* (to lie down). He also uses his theological background in his wordplay. For example, Franco's death inspired him to use the beginning of the Gospel according to John to create a humorous parody, treating Franco as God, who created everything and then died in the end:

Zugatik egin da dena
eta zu gabe ez da ezer egin
baina zureak ere egin du . . .
zautza hor eta zaude
sekulorum sekularen sekularioan.[36]

Everything was created by you,
and nothing was created without you,
but you have died, too . . .
lie down and rest in peace
for century after century.

For his similes and images, Amuriza employs nature (zoology and botany) as his source of inspiration. Once when he was assigned the theme of "robin redbreast," he confessed the influence nature had on him:

Negua horra dago
Jaunak etorria

txoritxo bat saltoka
ez da berria
lumak harroak eta
paparra gorria
horixe da neronen
amets iturria.[37]

Gentlemen,
winter has arrived,
it is nothing new
[to see] a bird hopping about
with its fluffed-up feathers
and its red chest,
that is the source
of my inspiration.

Amuriza is also very careful about the stylistic aspect of his verses. When assigned a theme to develop in three verses, he tries to respect logical structure and avoid betelana (meaningless, unnecessary fillers). As an example we have the three verses he improvised during the 1980 txapelketa on the theme "Man does not live by bread alone." He divided the theme into three parts: introduction, body, and epilogue. He positions the theme in the first verse, and creates an on-the-spot composition:

Ogiaz gain gizonari
anitz gauza zaio zor.[38]

Many things other than bread
are owed to man.

From this general edict he moves on to state that along with bread, justice is owed him.

In the second verse he develops the theme by giving examples and using similes such as the one of the human body. The heart and ribs are necessary to the integral formation of the human being:

Ogi utsez bizitzerik
nik ez nezake sinets.[39]

I do not believe that man
could live on bread alone.

In the third verse he delves more deeply into the theme by using simple images of country life (a pair of oxen and their yoke). The yoke symbolizes the Basque people's lack of freedom. He ends the verse with a humorous allusion to the "Semaforo Gorria" section of the newspaper Egin. He saves the last two lines to elicit applause from the audience, like a bullfighter's final moves; the applause was deafening:

Betiko berdetuko da
semaforo gorria.[40]

The red light
will turn green forever.

As a bertsolari, Amuriza is full of surprises. Sometimes he startles his audience with a new melody, and at other times with the dramatic tone of his verses or with the variety of his rhythms. He does not limit himself to the *zortzikoak*, or eight-line verses, but often employs very short rhythms in the manner of the kopla zaharrak—rhythms that enliven the competitions and break the monotony. He is also not afraid of such difficult rhythms as the bederatzi puntuko bertsoa, and he even uses them in his free-form themes. He is very sure of himself and has a beautiful voice and a fine ear for music.

In his renewal of the bertsolaritza style, he has managed to imbue his poetic creations with symbolism, drama, and lyricism. He is careful about logic, detail, knowledge, and the language he uses.

At times his style is grating, caustic, and harsh when dealing with themes of violence, politics, and sex. The crudity of his expressions can shock some individuals in the audience. No bertsolari takes his adversary's jokes seriously. Everyone accepts the fact that bertsolaritza is entertainment. Once Amuriza called his companion Jon Azpillaga a thief in verse, and he called Gorrotxategi an ass:

Zu jaio zinan egun haretan
lapur galanta sortu zen.[41]

On the day you were born
a great thief appeared.

Astorik bear bada
naiko asto aiz i.[42]

If somebody needs an ass,
you are ass enough yourself.

He uses much ironic, and sometimes biting, humor, but it is not that of Mattin and Lazkao Txiki, a humor that provokes a laugh without forcing one to think about the double meaning. Within the framework of a contest Amuriza's humor is normally ironic and satirical, but in other situations his wit is in a lighter and joking vein.

Amuriza is also gifted with quick thinking and he adapts immediately to the bertsolari role assigned to him. In the 1982 txapelketa he was given the theme of clean and dirty hands. Jon Azpillaga, who in real life is a mechanic, had the clean hands, and Amuriza, the former priest, had the dirty hands. Amuriza improvised the following verse:

Paperak orain aldatu behar
hau da komeri sorgina
nire laguna guri dagota
lengo apaiza zikina
esku horiei begiraturik
etzaude langile fina.[43]

Now we have to change roles,
this is a bewitching comedy,
my friend is clean
and the former priest is dirty,
looking at these hands,
you are not a good worker.

Since Amuriza possesses a special talent for music, on more than one occasion he has confessed that he prefers music over literature. During one period of his life, after his imprisonment, he dedicated himself to the *kantaldiak*, or public singing sessions, in addition to bertsolaritza.[44] Amuriza looks for new melodies in traditional music, just as did Resurrección María de Azkue and Padre Donostia before him. He sometimes contributes compositions of his own creation and has been rated highly when he uses them in the competitions.

In the 1982 txapelketa Jon Lopategi and Amuriza were tied. To break the tie they were assigned the following dramatic theme: A shipwrecked sailor sees a passing ship and calls for help, but since its captain refuses, the shipwrecked sailor must drown. Lopategi improvised three masterful verses that appeared unbeatable. Amuriza skillfully improvised another three verses, full of emotion and drama. But in addition he used a melody he had created in a minor key to suit the tragic moment he was trying to capture. The audience applauded him as few bertsolariak have been applauded in the recent history of performances. The following is his last verse:

Urak bete dit ia sabela
ito zorian nago honela
untzi haundi bat pasatzen eta
niri ukatu batela
hau da hilaren eskela
edo zer esan bestela
hori da bihotz ustela
biziagatik oso gustora
galduko nuke txapela
baina munduak hor jakingo du
kriminalak zeratela.[45]

My stomach is full of water,
I am about to drown,
a big ship passes by and

refuses me a lifeboat,
this is my obituary,
what else can I say,
that man has a rotten heart,
I would gladly lose the championship
in exchange for my life,
but the people will know
that you are assassins.

For Amuriza words and music go hand in hand. He is capable of singing for hours without stopping. He inherited the affinity for singing from his father and he believes he will carry this love with him to the grave:

Eman aurretik lurrari
hilkutxa zabalik jarri
azken bertsoa kanta dezadan
zuen negarrari.[46]

Before you bury me,
leave my coffin open
so that I may sing my last verse
to your tears.

Amuriza is decidedly one of the best bertsolariak in the modern history of this artistic phenomenon, and perhaps the one who has contributed the most to the future of the art form. Someday when extraliterary arguments disappear and the quality of Amuriza's art is objectively examined, he will be appreciated as he should be. His contribution differs in certain aspects from traditional bertsolariak, and nothing negative is implied by this statement. Basques in general are very traditional and loath to accept new things, but Amuriza's innovations will be accepted on the strength of the quality of his verses.

In conclusion, I should add that bertsolaritza is not an exclusive, isolated phenomenon belonging to one province, as are the pastorales of Zuberoa, nor does it belong to any single century. On the contrary, it is an artistic phenomenon that has spread throughout the Basque Country in a living and stable form since at least the beginning of recorded history. The four bertsolariak discussed are no more than representative examples, albeit highly exemplary ones, of the richness and variety of bertsolaritza in the Basque Country over the last two centuries.

CONCLUSION

The Future of Bertsolaritza

I am aware of the risks involved in predicting the future. Nevertheless, speculation is unavoidable. Until now, bertsolaritza has been evolving and adapting to the realities of every age, and it is logical to believe that it will continue to do so. The future of this oral literature will depend to a great extent on several factors: the Basque language, the ikastolak (Basque schools for children), the gau eskolak (night schools for adults), and above all the schools of bertsolaritza, which are dependent upon other unpredictable factors. However, some nonliterary circumstances, such as a coup d'état (so frequent in the last 150 years of Spain's history), could retard the development of both Euskara and bertsolaritza.

With these qualifiers in mind and with the data we have today, it is possible to deduce a few probable outcomes. Unlike similar phenomena that I have analyzed, the majority of which are headed for extinction, bertsolaritza is reaching levels previously unknown. According to Jon Juaristi, a critic of Basque literature,

> Bertsolaritza, the oral improvisation of the verses, is without a doubt the most well known and widely spread of all Basque folk literature. The status enjoyed today by bertsolariak is far greater

than that enjoyed by our own writers in Euskara. The public contests of improvisers can acquire the dimensions of true mass spectacles. The regard that Basque society holds for this activity does not diminish. On the contrary, the rise in the teaching of Euskara and the adult literacy rate are accompanied by the creation of bertsolaritza schools in large urban centers as well as publication of manuals to teach the techniques of improvisation.[1]

New facets of bertsolaritza became evident in the 1986 competition; the organizing committee had been restructured; young bertsolariak competed; a woman participated; contestants were evaluated on the basis of scores; a large audience attended; and the elimination rounds were held for the first time in the province of Araba. These new features are attributable to one principal factor: the process of institutionalization has begun for bertsolaritza. Consequently, I believe there will be additional organizational, linguistic, social, and technical changes.

On the organizational level, the Academy of the Basque Language has played a major role in these competitions since the end of World War II. The academy assumed complete responsibility for them and excluded all other groups, including the bertsolariak themselves. This has again changed drastically. Since the last txapelketa, the bertsolariak themselves have become responsible for the organizational process.

Moreover, on June 18, 1987, the bertsolariak became a formalized legal group with 150 members. Statutory approval of this new entity will undoubtedly provide stability for bertsolaritza.[2] More than fifteen years ago a smaller group of Basque bards met in Loyola (Gipuzkoa) to discuss their problems.[3] The society of bertsolariak is aware of the importance of preparing their competitions and it recognizes that the goals are much greater. The members want the new association to continue to act in other fields related to bertsolaritza. For example, they have decided to support the schools of bertsolaritza and to create an archive to preserve all the verses that are improvised. It is their intent to avoid the lamentable loss of their bertsolaritza art. Thousands of verses from the nineteenth century and part of the twentieth have already been lost forever.

From a linguistic viewpoint, bertsolaritza will rely on Euskara Batua in the future. It will be necessary to arrive at a standardized Euskara that will be understood both in the north and the south of the Basque Country.

Literacy campaigns and the ikastolak have created yet another group of young bertsolariak who are capable of using the unified dialect. In the txapelketa of 1986, several young bards improvised verses in Euskara Batua.

Currently, both Basque literature and bertsolaritza are taught in schools and universities. Just a quarter of a century ago the great majority of Basques did not even know that a Basque literature existed. The bertsolaritza of the future will be more thoughtful, more technical, and more learned. The Euskara used in these competitions will be purer and more refined. This literary expression has always managed to respond to current realities and to treat the problems of the people in its themes. Logically, we can hope that the bertso- lariak will gradually use better Euskara, as is the trend in publishing and in schools.[4] Bertsolaritza will last as long as the language endures. This is the only certainty we have about the future of the phenomenon.

From a sociological point of view, I assume that bertsolaritza will also change significantly. The most important change will be the active participa- tion of women. Basque society has been evolving, and many tasks that were considered exclusively male in the past are today shared by women. The same is happening in the field of bertsolaritza. In the past there were few female bertsolariak because, unfortunately, the society in which they lived did not permit them to perform in public or grant them the freedom to be themselves. In addition to the few female bertsolariak mentioned earlier, we should add the names of the sister and daughter, respectively, of Pello Errota, Sabina Elizegi (1842-1932) and Mikela Elizegi (1869-1967).

Furthermore, today nearly half of the participants in the children's bertso- lariak competitions, such as those organized in the schools of bertsolaritza, are female. This activity is beginning to bear its first fruit. In 1986 a woman— Bizkaian Cristina Mardaraz (1948-   )—participated for the first time in the txapelketa. We should also mention Arantza Loidi (1967-   ), who competes in official contests. A door that has long been closed to women is finally opening.

Changes are also taking place for audiences. Bertsolaritza has become a spectacle for the masses. Modern bertsolariak have available to them better means of communication for their events. Moreover, Basque radio and tele- vision can now broadcast the performances to the most remote farmhouses in the Basque Country. In addition to the ten or twelve thousand people who attend the performances, thousands of others follow the competitions on tele- vision. Although the spirit of battle and challenge that prevailed in the nine- teenth century is diminishing, the enthusiasm for the genre is increasing. Hardly any bertso-paperak are produced anymore, but the number of fans attending the improvisational performances is growing rapidly. The hope for their future lies in the classes that are given on this difficult art form and upon a considerable increase in Basque speakers.

Modern bertsolariak have also ignored the political barrier posed by the Pyrenees. As far as they are concerned these obstacles created by politicians do not exist. For them there exists only one united Basque Country, and they feel like members of the same family. Where once the work of the great bertsolari Etxahun was unknown in the southern part of the Basque Country, today such a situation is inconceivable. The existence of a dozen professional bards in the three northern provinces assures a bright future for bertsolaritza.

Finally, some changes in the technical area of bertsolaritza can be ex- pected. The txapelketak before large crowds will shape future bertsolaritza performances to a great extent. For example, the need for loudspeakers to enhance the performance are now indispensable for audiences. Bertsolaritza will persist because there is a demand to preserve the literary beauty of the verses on tapes and cassettes.

All these things will have their effect on the improvisational nature of bertsolaritza. The speed of improvisation can be fairly rapid when one is singing without a microphone or loudspeaker, but the reverse is not true. Bertsolariak like Xabier Amuriza and Jon Enbeita are occasionally attacked for singing more slowly than the old bertsolariak did, a fact of life imposed by modern technology. It is better to sing a little more slowly so that the audience will understand than to improvise a verse in fifteen seconds and have it garbled by sound system interference.

Today there are plans to bring performances to more urban areas, even to such noisy open squares as the Arenal in Bilbo. The bertsolariak are abandoning the traditional farmhouse and moving to the urban arenas where the future of both Euskara and bertsolaritza will be determined.

BASQUE PLACE NAMES AND
THEIR OFFICIAL EQUIVALENTS

Basque Name	Official Name
Aia (Gipuzkoa)	Aya
Altza (Gipuzkoa)	Alza
Amezketa (Gipuzkoa)	Amezqueta
Areatza (Bizkaia)	Las Arenas
Arrate (Gipuzkoa)	Mondragón
Baiona (Lapurdi)	Bayonne
Bergara (Gipuzkoa)	Vergara
Berriatu (Bizkaia)	Berriatua
Biasteri (Araba)	Laguardia
Bilbo (Bizkaia)	Bilbao
Billabona (Gipuzkoa)	Villabona
Bizkaia	Vizcaya
Deba (Gipuzkoa)	Deva
Donibane-Lohizune (Lapurdi)	Saint-Jean-de-Luz
Donostia (Gipuzkoa)	San Sebastián
Errenteria (Gipuzkoa)	Rentería
Errezil (Gipuzkoa)	Régil
Eskiula (Zuberoa)	Esquiule
Garindañe (Zuberoa)	Garindein
Gasteiz (Araba)	Vitoria
Gernika (Bizkaia)	Guernica
Getaria (Gipuzkoa)	Guetaria
Gipuzkoa	Guipúzcoa
Gizaburuaga (Bizkaia)	Guizaburuaga
Hondarribia (Gipuzkoa)	Fuenterrabia
Iruñea (Nafarroa)	Pamplona
Lapurdi	Labourd
Lazkao (Gipuzkoa)	Lazcano
Leitza (Nafarroa)	Leiza
Markina (Bizkaia)	Marquina
Mungia (Bizkaia)	Munguía
Munitibar (Bizkaia)	Arbácegui y Gerricaiz
Muxika (Bizkaia)	Múgica

Nafarroa	Navarra
Nafarroa Beherea	Baja Navarra
Oiartzun (Gipuzkoa)	Oyarzun
Ondarru (Bizkaia)	Ondárroa
Pasaia (Gipuzkoa)	Pasajes
Sara (Lapurdi)	Sare
Urepel (Nafarroa Beherea)	Urepele
Urretxu (Gipuzkoa)	Villareal de Urrechua
Usurbil (Gipuzkoa)	Usúrbil
Zaldibia (Gipuzkoa)	Zaldivia
Zarautz (Gipuzkoa)	Zarauz
Zestoa (Gipuzkoa)	Cestona
Ziburu (Lapurdi)	Ciboure
Zizurkil (Gipuzkoa)	Cizúrquil
Zornotza (Bizkaia)	Amorebieta
Zuberoa	Soule
Zumaia (Gipuzkoa)	Zumaya

NOTES

Introduction

1. Michelena, *1545 Bernat Detxepare*.
2. Ong, *The Presence of the Word*, 22.
3. Foley, *Oral Tradition in Literature*, 1–2.
4. Adam Parry, *The Making of Homeric Verse*, 272.
5. See Parry's *Serbo-Croatian Heroic Song*.
6. Lord, "Homer and Huso II," 440.
7. There are eleven works by Ruth Finnegan dealing with oral literature. See John Miles Foley's bibliography of *Oral-Formulaic Theory and Research*.
8. Finnegan, "What's Oral Literature Anyway?" 143–144.
9. Michelena, *Historia de la literatura vasca*, 11.
10. Urkizu, *Euskal antzertia*, 33.
11. Celaya, *Fuero nuevo de Vizcaya*, vii.

Chapter One. The Concept of Oral Tradition and Basque Oral Literature

1. Juan Mari Lekuona, "Oralidad y poesía," 127.
2. Gallop, *A Book of the Basques*, 109.
3. Ong, *Orality and Literacy*, 7.
4. Ormaetxea, *Euskaldunak*, 45.

Chapter Two. Definition and Qualities of a Bertsolari

1. Manuel Lekuona, "Gure bertsolariak," 5.
2. This recorded tape is located in the Basque Studies Program at the University of Nevada, Reno, and is the property of Dr. William A. Douglass.
3. Riquer, *Los Trovadores*, 1:67.
4. Amuriza, *Hitzaren kirol nazionala*, 12.
5. Akelarre, "Abestiak," *Habe* 93 (September 1986): 29.
6. There are two systems in use for expressing the structure of verses. In the southern Basque Country lines are defined by their caesuras, while in the north they are defined by their rhymes. What is hemistich for some, is stich for others.
7. Zubimendi, "Bigarren bertsolari eguna," 4:151.

8. Bertsolariak, *Bertsolari txapelketa 1980*, 49–50.

9. Ibid., 14.

10. Bertsolariak, *Bertsolari txapelketa 1962*, 146.

11. Zavala, *Xenpelar bertsolaria*, 298.

12. *Bertsolariya*, "Oraingo neskatxen Jazkera," 33.

13. Notes written by the bertsolari Jon Lopategi during a summer course on bertsolaritza at the Basque University summer school in Iruñea in 1986.

14. Viaud, *Le Pays Basque*, 128.

15. Agustín González, "Agustín González Acilu," *Berriak* 19 (January 1977): 33.

16. Arana Martija, *Música vasca*, 261.

17. Ibid., 244.

18. *Bertsolaritza, Formarik gabeko heziketa*, 114.

19. Ibid.

20. Xabier Amuriza, "Bertsolaritza arte informala?" *Punto y Hora* 333 (December–January 1984): 50.

21. Xabier Amuriza, "Etxean ezin kantatu," *Punto y Hora* 325 (October–November 1983): 50.

22. Joxe Zapirain recounts the death of his wife in seventeen verses. She left him a widower with nine children, the youngest only forty days old. The dialogue between husband and wife shortly before she dies makes many people weep. Zavala, *Zapirain anaiak*, 206–213.

23. *Bertsolarien txapelketa 1960*, 11.

24. In the 1986 txapelketa, in a section called "kartzelako gaia" (where all the bertsolariak sing about the same theme), they were given a difficult topic. In three verses they had to present a proclamation announcing decisions made at city hall. Several bertsolariak floundered in this section.

25. Amuriza, *Menditik mundura*, 172–173.

26. On more than one occasion Juan Ignacio Iztueta, alias "Lazkao Txiki," praised the quality of Juan Cruz Zapirain's verses. Zapirain narrated the life of Saint Genevieve in 163 verses. Zapirain's influence, especially the influence of his verses, was the basis for Lazkao Txiki's artistic vocation. Zavala, *Zapirain anaiak*, 61–132.

27. Kartzelako gaia can be a misleading term. The word *kartzela* (prison) does not mean that the theme must have to do with prison, but rather that everyone must sing about the same theme. The one who is singing does not know what his predecessors have sung. In order to keep the singers from hearing each other, they must go outside and remain there in isolation, as if they were in prison.

28. Caro Baroja, *Los vascos*, 352.

29. Bertsolariak, *Bertsolari txapelketa 1982*, 170–172. The following is a translation of the "shocking" words: panderoa (buttocks), iturri automatikoa (vibrator), plumeroa (penis), busti nere florerua (to wet the vagina), and uxola (ejaculation).

30. Ibid., 221–223.

31. Aire, *Odolaren mintzoa*, 61.

32. Xabier Amuriza, "Gauerditik aurrera," *Punto y Hora* 323 (October 1983): 50.

33. The festival of Saint Agate on February 5 is an occasion when groups of young friends go from farmhouse to farmhouse singing about the glories of the saint. These rounds last all night, from the evening of the fourth to the morning of the fifth. The verses they sing are not improvised, but there is always one person who takes advantage of the occasion to improvise a verse. Many bertsolariak make their debut on this occasion.

34. Balendin Enbeita says of Jon Lopategi (one of the best modern bertsolariak) that in the beginning he had a bad ear, but that little by little he improved. Josu Landa and Edorta Jiménez, "Bizitzari errepasoa eginez," *Argia* 1119 (October 1986): 39.

Chapter Three. Bertsolaritza Performance Types

1. Iztueta, *Guipuzkoako dantzak*, 186.

2. Ibid., 189.

3. Olaizola, *Lengo egunak gogoan*, 215.

4. Ignacio "Basarri" Eizmendi, "Sara'ko bertsolari txapelketa," *Aranzazu* (May 1960): 153.

5. Hnos. Estornés Lasa, *Enciclopedia general ilustrada del País Vasco*, 1:334–350.

6. Aita L. Villasante, *Aranzazu* 415 (January 1963): 18.

7. Xabier Amuriza, "Dibertsio eta desafioa," *Punto y Hora* 348 (April 1984): 50.

8. Aitzol was the soul of the Basque cultural renaissance that occurred in the early twentieth century in Euskal Herria, especially in Gipuzkoa. Aitzol was born in Tolosa and was killed by Franco's troops in the Hernani cemetery on October 17, 1936. In 1927 he founded the Euskaltzaleak society in an attempt to recover the rights of Euskara. He organized numerous cultural events among which are counted the "Euskal olerti eguna" (Day of Basque poetry), the "Antzerki egunak" (Competitions for theatrical works), and the bertsolariak competitions. In view of the fact that refined poetry was not very popular with the Basque public, Aitzol focused his efforts on those competitions that attracted large numbers of people. He was the arbiter of literary elegance in the prewar period and inspired the creation of the newspaper *El Día* as well as the magazine *Yakintza*. These publications reinforced the cultural renaissance initiated by Sabino Arana at the beginning of the century. In Aitzol's opinion, the Basque language was the soul of the Basque Country and it had to be saved. He also defended the social changes proposed by the independence and autonomy movement. He was a great student of nationalities without a state. According to Aiztol, literature could give a people prestige and independence, as it had done in Finland and Latvia.

9. Ignacio Eizmendi, "Lenengo bertsolari Eguna," *Yakintza* 3 (1977): 143.

10. Ibid., 146.

11. According to the oral testimony I collected from his family in the summer of 1986, this was the worst day of his life as a bertsolari. He wept bitterly, but the applause and affection that the city of Donostia always showed him made him forget his misfortune. For his part, he knew how to overcome the circumstances in that event as well. His simple, humble attitude earned him the applause of the majority of those attending that txapelketa.

12. Basarri agrees. In the article cited in note 4 about the problem of the excessive length of the bertsolaritza performances, he points out the problem of the lack of communication among the bertsolariak of the different provinces because of unfamiliarity with the dialects. He expresses this difficulty with a simile: "Ezin ondo uztartu" (They cannot be yoked together well). Like two oxen that work poorly if they are not well yoked, the pair of bertsolariak Joaquín Mitxelena and Balendin Enbeita do not make a good team because they use different dialects. This was evident when the Xalbador-Mattin team from the north won the competition.

13. Olaizola, *Lengo egunak gogoan*, 215.

14. The young Gipuzkoan Jon Sarasua was happy "because a Gipuzkoan had won." Iñaki Camino and Josu Landa, "Aurtengo txapela Gipuzkoan gelditu da: Sebastian Lizaso txapeldun," *Argia* 1096 (March 1986): 39.

15. The first militant ETA member assassinated was the Bizkaian Txabi Etxebarrieta (1944–1968), on June 7, 1968. Like Che Guevara, Etxebarrieta became a legend because of his revolutionary contribution. The ETA, in turn, assassinated Melitón Manzanas, commissioner and chief of the sociopolitical brigade of Donostia, a known torturer, in his Villa Arana in Irun (Gipuzkoa) in August 1968.

16. On February 4 and 11, 1968, there was a bertsolari competition in the Anoeta fronton. Sixteen bertsolariak took part. The prize of 100,000 pesetas was divided among the first- and second-place winners. Basarri won first place with 602 points; Xalbador was second with 598. Aire, *Herria gogoan*, 43.

17. Juan Mari Lekuona, "Oralidad y poesía," 190.

18. This collection is part of what was published on bertsolaritza by this simple, humble hard worker who had a small press in Errenteria (Gipuzkoa). From September 1931 to December 1932, Makazaga published four leaflets a week on the bertsolariak. He also published three small volumes entitled *Euskal erriko kanta zarrak*.

19. He has some verses entitled "Komeni zaigu erdera" (Spanish suits us). Zavala, *Mendaro Txirristaka bertsolaria*, 337–340.

20. Juan Mari Lekuona, *Euskaldunak*, 5:154.

21. It is an epic theme written in the Zuberoan dialect about an assassination that happened in 1440. Lakarra, *Euskal baladak*, 2:79–81.

22. Hnos. Estornés Lasa, *Cancionero popular del País Vasco*, 2:101.

23. Azkue, *Euskalerriaren yakintza*, 4:43.

24. Ormaetxea, *Euskaldunak*, 54–55.

Chapter Four. The Basque Language and Bertsolaritza

1. *Diccionario de la lengua española* (Madrid: Espasa Calpe, 1984), 1368.
2. Bertsolariak, *Bertsolarien txapelketa 1960*, 23.
3. Zavala, *Udarregi bertsolaria*, 36.
4. Jon Azpillaga says that in one year he performed in 178 different towns. "Herriak erretirorik eman gabeko bertsolaria," *Argia* 1133 (January 1987): 39.
5. "Sara'ko bertsolaria txapelketa," *Aranzazu* 384 (May 1960): 153.
6. "Pellokeriak ere ugari," *Punto y Hora* 343 (March 1984): 50.
7. Zavala, *"Bilintx." Indalecio Bizcarrondo. (1831–1876)*, 173.
8. Bertsolariak, *Bertsolarien txapelketa 1962*, 116.

Chapter Five. Origins of Bertsolaritza

1. Manuel Lekuona, *Literatura oral vasca*, 59–60.
2. Manuel Lekuona's position has been characterized by a lack of historical data and rejected by certain Basque writers. Joxe Azurmendi, in a round-table discussion said:

> Zergaitik esan behar dugu bertsolaritzan dagoen guztia dela artzaina, lirikoa, bakarka kantatzen duena eta gero dialektikoa nekazari- tzarekin hasi omen zena? Eskema hau Manuel Lekuonarena da. Zer- gatik esan behar dugu bata bestean ondoren etorriak balira bezala?

> Why must we say that everything that exists within bertsolaritza— the shepherd, lyricism, solitary singing, and later the emergence of another type of dialectic bertsolari—began in the agricultural era? That is Manuel Lekuona's plan. Why must we affirm this as if [these two types of bertsolaritza] had occurred one after the other?

Bertsolaritza, Formarik gabeko heziketa, 189.
3. Juan Mari Lekuona, *Ahozko euskal literatura*, 95–96.
4. Zavala, *Bosquejo de historia del bertsolarismo*, 17.
5. Guerra, *Los cantares antiguos del euskera*, 39.
6. Gorostiaga, *Antología de poesía popular vasca*, 113.
7. Ibid., 113–114.
8. Michelena, *Historia de la literatura vasca*, 42.
9. Guerra, *Los cantares antiguos del euskera*, 36.
10. Lindstrom, *A Concise History of Russian Literature*, 1:37.
11. *Bizkai'ko forua*, 419.
12. Ibid., 113.
13. Iztueta, *Guipuzkoako dantzak*, 185.
14. Iztueta, *Guipuzcoaco provinciaren condaira edo historia*, 12.

Chapter Six. Characteristics of Great Bertsolariak

1. Iztueta, *Guipuzkoako dantzak*, 190.
2. Arruti's memory was famous. In one competition he was tied with his opponent. To break the tie, the bertsolariak were asked to repeat from memory all the verses improvised during the competition. The shepherd won by being able to repeat fifty verses word for word. Zavala, *Pastor Izuela (1780-1837): Ezkioko ta Segurako itxuak*, 22-23.
3. Satrústegi, *Bordel bertsularia*, 1965.
4. "Bertsolaritza Pernando Amezketarraren garaian," *Egan* (July–December 1969): 23.
5. Dorronsoro, *Bertsotan (1789-1936)*, 7.
6. The Basque poet Jules Moulier, alias "Oxobi" (1888-1958), says of Otxalde that, in the northern part of the Basque Country, there were no bertsolaritza festivals at which he did not perform.
7. Xabier Lete, "Xenpelar," *Garaia* (October 1976): 44.
8. For the Basques the word *fuero* meant freedom. The foral spirit encompassed the administrative and political rights that the Basques had enjoyed for several centuries: the election of Basque representatives, exemption from military service, respect for Basque culture, and the possibility of having Basque teachers in their schools. A written pact existed as a juridical source between the Spanish kings and the Basques. The fueros were not privileges that sprang from a gratuitous act (*gratia*) on the part of the king but were rights (*jus*). This pact was radically modified unilaterally by one of the contractual parties by the Spanish law of October 25, 1839. According to the new legal precept, the crown was no longer the repository of power; power now passed to the nation.
9. Zavala, *Xenpelar bertsolaria*, 410-411.
10. Ibid., 224.
11. Castresana, *Vida y obra de Iparragirre*, 232.
12. Xenpelar treated him like a comedian interested in the money. "Atoz gure kalera . . . musika oiek utzita" (Come to our street . . . leave this music behind). Zavala, *Xenpelar bertsolaria*, 121.
13. Martín Ugalde, *Historia de Euskadi* (Madrid: Cupsa, 1982), 4: 224.
14. After fleeing the country he spent the greater part of his life abroad. With the exception of his childhood years and two other time periods (1852-1858 and 1878-1881), he spent the rest of his life traveling throughout France, Italy, Switzerland, Germany, England, Portugal, Argentina, and Uruguay, where he frequented theaters, palaces, and hovels.
15. There were constant political dramas in Spain throughout the nineteenth century. Not a single governmental change was brought about democratically. Everything was resolved by military coups, mutinies, palace intrigues, and assassinations.
16. Castresana, *Vida y obra de Iparragirre*, 236.
17. Ibid., 242.
18. Ibid., 103.

19. Becerro, "Un recuerdo del bardo guipuzcoano en 1877," 353.

20. Castresana, *Vida y obra de Iparragirre*, 270.

21. Ibid., 256.

22. Ibid., 234.

23. Ibid., 310.

24. Unamuno, *Obras completas*, 4:207.

25. The grenade tossed by Carlist artillery personnel completely destroyed his right leg, and it had to be amputated that afternoon. The left leg was also broken in the blast and had to be amputated later. Zavala, *"Bilintx," Indalecio Bizcarrondo (1831–1876)*, 363.

26. José de Manterola (1849-1884) was born in Donostia. Although he died at the age of thirty-five, he was the inspiration for the cultural renaissance in Gipuzkoa at the time. He was enterprising and restless. He initiated poetry competitions in Gipuzkoa and wrote several books. His two most outstanding works are the *Cancionero vasco*, in which he published a beautiful anthology of verses by the bertsolariak, and the magazine *Euskal Erria*, which he began publishing in 1880 and edited until his death.

27. Unamuno, *Obras completas*, 6:207.

28. Benito Jamar was a Nafarroan who lived in Donostia as a small child. Zavala, *"Bilintx." Indalecio Bizcarrondo (1831–1876)*, 352.

29. Amuriza maintained that those verses were not improvised. Similar critics have asserted that the verses could have been previously prepared because Domingo Kanpaña worked in the same carpenter's shop as Bilintx. They contend that the beauty of the verses could not have been created without ample preparation. I personally believe that Bilintx was capable of improvising the verses on his own. On one occasion I discussed with Amuriza his reason for thinking thus (personal communication, 1986, in Iruñea), indicating to him the great beauty of his improvised verses dedicated to his father. Zavala relates another encounter between Bilintx and the great bertsolari Udarregi in which both were improvising. Zavala, *"Bilintx." Indalecio Bizcarrondo (1831–1876)*, 348.

30. Bizcarrondo, *Bertso ta lan guztiak*, 154.

31. Zavala, *"Bilintx." Indalecio Bizcarrondo (1831–1876)*, 352.

32. The Basque representative from Araba, Mateo Benigno Moraza (1816-1878), addressed the members of the Spanish parliament: "Gentlemen, consider the great act you are about to commit. You are going to do away with the most ancient liberties in the world." Mateo Benigno de Moraza, *Discursos de Mateo Benigno de Moraza* (Vitoria: Diputación Foral de Alava: 1976), 178. Spanish orator Emilio Castelar (1832-1899) noted: "Something great dies in Spain today." Madrid's centralism intended to smother the democratic spirit of an ancient nation, but the Basques, like José de Manterola, cried, "The fueros are dead! Long live the fueros!" (ibid., 366).

33. Otaño, *Pedro Mari Otaño'ren bertsoak*, 7.

34. Zavala, *"Txapel" bertsolaria*, 1969.

35. Zavala, *Zepai bertsolaria*, 1971.

36. Zavala, *Udarregi bertsolaria*, 21.

37. Zavala, *Azpeitiko premiyoaren bertsoak (1893–1895)*.

38. Zavala, *Udarregi bertsolaria*, 36.

39. Zavala, *Azpeitiko premiyoaren bertsoak (1893–1895)*, 30.

40. Zavala, *Pello Errotaren itzala*, 85.

41. Numbers 101, 102, 103, 104, and 126 of the *Auspoa* collection.

42. Zavala, *Txirritaren bertsoak*, 2:129.

43. Ibid., 1:132.

44. Ibid., 2:169.

45. Zavala, *Ustu ezin zan ganbara*, 62.

46. Zavala, *Txirritaren bertsoak*, 1:50.

47. The tree of Malato was located in the Encartaciones, near the border with Santander. Basque soldiers were prohibited from crossing that border during wartime.

48. Zavala, *Txirritaren bertsoak*, 2:84.

49. Ibid.

50. Ibid., 85.

51. Ibid., 1:102–107.

52. Ibid., 114.

53. Gabriel Aresti, "José Manuel Lujanbio Retegi 'Txirrita'," *Anaitasuna* 209 (April 1971): 8.

54. Zavala, *Txirritaren bertsoak*, 1:253.

55. Ibid., 2:116.

56. Joxe Manuel Lujanbio, "Pello eta Txirrita," *Punto y Hora* 320 (September 1983): 50.

57. Zavala, *Ustu ezin zan ganbara*, 50.

58. In addition to Urretxindor, the most prominent members of his family were his son Balendin, Bizkaian champion in 1958 and 1959; and his grandson Jon (1950–   ), runner-up in the 1980 national championship. Urretxindor's brothers Imanol and Xanti were also very good, especially with bertso jarriak. Kepa Enbeita, *Gure Urretxindorra*, 124–126.

59. There was another bertsolari from Bizkaia, Esteban Uriarte, who was born in Dima but settled in Bermeo. He took part in the 1935 national championship in Donostia and later performed several times with Urretxindor. He never achieved the latter's artistic caliber, nor did he enjoy Urretxindor's fame.

60. Kepa Enbeita, *Gure Urretxindorra*, 161.

61. Oleskari is a difficult word to translate. An oleskari is similar to a bertsolari who goes from farmhouse to farmhouse singing.

62. Juan Bautista Arrospide was born on the Eskibel farm in Busturia (Bizkaia) in 1869. He studied medicine in Zaragoza. He was a dedicated doctor for fifty years, a close friend of Sabino Arana, founder of the Basque Nationalist Party (PNV), and one of the first proponents of Arana's nationalism in the Gernika area. Until the age of twenty-five, Kepa Enbeita knew very little about this new radical nationalism. Balendin Enbeita, *Bizitzaren joanean*, 102–105.

63. Arana's linguistic reform was fundamentally marked by purism. He stayed away from Basque words derived from Spanish. His linguistic reform

covered lexicon, grammar, proper names, phonetics, syntax, and the calendar. Putting purism before antiquity, he invented new words such as *txadon* (church), *gentza* (peace), and *ludi* (world). He wanted a pure Basque, free from any traces of other languages.

64. Kepa Enbeita, *Gure Urretxindorra*, 47.

65. Ibid.

66. Ibid., 144.

67. Leopoldo Lugones, along with Rubén Darío, is considered one of Latin American's best modernist poets of the early twentieth century.

68. Lugones, *Obras poéticas completas*, 839-843.

69. Zavala, *Gaztelu bertsolaria*.

70. Interview from "Euskara bukatu egingo da," *Habe* 64 (May 1985): 6-9.

71. Ibid., 9. He has many biographies in his library as well as several books by Seneca (2 B.C.-65 A.D.), Benito Pérez Galdós (1843-1920), Pío Baroja (1872-1956), and Miguel de Unamuno (1864-1936).

72. Eizmendi, *Laugarren txinpartak*, 44-45.

73. Eizmendi, *Kantari nator*, xix.

74. Aire, *Odolaren mintzoa*, 311.

75. One member of the jury confessed to the young Uztapide that he in actuality had won first place but because of Txirrita's advanced age, it was given to the old bertsolari. Olaizola, *Lengo egunak gogoan*, 219.

76. Aire, *Odolaren mintzoa*, 311.

77. Manuel "Uztapide" Olaizola, "Gure bertsolariak," *Aranzazu* 417 (March 1963): 78.

78. Bertsolariak, *Bertsolarien txapelketa 1962*, 145-146; *Bertsolari txapelketa 1965*, 119.

79. Balendin Enbeita, *Bizitzaren joanean*, 66-69.

80. While working at the Zabale-Ormaetxe farm, he fell from the loft and broke several ribs. Other complications arose later while he was in the hospital at Galdakao (Bizkaia).

81. M. Uzkia, "Balendin Enbeita, euskara eta aberria maite zituen gizona," *Punto y Hora* 454 (November 1986): 37.

82. On October 7, 1979, he had an accident with his tractor. Later he developed gangrene in one leg. *Deia*, July 24, 1981.

83. Ibid., 40.

84. Aire, *Odolaren mintzoa*, 118.

85. Aire, *Herria gogoan*, 86.

86. Ignacio "Basarri" Eizmendi, "Nere bordatxotik," *Aranzazu* 493 (February 1972): 11.

87. Hernández, *Martín Fierro*, 30.

88. Lasarte, *Gordean neuzkanak*, 13.

89. Manuel Lasarte published some verses in the May 1982 issue of the magazine *Aranzazu*, in which the word *dizuna* appeared twice as a rhyme in the third stanza. Some readers of the magazine could not believe Lasarte was capable of such an error and sent letters to the editor. As it turned out, it was

a typographical error and a note of explanation was later printed. *Aranzazu* (September 1982): 13.

90. Ignacio "Basarri" Eizmendi, "Danetik zerbait," *Aranzazu* 482 (March 1971): 25.

91. Bertsolariak, *Bertsolari txapelketa 1965*, 31.

92. "Lazkao Txiki," *Goiz Argi* 277 (January 1976): 2.

93. The new Basque songs arose because of Mixel Labeguerie's personal efforts during 1963–1964. In a simple, direct style, Labeguerie sang about the Basque people's struggle for freedom; his songs heightened cultural awareness and had a tremendous impact on the people's political consciousness. In 1965 a musical group, Ez dok amairu, was created by Mikel Laboa, Benito Lertxundi, Xabier Lete, Lurdes Iriondo, Julen Lekuona, and Antton Valverde to expose the collective political and cultural unrest of the culturally alienated and colonized Basque nation. Later, many other groups and singers of young men and women followed their lead. Aristi, *Euskal kantagintza berria*, 11–83.

94. In May 1960, 339 priests signed a letter condemning, among other things, the Franco government's persecution of the Basque people and culture. In that letter, they used the word *genocide*. The ecclesiastical authorities in Madrid (the Nuncio and the bishops of the Basque dioceses) condemned the letter harshly without publishing it.

95. Juan Mari Lekuona, "Oralidad y poesía," 214.

96. In a conversation I had with his brother Jesús in Boise, Idaho (personal communication, June 1987), I asked Jesús if he knew how to improvise verses. He answered that he could not even though he was Jon's brother. According to Jesús, his brother would not have reached the level he has attained if it were not for the Enbeita family.

97. Xalbador loved the other Basque dialects. He was very fond of young Jon Lopategi's verses composed in Bizkaian.

98. Jon Azpillaga's father was from Ondarru and his mother from Berriatua. Because of his father's work, they had to move to Pasaia, where Jon was born. Later he went to school in Berriatua and lived there for many years. His wife is from Motriku (Gipuzkoa), where his house is, but he works in his factory in the port of Ondarru (Bizkaia).

99. Jon Azpillaga follows the Partido Nacionalista Vasco's (PNV) Christian democratic platform. In contrast, Jon Lopategi supports the Herri Batasuna (HB), a radical party fighting for the independence of Euskadi.

00. The public attended the 1959 txapelketa in great numbers; the crowd was estimated at twelve thousand. "Gernikako arbola" was sung at the end of the performance. This did not please the Spanish authorities and future competitions were held in bullfighting rings or in the courtyard of the Institute of Bilbo. One order from the governor of Bizkaia was enough to negate the bertsolariak's efforts. Balendin Enbeita, *Bizitzaren joanean*, 65–66.

Chapter Seven. Regard for Bertsolaritza

1. The following lists some of those writers: Agustín Cardaberaz (1703-1770), Juan Antonio Ubillos (1707-1789), Sebastián Mendiburu (1708-1782), José Ignacio Guerrico (1740-1824), Juan Bautista Aguirre (1743-1823), Juan Antonio Moguel (1745-1804), Pedro Astarloa (1751-1821), Pablo Pedro Astarloa (1752-1806), Juan Ignacio Iztueta (1767-1845), Fray Bartolomé Madariaga (1768-1853). Villasante, *Historia de la literatura Vasca*, 4-5, 103-109.

2. Larramendi, *El Impossible Vencido*, 373-374.

3. Ibid., 374.

4. Iztueta, *Guipuzkoako dantzak*, 188.

5. Ibid., 190.

6. Haritschelhar, "L'antibertsolaritza dans basa-koplariari (1838) de Jean Baptiste Camoussarry (1815-1842)," *Revista Internacional de los Estudios Vascos* (January-June): 97; 112.

7. Gorosábel, *Noticia de las cosas memorables de Guipúzcoa*, 364.

8. Carmelo de Echegaray, *Apéndice a la obra Noticia de las cosas memorables de Guipúzcoa* (Tolosa: N.p., 1901).

9. Zavala, *Bosquejo de historia del bertsolarismo*, 97.

10. Ibid., 153.

11. Aguirre, *Garoa*, 89-90.

12. The Spanish equivalents of these Basque words are *preparar* (to prepare), *pasar* (to pass), *portarse* (to behave), *importancia* (importance), *sustancia* (substance), *bolsillo* (pocket), and *alegría* (joy).

13. Gregorio de Mújica, "Gure gauzak. Bertsolariak," *Revista Internacional de Estudios Vascos* 1 (January-February 1908): 428-429.

14. Gabriel Aresti, "Poesía eta Euskal poesia," *Egan* 3-6 (May-December 1960): 159.

15. Oteiza, *Quousque tandem . . . !*, 9.

16. Michelena, *Historia de la literatura vasca*, 148.

17. Nicolás Ormaetxea, "Euskeraren edertasunak," *Euskal Esnalea* 284 (August 1927): 172-173.

18. Luis Villasante, former president of the Academy of the Basque Language, did not include bertsolaritza in his lengthy and interesting *Historia de la literatura vasca* (1961).

19. Nicolás Ormaetxea, "Poesi erritarra," *Euskal Esnalea* 284 (August 1927): 173.

20. Ibid.

21. Goikoetxea, *Musika ixilla*, 19.

22. Aresti, *Obra guztiak. Poemak*, 1:532.

23. Xanti "Errialde" Onaindia, "Poesia da herria gehienik zuzpertzen duena," *Zeruko Argia* 610 (November 1974): 7.

Chapter Eight. Phenomena Similar to Bertsolaritza

1. Armistead, "Folk Poetry of Modern Greece," 91.
2. Galicia is in northwest Spain. It consists of four provinces with an area of 29,434 km² and a population of two million. Galicia's economy is essentially agriculture-based in the interior, while fishing is very important along the coast.
3. This death occurred in the province of Lugo.
4. Tolosana, *Folklore in the Modern World*, 289.
5. García Cotorruelo, *Anejos del Boletín de la Real Academia Española*, 136.
6. The aviators Ramón Franco (brother of General Franco), Durán, Alda, and Rada were the first to cross the southern Atlantic in the plane *Non Plus Ultra*. They used a Dornier seaplane. Like Christopher Columbus, they departed from the port of Palos (Huelva). After landing in the Atlantic four times, they were able to set down in Pernambuco (Brazil) on February 2, 1926. Later they continued to Montevideo and Buenos Aires. Before this trip, pilots Alcock and Brown had crossed the northern Atlantic. Trythall, *Franco*, 52.
7. Along with slavery established by the Spaniards at the beginning of the sixteenth century, there existed a set of feudal socioeconomic relationships in Cuba. The plantation owners, commercial and industrial impresarios, the military, and the administrative and ecclesiastical hierarchies (mostly Spaniards) controlled politics and the economy. Generally speaking, Creoles were not admitted to important administrative posts. The poor and middle-class white peasants were called *guajiros*. Lukin, "Testimonios sobre la poesía popular Cubana del segundo tercio del siglo XIX."
8. Ibid., 78.
9. The word *payador* or *pallador* comes from the Quechua word *paclla*, which means peasant.
10. Uribe Echevarria, *Flor de canto a lo humano*, 22.
11. Hernández, *Martín Fierro*, 30.
12. Ibid., 120.
13. Guerrero Cárpena, "Santos Vega y Poca Ropa, payadores ríoplatenes," 647.
14. De La Fuente, *El payador en la cultura nacional*.
15. Ibid., 23.
16. Ibid., 69.
17. Suassuna, "Coletânea da poesia popular nordestina," 16.
18. Aulestia, "A Comparative Study of Basque and Yugoslav Troubadourism," 382; Adam Parry, *The Making of Homeric Verse*.
19. Lord, *The Singer of Tales*, 43.
20. Albert B. Lord, "Avdo Međedović, Guslar," in *Slavic Folklore* (Philadelphia: American Folklore Society, 1956), 129.
21. Abu-Lughod, "A Community of Secrets," 653.
22. Angel María Castell, "Bertsolaris . . . Ingleses," *Euskal Erria* 35 (1896): 543.

Chapter Nine. Pierre Topet, Alias "Etxahun"

1. Lhande, "Le bard Etchahun," 542.
2. Interview, July 1985, Iruñea.
3. Etxaide, *Etxahun'en bertsoak Gipuzkeraz*, 23.
4. Jean Haritschelhar, professor and current president of the Basque Academy, has devoted more than ten years to this subject for his doctorate. Two books have resulted from his intensive labors: *Le poète souletin Pierre Topet-Etchahun (1786–1862)* and "L'oeuvre poétique de Pierre Topet-Etchahun," XIV-XV, 1969-1970, Bilbao.
5. Haritschelhar, *Le poète souletin Pierre Topet-Etchahun (1786–1862)*, 14.
6. Lhande, "Le barde Etchahun," 420-421.
7. Jean Baptiste Otxalde, "Etchahun eta Otxalde," *Gure Herria* 2 (1967): 68.
8. Lafitte, *Le Basque et la littérature d'expression basque en Labourd, Basse-Navarre et Soule*, 48-49.
9. The title of the novel is *Etchahun le Malchanceux* by Pierre Espil. The play *Etchahun* was written by Pierre Larzabal (1915-   ).
10. Diharce, *Zeru menditik*, 90-91.
11. Haritschelhar, *Le poète souletin Pierre Topet-Etchahun (1786–1862)*, 15.
12. Lafitte, *Le Basque et la littérature d'expression basque en Labourd, Basse-Navarre et Soule*, 48.
13. Haritschelhar, "L'oeuvre poétique de Pierre Topet-Etchahun," 140.
14. Ibid.
15. Ibid., 172.
16. Ibid., 176.
17. Ibid., 80.
18. Haritschelhar, *Le poète souletin Pierre Topet-Etchahun (1786–1862)*, 116.
19. Haritschelhar, "L'oeuvre poétique de Pierre Topet-Etchahun," 80.
20. Ibid., 78.
21. The great German poet was of French origin. As a small child he accompanied his parents into exile during the French Revolution (1789). He found himself astride two centuries, two traditions, and two nations (France and the young, still-forming Germany). He lived in the midst of the resurgence of nationalism and the beginning of German romanticism. He was considered a classical representative of that movement because of his novel *Peter Schlemihls wundersame Geschichte* (1814) and his book of poems *Frauenliebe und Leben*. In the latter collection, he published the poem about the assassination of Dominque Etchegoyhen and the subsequent Etxahun trial. The poem is entitled "Des Basken Etchahon Klage" (The Lament of Etxahun the Basque). Some of his poems became folk songs. Haritschelhar, "Etchahun et Chamisso," *Boletín de la Real Sociedad Vascongada de los Amigos del País*, xvi, 71-83.
22. Haritschelhar, "L'oeuvre poétique de Pierre Topet-Etchahun," 186.
23. Ibid., 144.
24. Ibid., 138-153.
25. Ibid., 246.

26. Ibid., 234.

27. Ibid., 240.

28. Ibid., 242.

29. "A propos de Topet-Etchahun," *Gure Herria* (1950): 178-181.

30. Haritschelhar, "L'oeuvre poétique de Pierre Topet-Etchahun," 242.

31. Ithurriague, *Un peuple qui chante*, 71-72.

32. Louis Dassance, "De la léngende d'Etchahun à son histoire," *Gure Herria* (1962): 115-116.

33. Etxaide, *Amasei seme euskalerriko*, 47.

34. The priest was son of an officer in Napoleon's army who had married a Basque. The priest's Alsatian name explains Etxahun's xenophobia. Jon Mirande, "L'oeuvre poétique de Etxahun," *Euskera* (1969-1970): 485.

35. Ibid., 460.

36. Ibid., 642.

37. In order to disseminate Etxahun's work more widely among the Basque people, Jon Etxaide translated his poems into the Gipuzkoan dialect with the collaboration of Jon Mirande, a native of that province.

38. Villasante, *Historia de la literatura vasca*, 173.

39. Nicolás Ormaetxea, "Euskal-literatur'ren atze edo edesti laburra," *Euskal-Esnalea* 285 (1927): 214.

40. Jokin "Udalaizpe" Zaitegi, "Villon eta Etxahun," *Euzko Gogoa* 3-4 (1955): 44.

41. Artaso, "Etxahun koblalari pastorala ia pronto daukate barkoxtarrek," *Argia* 1106 (1986): 24-26.

Chapter Ten. Pello Mari Otaño, Alias "Katarro"

1. The theme of returning home is emotionally reflected in the songs "Ara nun diran" by José María Iparragirre and "Urrundik" by Jean Baptiste Elizanburu. The first song is reprinted in Castresana's *Vida y obra de Iparragirre*, p. 256; the second is in Labayen's *Elizanburu: bere bizitza ta lanak. Su vida y obras*, p. 183.

2. In 1521 the Portuguese Ferdinand Magellan was assassinated by natives of the Philippines. His first officer, the Basque Juan Sebastian Elcano, a native of Getaria (Gipuzkoa) assumed command of the ship and became the first to circumnavigate the world in 1522. *The New Encyclopaedia Britannica*, 15 ed., (Chicago: Encyclopaedia Britannica, 1981), 669.

3. Azkue, *Cancionero popular vasco*, 1:76.

4. Ibid., 75.

5. In the summer of 1985 I visited Zizurquil. In the square there is a small monument erected in honor of this bertsolari. Close by, there is a bar where I asked the owner about Pello Mari Otaño's life. I was surprised to hear from him that that man depicted by the statue was Nafarroan.

6. In the history of bertsolaritza there have been three outstanding families. We have already discussed the Enbeitas. There were also the Otaños and

the Elizegis; Pello Errota and several women who improvised verses came from the latter family.

7. In Zavala's book *Azpeitiko premiyoaren bertsoak (1893–1895)*, there are eleven of his verses in bederatzi puntuko bertsoak.

8. Félix Ortiz y Pelayo composed the music for that opera. In 1906 it was performed at the Victoria theater, and twenty years later at the Colón in Buenos Aires. Koldo Azkarate, "Pedro Mari Otañoren 75. Urteurrena Zizurkilen," *Argia* 1,057 (1985): 32-33.

9. Otaño, *Pedro Mari Otaño'ren bertsoak*, 66.

10. Ibid., 67-69.

11. Ibid., 65-66.

12. Ibid., 103-107.

13. Otaño, *Otaño'tar Pedro M'ren olerki onenak*, 97-98.

14. Ibid., 94-96.

15. Luis Michelena, "Pedro Mari Otañoren bertsoak," *Egan* 1-2 (1960): 118.

16. Emeterio Arrese, "Otaño'tar Pello Mari," *Euzko Gogoa* 9-10 (September-October 1952): 15.

17. Otaño, *Otaño'tar Pedro M'ren olerki onenak*, 39-49.

18. Ibid., 35-37.

19. Otaño, *Pedro Mari Otaño'ren bertsoak*, 59-60.

20. Otaño, *Otaño'tar Pedro M'ren olerki onenak*, 13-14.

21. Otaño, *Pedro María Otaño*.

Chapter Eleven. Fernando Aire, Alias "Xalbador"

1. This book contains a brief prologue by Emile Larre (1926-   ). According to José María Aranalde, a specialist in this field, it is the best book written to date about this form of artistic expression.

2. This opinion is shared by the great majority of bertsolariak and fans. Mattin, who has accompanied Xalbador from plaza to plaza since 1946, states: "Bertso jartzen, berriz, ez zuen parekorik" (Then again, there was no other to equal him in the writing of verses). *Deia*, November 6, 1977.

3. Long ago Nafarroa was divided into six *merindades*, or counties. The county of Ultrapuertos is currently in Nafarroa Beherea, located in France in the region of Cize. In 1512 the Spanish troops of the Catholic king and queen Ferdinand and Isabella occupied all of Nafarroa, which resulted in the current division. Jean Louis Davant, *Histoire du Pays Basque* (Goiztiri: Bayonne, 1968), 30.

4. Editorial entitled "Agur Xalbador," *Zeruko Argia* 712 (November 1976): 2.

5. Aire, *Odolaren mintzoa*, 25-27.

6. Ibid., 222.

7. Ibid., 83.

8. Ibid., 102.

9. Ibid., 103-104.

10. Ibid., 37.

11. Ibid., 41.

12. Aire, *Herria gogoan*, 64.

13. Aire, *Odolaren mintzoa*, 37.

14. Ibid., 39.

15. "Aurpegi iluna" is from the poem *Ni Naiz* in ibid., 345.

16. Ibid., 337.

17. Aztiri, "Xalbador hil da," *Aranzazu* 547 (December 1976): 381.

18. We should also keep in mind his two other books, *Ezin bertzean* and *Herria gogoan* as well as many of his verses in different txapelketak and public performances.

19. Aire, *Odolaren mintzoa*, 348.

20. Ibid., 343.

21. He learned from this priest to love the Basque language. Bascans was a fervent admirer of Euskara but was not a Basque nationalist. Ibid., 214-215.

22. According to the current parish priest, Jean Baptiste Bascarans, this poem was composed after Xalbador had heard a sermon on this theme. Ibid., 265.

23. Ibid., 270.

24. Ibid., 299.

25. Ibid., 114-115.

26. Uztapide was also very much loved among the bertsolariak. The two of them were great friends; even their constant competition for first place did not cool their friendship. Xalbador dedicated a poem to Uztapide in which he says: "Zu baino lagun hoberik ez det aurkitu ene bizitzan" (I have never found a better friend than you in all my life). Ibid., 311.

27. Some of the photos, such as the one on page 280 of Aire's *Odolaren mintzoa*, reveal this mood. According to family members, he could spend an entire week distracted and pensive. In contrast, when he had a scheduled bertsolari performance, he was much happier.

28. Aztiri, "Xalbador hil da."

29. Jon Azpillaga, *Egin*, November 8, 1977. We must bear in mind that Azpillaga spent a quarter of a century competing with the bard from Urepel.

30. We often see in the Basque Country individuals like Xalbador and Mattin. They were quite different; perhaps that is why they got along so well. One was as serious as Don Quixote while the other was as humorous as Sancho Panza. Generally speaking, Xalbador did not talk much because he felt conversation required the right atmosphere. He would open up, however, in a group of friends and was often the best *kontulari* (storyteller). Basarri tells us that on a trip with Xalbador to Paris, the fellow never stopped talking: "Appearances can be deceiving . . . underneath he was happy and entertaining. He had a special gift of humor for telling jokes and relating events. . . . We really enjoyed ourselves!" *La Voz de España*, November 9, 1976.

31. Aire, *Odolaren mintzoa*, 144.

32. Ibid.

33. Ibid., 345.

34. Aire, *Herria gogoan*, 124.

35. Ibid., 85.

36. *Bertsolari txapelketa 1965*, 93–94.

37. *Bertsolari txapelketa 1967*, 71.

38. Aire, *Xalbador.*

39. According to a personal interview in 1985 with Marie Claude, the daughter-in-law who lived with Xalbador during his final years, he became completely distracted. Xalbador needed to be left alone in his inner world when he began to think. He made a small, constant noise that was an unmistakable sign that he was submerged in his inner world.

40. Diharce, *Biziaren olerkia*, 492.

41. Ernest Alkat, "Xalbadoren omenaldia," *Goiz Argi* 314 (October 1976): 21.

42. Aire, *Odolaren mintzoa*, 119.

43. José María Satrústegi, "Ez adiorik," *Punto y Hora* 17 (December 1976): 29.

44. Aire, *Odolaren mintzoa*, 59.

45. Aire, "Xalbador."

46. Aire, *Odolaren mintzoa*, 67.

47. Errialde, "Xalbador artzain bertsolaria," *Zeruko Argia* 478 (April 1872): 1.

48. Elizanburu was born in Sara (Lapurdi). He became known as a great poet during the literary competitions organized by Antoine d'Abbadie. In the 1860s he won first prize. Some of his poems, such as "Nere etxea," "Agur herriari," and "Lau andren besta," became well-known popular songs. Labayen, *Elizanburu. Bere bizitza ta lanak*, 179–221.

49. Aire, *Odolaren mintzoa*, 114.

50. Ibid., 186.

51. His library reflects his interests and concerns. There are several books from the *Auspoa* collection about bertsolaritza (in particular, works from Uztapide, Lasarte, Zepai, and Bilintx). There are also some books on Basque literature, such as *Euskaldunak* by Nicolás Ormaetxea and works by Victor Hugo and Prosper Mérimée (1803–1870).

52. Bertsolariak, *Errege eguneko bertso-sayoa (1962)*, 89.

53. Aire, *Odolaren mintzoa*, 339.

54. Ibid., 341.

55. Peillen, "Amodiozko baratzetan."

Chapter Twelve. Xabier Amuriza

1. Xabier Amuriza, "Amuriza gizona eta bertsolaria," *Anaitasuna* 410 (April 1981): 27.

2. Ibid.

3. Jules "Oxobi" Moulier, "Pertsularien dohain-eginbideak," *Gure Herria* (September–October 1952): 317.

4. Aire, *Odolaren mintzoa*, 34.

5. See note 1 above, 25.

6. It was a time when even instruction in the seminaries was directly or indirectly controlled by Franco's government. Speakers of the Basque language were persecuted, and the language was allowed to languish as a cultural remnant that did not deserve much attention.

7. Xabier Amuriza, "Kateak eta kate markak," *Zeruko Argia* 758 (October 1977): 20.

8. The concordat, signed in 1953 between the Holy See and Franco's government, established at Zamora a special prison for priests. Many priests were sent there, including Amuriza, whose long imprisonment also coincided with that of four Basque priests and a priest from Madrid.

9. Xabier Amuriza, "Gogor," Baiona, Agorila, AG 30-15, 1968. Sound recording.

10. Their messages urged a more humble and autochthonous church. They requested of Rome that the bishops of Basque dioceses be Basque and know Euskara. They also protested Franco's authority in the presentation of the *terna* (or list of three candidates) for naming bishops, and asked that these nominations come directly from the pope.

11. The bishop in charge of the diocese at the time was the Bizkaian José María Cirarda.

12. The five Bizkaian priests were Nikola Telleria, Xabier Amuriza, Julen Calzada, Alberto Gabikagogeaskoa, and Jesús Naberan. Amuriza, *Menditik mundura*, 180; idem, "Kateak eta kate markak," *Zeruko Argia* 758 (October 1977): 20.

13. Amuriza, *Menditik mundura*, 175-179.

14. Ibid., 182-185.

15. The same incident occurred with Julen Calzada and Alberto Gabikagogeaskoa, when Calzada's mother died in Busturia and Gabikagogeaskoa's father died in Lekeitio.

16. *Bertsolari txapelketa nagusia 1980* (Tolosa: Auspoa, 1980), 97.

17. Antonio Añoveros, a Nafarroan and bishop of Bilbo, has been one of the most noteworthy bishops the diocese has had since its creation in 1950. He tried to act independently of Franco's government. His famous pastoral, "El cristianismo: mensaje de salvación para los pueblos," preached in the parishes of the diocese in February 1974 in Bizkaia, resulted in a government order calling for his expulsion from Spain. The order, however, was never carried out because of the pressure exerted by the Bizkaian clergy and the Vatican.

18. Amuriza, *Menditik mundura*, 186.

19. His work on prefixation, "Euskal aurrizkiak" (Basque prefixes), was published in *Euskera*, and the work on rhymes can be found in *Hiztegi errimatua hitzaren kirol nazionala* (Rhyming dictionary: The national sport of words).

20. Amuriza, *Menditik mundura*, 244.

21. According to the information I collected from one of the leaders, the mouth of this tunnel was in a washroom. They dug it under dangerous and difficult circumstances because they lacked the proper tools for the job; on occasion they used their hands to remove the dirt. They were discovered by pure chance during a routine inspection.

22. Amuriza, *Menditik mundura*, 197-200.

23. Ibid., 207-208.

24. See note 1 above, 26.

25. Amuriza, *Menditik mundura*, 205.

26. The words "Haizelarreko Berrimetroa" and "Bertsolandia" are this bertsolari's creations. They are not found in any Basque dictionary.

27. "El rey en las vascongadas," *Punto y Hora* 213 (February 1981): 10. While King Juan Carlos was praising Spanish democracy in Gernika, young Joseba Arregi, suspected of being an ETA militant, was tortured to death in a police station in Madrid. "Lo reventaron," *Punto y Hora* 214 (February 1981): 9-15.

28. Some of Rufino Iraola's attacks included the following

Lotsagabekeriaz	Do not speak without shame
ez mugi mingaina . . .	do not deceive anyone . . .
ez da erraz baina	although it's not easy
inor ez engaina . . .	you are new to politics,
politikan lego	you are free to do what you
nahi duena esan	wish after saying what you
libre du gero.	want. [paraphrase]

"Xabier Amuriza bertsotan borbor," *Punto y Hora* 269 (June 1982): 15.

29. Amuriza, *Laurehun herri. Mila bertso berri*, 357.

30. See note 1 above, 27.

31. Amuriza, *Menditik mundura*, 172.

32. *Bertsolari txapelketa nagusia 1980*, 80.

33. Ibid., 35-36.

34. Amuriza, *Laurehun herri. Mila bertso berri*, 152-153.

35. Amuriza, *Menditik mundura*, 143.

36. Ibid., 168.

37. *Bertsolari txapelketa 1982*, 258.

38. *Bertsolari txapelketa nagusia*, 80.

39. Ibid.

40. Ibid., 81.

41. *Bertsolari txapelketa 1982*, 221.

42. *Bertsolari txapelketa nagusia*, 49.

43. *Bertsolari txapelketa 1982*, 221.

44. As a result of this work he prepared a sound recording entitled *Menditik mundura*. Many of the words on the record were taken from his book with the same title.

45. *Bertsolari txapelketa 1982*, 318.

46. *Bertso-paperak. Xenpelar saria*, 29.

Conclusion. The Future of Bertsolaritza

1. Juaristi, *Literatura vasca*, 23-24.

2. Imanol Lazkano has been elected president and other directors of the association have been selected. They have also designated Manuel Lekuona, Antonio Zavala, and Xabier Amuriza as honorary members. David Zuazalde, "Bertsolaritza," *Argia* 1157 (June 1987): 47.

3. This group of friends is becoming organized. The members are so close that even the wives of the bertsolariak meet to discuss their problems. They participate in events other than artistic ones as a way of becoming united. These bertsolariak have organized soccer games with bertsolaritza organizers and fans.

4. Today more than seven hundred books a year are published in Euskara in the Basque Country. A very high percentage of them are related to the Basque language itself and its literature. Eighty percent of the materials published in the Basque language are written in Euskara Batua.

GLOSSARY

adarra jo. To kid, to tease.

alboka. Type of Basque horn (musical instrument).

amaia da hasera; atzekoz aurrera. The end is the beginning; from back to front.

bapateko bertsoak. Improvised verses.

batua. Unified Basque language.

bederatzi puntuko. Stanza with fourteen verses and nine similar rhymes.

bel canto. Opera.

bertso. Stanza.

bertsoak. Plural form of *bertso.*

bertso-berriak. Although a literal translation is "new verses," the term refers to written verses common in Gipuzkoa during the nineteenth century.

bertso jarriak. Popular verses that are transcribed (see *jarri*).

bertso-paperak. See *bertso jarriak.*

bertsolari. Improviser of sung verses.

bertsolariak. Plural form of *bertsolari.*

bertsolaritza. Improvisation of verse art form.

bertsolaririk osona. The most competent bertsolari.

betelana. An error in the logic of the bertso that results from a bertsolari's ramblings.

bota. To improvise sung verses.

cuaderna via. Stanza composed of four alexandrine monorhythmic verses.

dulzaina. Basque end-blown flute made of wood and iron with nine holes and a wide bell.

eresi. Dirge or elegy.

eresiak. Plural form of *eresi.*

etxeko andre. Female head of the household.

etxola. Hut or cabin.

Euskaldun. Basque people and things.

Euskaltzale. Bascophile.

Euskaltzaleak. Plural form of *Euskaltzale.*

Euskara. Basque language.

Euskara Batua. Unified Basque language.

Euskera. See *Euskara*.

Euskera. Journal title or name of the Academy of the Basque Language.

fuero. Compilation of Basque laws; old Basque liberties.

gai-jartzaile. Moderator in a bertsolaritza competition who assigns themes and directs the performance.

gau eskolak. Night classes in Euskara for adults.

hamarreko handia. Stanza of ten verses in which odd verses have ten syllables and even verses have eight.

hamarreko txikia. Stanza of ten verses in which odd verses have seven syllables and even verses have six.

herri. People or audience.

herria betsolari. Bertsolaritza of the people. The art form is not possible without public participation.

herriaren kantuzko hitza. Sung word of the people. Bertsolaritza implies that the verses are sung in front of an audience.

ikastolak. Basque schools for children.

jarri. To write popular verses without improvisation.

jarriak. Written verses.

jendeaurreko bertsolaritza. Improvised bertsolaritza.

joko. Diversion, recreation, entertainment.

jolas. See *joko*.

kantaldi. Musical recital or performance.

kantaldiak. Plural form of *kantaldi*.

kartzelako gaia. Assigned themes provided to each bertsolariak just before the performance. (Artists are removed from the stage to ensure they do not hear the assigned subjects and to avoid advance preparation of verses. Thus total improvisation is guaranteed.)

kirol. Sport.

koblakari. Bertsolari; used by northern French Basques.

kopla. Old Basque sung verse.

koplak. Plural form of *kopla*.

koplari. A variant spelling of *koblakari*.

koplariak. Plural form of *koplari*.

kopla zaharrak. Although a literal translation is "old sung stanzas," this term means short stanzas, usually of two rhymes and four verses. (These stanzas are normally sung with an instrumental accompaniment, such as an accordion.)

lana bete. Opposite of *betelana;* following the rules in improvising the verses for the assigned theme.

langue d'oc. Provençal language spoken in the southeast of France and cultivated by the troubadours.

lorejaiak. Although the term literally means "floral games," it refers to the competition for Basque troubadours and poets.

manech. Term used by Zuberoan Basques to refer to Basques of other provinces.

nagusia. Verses or stanzas with eight to ten syllables.

olerkari. Poet.

pellokeria. Nonsense, silliness.

phastuala. Pastorale in the Zuberoan dialect.

plaza gizona. Showmanship or stage presence.

poeta culto. Opposite of bertsolari; a poet who follows different poetic techniques and always prepares verses in writing.

poto egin. Error that consists of repeated rhymes that have the same meaning in a verse.

puntu. Rhyme.

puntuak. Plural form of *puntu.*

sei puntukoa. Verse of six rhymes.

tenso. Provençal poetic composition involving a dispute between two or more poets on the subject of love.

trikitria. Accordion.

trovador. Poet-improvisor and singer of the Middle Ages.

txapelketa. Basque troubadour competition.

txapelketak. Plural form of *txapelketa.*

txikia. Although word means *small,* the term refers to verses with seven to six syllables.

txikiak. Plural form of *txikia.*

txistu. Basque wind instrument similar to the flute.

txistulari. *Txistu* players.

vascuence. Spanish word for the Basque language.

ziria sartu. To add difficulties, to trick.

zortzikoak. Stanzas of eight verses.

zorziko handia. Stanzas of eight verses in which the odd verses have ten syllables and the even verses have eight.

zortziko txikia. Stanzas of eight verses in which the odd verses have seven syllables and the even verses have six.

zortzi puntukoa. Verses with eight similar rhymes.

BIBLIOGRAPHY

Abu-Lughod, Lila. "A Community of Secrets." *Signs: Journal of Women in Culture and Society* (Summer 1985): 637-657.

Aguirre, Domingo. *Garoa.* Donostia: Euskerazaleak, 1935.

Aire, Fernando [Xalbador]. *Ezin bertzean.* Tolosa: Auspoa, 1969.

———. *Odolaren mintzoa.* Tolosa: Auspoa, 1976.

———. *Xalbador.* Elkar, K15. 1976. Sound cassette no. 3.

———. *Herria gogoan.* Tolosa: Auspoa, 1981.

———. "Xalbador." On recording of *Iparraldeko kantu zaharrak.* Edigsa. Herri Gogoa 155/456L.

Akesolo, Lino. "Bertsolaritza Pernando Amezketarraren garaian." *Egan* (July–December 1969): 3-24.

Altadill, Julio. *Memorias de Sarasate.* Pamplona: Aramendi y Onsalo, 1909.

Alvar, Carlos. *La poesía trovadoresca en España y Portugal.* Madrid: Cupsa, 1977.

Amezketarra, Fernando. *Fernando Amezketarra bertsolaria.* Tolosa: Auspoa, 1966.

Amuriza, Xabier. "Euskal aurrizkiak." *Euskera* 19 (1974): 9-104.

———. *Menditik mundura.* Bilbao: Printzen, 1977.

———. "Bertsolarien barne-prozesua." *Jakin* 14-15 (April–September 1981): 134-138.

———. *Hitzaren kirol nazionala.* Euskadi: AEK, 1981.

———. *Hiztegi errimatua.* Euskadi: AEK, 1981.

———. "Iparraguirre bertsolari." *Jakin* 19-20 (August–December 1981): 149-158.

———. *Laurehun herri. Mila bertso berri.* Donostia: Elkar, 1982.

———. *Zu ere bertsolari.* Donostia: Elkar, 1982.

———. *Menditik mundura IZ.* 109-C. Sound recording.

Arana Goiri, Sabino de. *Lecciones de ortografía del euskera Bizkaino.* Bilbao: Sebastián de Amorrortu, 1896.

Aranalde, José María. "Bertsolari haundi deklaratua." *Jakin* 28 (July–September 1983): 195-196.

Arana Martija, José Antonio. *Música vasca.* San Sebastián: Caja de Ahorros Municipal de San Sebastián, 1976.

———. "Bertsoen doinua." *Jakin* 14-15 (April–September 1980): 80-98.

Aresti, Gabriel. *Obra guztiak. Poemak.* 2 vols. Donostia: Kriselu, 1976.

Aristi, Pako. *Euskal kantagintza berria.* Donostia: Erein, 1985.

Aristimuño, José de [Aitzol]. "Eusko olerti-kera berezia." *Yakintza* 2 (1934): 243-255.

Armistead, Samuel G. *Judeo-Spanish Ballads from New York.* Berkeley & Los Angeles: University of California Press, 1981.

———. "Folk Poetry of Modern Greece." *Comparative Literature* 35 (Winter 1983): 89-95.

Arozamena, Jesús María de. *Jesús Guridi.* Madrid: Editora Nacional, 1967.

———. *Joshemari Usandizaga y la bella época donostiarra.* San Sebastián: Caja de Ahorros Municipal de San Sebastián, 1969.

Arozamena, Mikel. *Nere aldia.* Tolosa: Auspoa, 1976.

Arrillaga, Antonio. *Lo que se ha dicho de Iparraguirre.* Elgoibar: Publicaciones de la Junta de Cultura de Vizcaya, 1953.

Aulestia, Gorka. "A Comparative Study of Basque and Yugoslav Troubadourism." *World Literature Today* 59 (Summer 1985): 382-385.

Azkue, Resurrección María de. *Euskalerriaren yakintza.* 4 vols. Madrid: Real Academia Española, 1959.

———. *Cancionero popular vasco.* 2 vols. Bilbao: La Gran Enciclopedia Vasca, 1968.

Azurmendi, Joxe. "Bertsolaritzaren estudiorako." *Jakin* 14-15 (April-September 1980): 139-164.

Baraiazarra, Luis. "Bertsolari txapelketaren ondoko galbahaketa." *Karmel* 177 (April-June 1986): 6-22.

Barandiaran, Emiliano. *Euskal musikalari bikaiñak.* Zarauz: Itxaropena, 1967.

Barandiarán, José Miguel. *Euskalerri'ko leen-gizona.* Donostia: Zarautz: Itxaropena, 1934.

———. *El mundo en la mente popular vasca.* 2 vols. San Sebastián: Auñamendi, 1961.

———. "Cuentos y leyendas." In *Obras completas,* vol. 2, 238-353. Bilbo: La Gran Enciclopedia Vasca, 1973.

Becerro, Ricardo. "Un recuerdo del bardo guipuzcoano en 1877." *Euskal Erria* (April 1905): 353-361.

Bertsolariak. *Bertsolarien txapelketa 1960.* Zarautz: Itxaropena, 1961.

———. *Errege eguneko bertso-sayoa (1962).* Tolosa: Auspoa, 1962.

———. *Bertsolarien txapelketa 1962.* Tolosa: Auspoa, 1962.

———. *Bertsolari txapelketa 1965.* Tolosa: Auspoa, 1965.

———. *Amar urteko bertso-paperak (1954-1963).* Tolosa: Auspoa, 1964.

———. *Bertsolari txapelketa 1967.* Tolosa: Auspoa, 1967.

———. *Bertsolari txapelketa 1980.* Tolosa: Auspoa, 1980.

———. *Bertsolari txapelketa 1982.* Bilbao: Euskaltzaindia, 1983.

Bertsolaritza, formarik gabeko heziketa. Bilbao: Euskal Herriko Unibertsitatea, n.d.

Bertsolariya. Donosti: Sendoa, 1981.

Bertso-paperak. Xenpelar saria. Donostia: Gipuzkoako Aurrezki Kutxa Probintziala, 1985.

Bizcarrondo, Indalecio [Bilintx]. *Bertso ta lan guztiak.* Tolosa: Auspoa, 1962.

Bizkai'ko forua. Bilbao: Estornés Lasa, 1984.

Câmara Cascudo, Luis da. *Literatura oral no Brasil*. Rio de Janeiro: José Olympio, 1978.

Caro Baroja, Julio. *Los vascos*. Madrid: Minotauro, 1958.

Castresana, Luis de. *Vida y obra de Iparragirre*. Bilbao: La Gran Enciclopedia Vasca, 1971.

————. *Iparragirre'ren bizitza*. Bilbao: La Gran Enciclopedia Vasca, 1978.

Celaya, Adrián. *Fuero nuevo de Vizcaya*. Durango: Leopoldo Zugazaga, 1976.

Chaho, Augustin. *Biarritz entre les Pyrénées et l'Océan*. Bayonne: "Lespés," n.d.

Chamisso, Adelbert von. *Peter Schlemihls wundersame Geschichte*. Berlin: 1814.

Cid, J. Antonio. "Peru Gurea." *Anuario: Seminario de filología vasca "Julio de Urquijo"* 19, no. 2 (1985): 289-404.

De La Fuente, Alfredo. *El payador en la cultura nacional*. Buenos Aires: Corregidor, 1986.

Díaz Plaja, Guillermo. *Tesoro breve de las letras hispánicas*. Vol. 6. Madrid: Magisterio Español, 1972.

Diharce, Jean [Iratzeder]. *Zeru menditik*. Belloc: Eskila, 1959.

————. *Biziaren olerkia*. Bilbo: Gero, 1984.

Dorronsoro, Joanito. *Bertsotan: 1789-1936*. Bilbao: Ediciones Elexpuru, 1981.

————. *Bertsotan: 1936-1980*. Zarauz: Itxaropena, 1988.

Eizmendi, Ignacio [Basarri]. *Ataño III*. Zarautz: Icharopena, 1949.

————. *Basarriren bertso-sorta*. Zarautz: Itxaropena, 1950.

————. *Kantari nator*. Zarautz: Itxaropena, 1960.

————. *Laugarren txinpartak*. Tolosa: Auspoa, 1966.

————. *Sortu zaizkidanak*. Tolosa: Auspoa, 1973.

————. *Kezka giroan*. Tolosa: Auspoa, 1983.

————. *Bertsolaritzari buruz*. Tolosa: Auspoa, 1984.

————. "Herriaren anima da bertsoa." *Argia* 1015 (May 1984): 22-25.

————. "Euskara bukatu egingo da." *Habe* 64 (May 1985): 6-9.

Elicegui, Mikela. *Pello Errotak jarritako bertsoak*. Tolosa: Auspoa, 1963.

————. *Pello Errotaren bizitza*. 2 vols. Tolosa: Auspoa, 1963.

Elósegui, Jesús. *Juan Ignacio de Iztueta Echeberria (1767-1845)*. San Sebastián: Auñamendi, 1969.

Enbeita, Balendin. *Nere apurra*. Tolosa: Auspoa, 1974.

————. *Bizitzaren joanean*. Donostia: Elkar, 1986.

Enbeita, Jon. *Inguruaren arduraz*. Donostia: Hordago, 1980.

Enbeita, Kepa. *Gure Urretxindorra*. Buenos Aires: Ekin, 1971.

Erauskin, José Ramón. *Aien garaia*. Tolosa: Auspoa, 1975.

Erkoreka, Ramón. "Bertsolari txapelketa nagusiaren historia." *Argia* 1096 (March 1986): 27-34.

Espil, Pierre. *Etchahun le Malchanceux*. Bayonne: Euskadi, 1947.

Estornés Lasa, Bernardo. *Estética vasca*. Buenos Aires: Editorial Vasca, 1952.

Estornés Lasa, Hnos. *Cancionero popular del País Vasco*. 3 vols. San Sebastián: Auñamendi, 1968.

————. *Enciclopedia general ilustrada del País Vasco*. Vol. 1. San Sebastián: Auñamendi, 1981.

Etxaide, Jon. *Amasei seme euskalerriko*. Zarauz: Itxaropena, 1958.

——. *Etxahun'en bertsoak Gipuzkeraz*. Zarauz: Itxaropena, 1969.

Euskal Herria. 2 vols. Donostia: Jakin, 1984.

Fagoaga, Isidoro de. *Pedro Garat "El Orfeo de Francia."* Buenos Aires: Editorial Vasca Ekin, 1948.

——. *Los poetas y el País Vasco*. San Sebastián: Sociedad Guipuzcoana de Ediciones y Publicaciones, 1969.

Ferrero, José. *Luis Iruarrizaga*. Bilbao: La Gran Enciclopedia Vasca, 1977.

Finnegan, Ruth. "What's Oral Literature Anyway?" In *Oral Literature and the Formula*. Ann Arbor: University of Michigan Press, 1976.

——. *Oral Poetry: Its Nature, Significance and Social Context*. Cambridge: Cambridge University Press, 1977.

Foley, John Miles. *Oral Formulaic Theory and Research*. New York and London: Garland Publishing, 1985.

——, ed. *Oral Tradition in Literature*. Columbia: University of Missouri Press, 1986.

Gallop, Rodney. *A Book of the Basques*. London: Macmillan, 1930.

García Cotorruelo, Emilia. "Estudio sobre el habla de Cartagena y su comarca." In *Anejos del Boletín de la Real Academia Española*. Madrid: S. Aguirre Torre, 1959.

Garmendia, José. *Iztueta'ren olerkiak*. Tolosa: Kardaberaz Bilduma, 1978.

Garmendia, Txomin. *Bizitzaren arian*. Tolosa: Auspoa, 1982.

——. *Denbora pasa*. Tolosa: Auspoa, 1982.

——. *Bordaberri'ko gozo-mikatzak*. Tolosa: Auspoa, 1983.

——. *Erririk-erri*. Tolosa: Auspoa, 1984.

Gascue, F. *Origen de la música popular vascongada*. Paris: Honoré Champion, n.d.

Gogor (Record). Bayonne, Agorila, AG 30-15.

Goikoetxea, Joan Inazio [Gaztelu]. *Musika ixilla*. San Sebastián: Auñamendi, 1962.

González, Maite. *Bertan ikusia*. Donostia: Erein, 1984.

Goody, Jack. *Literacy in Traditional Societies*. Cambridge: Cambridge University Press, 1968.

Gorosábel, Pablo de. *Noticia de las cosas de Guipúzcoa*. Vol. 1. Bilbao: La Gran Enciclopedia Vasca, 1972.

Gorostiaga, Juan. *Antología de poesía popular vasca*. San Sebastián: Icharopena, 1955.

Guerra, Juan Carlos. *Los cantares antiguos del euskera*. San Sebastián: Martín y Mena, 1924.

Guerrero Cárpena, I. "Santos Vega y Poca Ropa, payadores rioplatenses." *Boletín de la Academia Argentina de Letras* 57 (October–December 1946): 637-669.

Haritschelhar, Jean. "Etchahun et Chamisso." In *Boletín de la Real Sociedad Vascongada de los Amigos del País Vasco*, 71-83. San Sebastián, 1960.

——. *Le poète souletin Pierre Topet-Etchahun (1786–1862)*. Bayonne: Société des Amis du Musée Basque, 1969.

——. "L'oeuvre poétique de Pierre Topet-Etchahun." *Euskera* 14-15 (1970): 1-170.

Hérelle, Georges. *Les pastorales basques*. Bayonne: Tavernier, 1903.

———. *Etudes sur le théatre basque. La représentation des pastorales à sujets tragiques*. Baiona: Foltzer, 1923.

Hernández Girbel, F. *Julián Gayarre*. Barcelona: Ediciones Lira, 1955.

Hernández, José. *Martín Fierro*. Buenos Aires: Editorial Vasca Ekin, 1972.

Historia de Euskadi. Vols. 3 and 6. Madrid: Planeta, 1981.

Ithurriague, Jean. *Un peuple qui chante. Les Basques*. Paris: Edimpres, 1947.

Iztueta, Juan Ignacio de. *Guipuzcoaco provinciaren condaira edo historia*. Donostia: Baroja, 1847.

———. *Guipuzkoako dantzak*. Tolosa: E. López, 1895.

Jaka, Angel Cruz. *Iparragirre*. Donostia: Donostiako Aurrezki Kutxa, 1982.

Jeanroy, Alfred. *Les origines de la poésie lyrique en France*. Paris: Honoré Champion, 1904.

Jousse, Marcel. *Le style oral rhythmique et mnémotechnique chez les verbo-moteurs*. Paris: Gabriel Beauchesne, 1925.

Juaristi, Jon. *Literatura vasca*. Madrid: Taurus, 1987.

Kantu kanta khantore. Baiona: Kordelerien Irarkolan, 1967.

Labayen, Antonio María. *Elizanburu. Bere bizitza ta lanak*. San Sebastián: Auñamendi, 1978.

Lafitte, Pierre. *Le Basque et la littérature d'expression basque en Labourd, Basse-Navarre et Soule*. Bayonne: Aintzina, 1941.

———. *Eskualdunen loretegia*. Baiona: Laserre, n.d.

Lakarra, Joseba. *Euskal baladak*. 2 vols. Donostia: Hordago, 1983.

Larramendi, Manuel. *El Impossible Vencido*. Salamanca: Arte de la Lengua Vascongada, 1729.

Larre, Emile. "Ipar euskadiko bertsulariak." *Jakin* 14-15 (April–September 1980): 30-37.

Larrondo, Jakes. *Etxahun-Iruri khantan*. Pau: Jakes Larrondo, 1977.

Larzabal, Pierre. *Etchahun*. Baiona: Herria, n.d.

Lasagabaster, Jesús María. "Literatura y vida literaria." In *Euskal Herria*. Vol. 2. Donostia: Jakin, 1984.

Lasarte, Manuel. *Bertso-mordoxka*. Tolosa: Auspoa, 1975.

———. "Kristau itxaropena." In *Gordean neuzkanak*. Tolosa: Auspoa, 1975.

Lázaro Carreter, Fernando. *Diccionario de términos filológicos*. Madrid: Gredos, 1984.

Leizaola, Jesús María de. *Estudios sobre la poesía vasca*. Buenos Aires: Editorial Vasca Ekin, 1951.

———. *1808-1814 en la poesía popular vasca*. Buenos Aires: Editorial Vasca Ekin, 1965.

———. *Romances vascos y literatura prehistórica*. Buenos Aires: Editorial Vasca Ekin, 1969.

———. *El refranero vasco antiguo y la poesía vasca*. Buenos Aires: Editorial Vasca Ekin, 1978.

Lekuona, Juan Mari. *Ilargiaren eskolan*. Bilbao: Mensajero, 1973.

———. "Bertsolari gazteen eskolatzea." *Zeruko Argia* 600 (September 1974): 5.

———. "Txirrita eta Basarri." *Euskera* 20 (1975): 333-339.

———. "Ahozko euskal literatura." In *Euskararen liburu zuria*. Bilbao: Euskaltzaindia, 1978.

———. "Literatura oral vasca." In *Cultura Vasca II*, 59-109. Zarauz: Erein, 1978.

———. *Muga beroak*. San Sebastián: Erein, 1979.

———. "Bertsolariak historian." *Jakin* 14-15 (April-September 1980): 6-16.

———. "Jendaurreko bertsolaritza." *Jakin* 14-15 (April-September 1980): 99-114.

———. *Ahozko euskal literatura*. Donostia: Erein, 1982.

———. "Lizardiren eskema metrikoak eta puntuak." *Jakin* 29 (October-December 1983): 53-88.

———. "Ahozko literaturaren historiaz." In *Euskal Herria*. Vol. 1. Donostia: Jakin, 1984.

———. *Euskaldunak*. Vol. 5. Bilbao: Etor, 1985.

———. "Oralidad y poesía." In *Euskaldunak*. Vol. 5. Bilbao: Etor, 1985.

———. *Mimodramak eta ikonoak*. Donostia: Erein, 1990.

Lekuona, Manuel. "De etnografía. Las toberas." *Euskalerriaren Alde* 194 (February 1920): 41-53.

———. "Gure bertsolariak." *Anaitasuna* 55 (October 1959): 5.

———. *Literatura oral vasca*. San Sebastián: Auñamendi, 1965.

———. "El misterio de la literatura oral euskérica." *Aranzazu* 452 (July 1967): 1-4.

———. "Ahozko literatura." In *Idaz-lan guztiak*. Gasteiz: Kardaberaz Bilduma, 1978.

———. *Idaz-lan guztiak*. Vol. 1. Gasteiz: Kardaberaz Bilduma, 1978.

———. *Lekuona'tar Manuel idaz-lan guztiak*. 12 vols. Tolosa: Gipuzkoako Foru Aldundia, 1978.

———. "Métric vasca." In *Lekuona'tar Manuel idaz-lan guztiak*, vol. 1, 131-157. Tolosa: Kardaberaz Bilduma, 1978. Tolosa: Kardaberaz Bilduma, 1978.

———. "Poesía popular." In *Lekuona'tar Manuel idaz-lan guztiak*, vol. 1, 187-257.

———. "Bertsoen metrika." *Jakin* 14-15 (April-September 1980): 60-79.

Lete, Xabier. "Xenpelar." *Garaia* (October 1976): 44.

Lhande, Pierre. "Le barde Etchahun." *Gure Herria* 2 (1923).

Lindstrom, Thaïs. *A Concise History of Russian Literature*. Vol. 1. New York: New York University Press, 1966.

Lison Tolosana, Carmelo. "Verbal Art in Modern Rural Galicia." In *Folklore in the Modern World*, 281-300. The Hague: Mouton, 1978.

Lord, Albert B. "Homer and Huso I: The Singer Rests in Greek and South Slavic Heroic Song." *TAPA* 67 (1936): 106.

———. "Homer and Huso II: Narrative Inconsistencies in Homer and Oral Poetry." *TAPA* 69 (1938): 439-445.

———. *The Singer of Tales*. Cambridge: Harvard University Press, 1960.

Lugones, Leopoldo. *Obras poéticas completas*. Madrid: Aguilar, 1959.

Lukin, Boris V. "Testimonios sobre la poesía popular Cubana del segundo tercio del siglo XIX." Santiago de Cuba: Departamento de Actividades Culturales. *Santiago: Revista de la Universidad de Oriente* 31 (September 1978): 61-80.

Makazaga, Juan José. *Bertsolariya*. Donostia: Sendoa, 1981.

Manterola, José de. *Cancionero vasco.* 3 vols. Donostia: Sendoa, 1981.

Mendiburu, Jean Pierre. *Bertsutan ariz ikasten.* Bayonne: Bertsolarien Lagunak, 1985.

Menéndez Pidal, Ramón. *Poesía juglaresca y juglares.* Madrid: Espasa-Calpe, 1962.

———. *El romancero.* Madrid: Paez, n.d.

Menocal, María Rosa. "The Etymology of Old Provençal Trobar, Trobador: A Return to the 'Third Solution.'" *Romance Philology* 36, no. 2 (November 1982): 137-153.

Michel, François. *Poesías populares de los vascos.* 2 vols. San Sebastián: Auñamendi, 1962.

———. *Le romancero du Pays Basque.* Paris: Firmin Didot Frères, n.d.

Michelena, Luis. *Historia de la literatura vasca.* Madrid: Minotauro, 1960.

———. *Textos arcaicos vascos.* Madrid: Minotauro, 1964.

———. *1545 Bernat Detxepare.* San Sebastián: Txertoa, 1978.

Mitxelena, Salbatore. *Arantzazu euskal sinismenaren poema.* Oñati: Jakin, 1977.

———. *Idazlan guztiak.* 2 vols. Oñati: Jakin, 1977.

Mujika, Luis Mari. *Historia de la literatura euskérika.* Donostia: Haramburu, 1979.

Muniategi, Abel. "Bertsolaritza Bizkaian." *Jakin* 14-15 (April–September 1980): 17-29.

Muxika, Gregorio. *Pernando Amezketarra.* Donostia: Iñaki Irarkola, 1927.

Niño, Angel. *Canciones populares.* Madrid: Publicaciones Españolas, 1976.

Oihenart, Arnaud. "L'Art poétique basque." *Gure Herria* (October 1967): 195-204.

———. *Atsotitzak eta neurtitzak.* Donostia: Herri-Gogoa, 1971.

Olaizola, Manuel [Uztapide]. *Noizbait.* Tolosa: Auspoa, 1964.

———. *Lengo egunak gogoan.* Tolosa: Auspoa, 1975.

———. *Sasoia joan da gero.* Tolosa: Auspoa, 1976.

Onaindia, Santiago. *Milla euskal olerki eder.* Zarauz: Karmeldar Idaztiak, 1954.

———. *Gure bertsolariak.* Bilbao: Aita Onaindia, 1964.

———. *Enbeita oleskaria.* Zarautz: Kuliska Sorta, 1966.

———. *Euskal literatura.* Vol. 1. Bilbao: Etor, 1972.

———. *Las cien mejores poesías de amor en lengua vasca.* Bilbo: La Gran Enciclopedia Vasca, 1975.

Ong, Walter J. *The Presence of the Word.* New Haven and London: Yale University Press, 1967.

———. *Orality and Literacy.* London and New York: Methuen, 1982.

Onnen, Frank. *Mauricio Ravel.* Barcelona: Juventud, 1951.

Ormaetxea, Nicolás [Orixe]. *Euskaldunak.* Donostia: Auñamendi, 1976. Originally published in 1950.

Otaño, Pedro Mari. *Otaño'tar Pedro M'ren olerki onenak.* Donostia: Alkar, 1930.

———. *Pedro Mari Otaño'ren bertsoak.* Zarautz: Itxaropena, 1959.

———. *Pedro María Otaño.* San Sebastián. HG 221 K.OTS. 1980. Sound cassette.

Oteiza, Jorge de. *Quousque tandem . . . !* San Sebastián: Auñamendi, 1963.

Parry, Adam. *The Making of Homeric Verse: The Collected Papers of Milman Parry.* Oxford: Clarendon, 1971.

Parry, Milman. *L'Epithète traditionelle dans Homère.* Paris: Les Belles Lettres, 1928.

———. *Les formules et la métrique d'Homère*. Paris: Les Belles Lettres, 1928.

———. *Serbo-Croatian Heroic Song*. Cambridge: Harvard University Press, 1953–1954.

Peillen, Dominique. "Amodiozko baratzetan." *Gure Herria* (May–June 1962): 74–96.

———. "Eske pertsuen bilduma." *Cuadernos de etnología y etnografía de Navarra* (1975): 407–442; (1976): 47–86.

Riezu, Jorge de. *Cartas al Padre Donostia*. San Sebastián: Caja de Ahorros Municipal de San Sebastián, 1980.

———. *Flor de canciones populares vascas*. Donostia: Sendoa, 1982.

Riquer, Martín de. *Los trovadores*. 3 vols. Barcelona: Planeta, 1975.

Rychner, Jean. *La chanson de Geste: Essai sur l'art épique des jongleurs*. Geneva and Lille: Droz and Guard, 1955.

Sallaberry, Jean Dominique Julien. *Chants populaires du Pays Basque*. Marseille: Lafitte Reprints, 1977.

San Martín, Juan. *Gogoz*. San Sebastián: Caja de Ahorros Provincial de Guipúzcoa, 1978.

———. *Bidez*. San Sebastián: Caja de Ahorros Provincial de Guipúzcoa, 1981.

———. *Landuz*. Donostia: Gipuzkoako Aurrezki Kutxa Probintziala, 1983.

———. "Manuel Olaizola, 'Uztapide' (1909–1983)." *Euskera* 28 (1983): 527–539.

Sarasola, Ibon. *Euskal literaturaren historia*. Donostia: Lur, 1971.

Satrústegi, José María. *Bordel bertsularia*. Tolosa: Auspoa, 1965.

———. *Luzaide'ko kantiak*. Tolosa: Auspoa, 1967.

———. "Literatura popular vasca." In *Tesoro breve de letras hispánicas*, vol. 6, 28–45. Madrid: Magisterio Español, 1972.

Stolz, Benjamin A. *Oral Literature and the Formula*. Ann Arbor: University of Michigan Press, 1976.

Suassuna, Ariano. "Coletânea da poesia popular nordestina." *Romances do Ciclo Heróico. Deca* (1962): 11–27.

Torrealday, Joan Mari. *Euskal idazleak gaur*. Oñati-Arantzazu: Jakin, 1977.

Treku, M. [Mattin]. *Etxe xokotik kantari*. Tolosa: Auspoa, 1981.

Trythall, J. W. D. *Franco*. London: Rupert Hart-Davis, 1970.

Unamuno, Miguel de. *Obras completas*. Vol. 6. Madrid: Afrodisio Aguado, 1958.

Uribe Echevarria, Juan. *Flor de canto a lo humano*. Santiago de Chile: Editora Nacional Gabriela Mistral, 1974.

Urkizu, Patri. *Lengua y literatura vasca*. Zarauz: Luis Haranburu, 1978.

———. *Euskal antzertia*. Donostia: Antzerti Saioak, 1984.

Urquijo, Julio de. *Refranero vasco*. 2 vols. San Sebastián: Auñamendi, 1964.

Valverde, Antonio [Ayalde]. *Con fondo de chistu*. San Sebastián: Auñamendi, 1965.

Veyrin, Philippe. *Les Basques*. France: Arthaud, 1975.

Viaud, Julien [Pierre Loti]. *Le Pays Basque*. Paris: Calman-Lévy, 1930.

Villasante, Luis. *Historia de la literatura vasca*. Bilbao: Sendo, 1961.

Vinson, Julien. *Le folk-lore du Pays Basque*. Paris: Maisonneuve, 1883.

Zabala, Enrike. *Euskal alfabetatzeko literatura*. Lazkao: Pax, 1981.

Zavala, Antonio. "Bertsolariak eta Europako lenengo gerratea (1914)." *Euskera* 4 (1959): 183-206.

———. *Azpeitiko premiyoaren bertsoak (1893-1895)*. Tolosa: Auspoa, 1963.

———. *Bosquejo de historia del bertsolarismo*. Tolosa: Auñamendi, 1964.

———. *Pello Errotaren itzala*. Tolosa: Auspoa, 1965.

———. *Gaztelu bertsolaria*. Tolosa: Auspoa, 1966.

———. *Pernando Amezketarra bertsolaria*. Tolosa: Auspoa, 1966.

———. *Udarregi bertsolaria*. Tolosa: Auspoa, 1966.

———. "Riquísimo tesoro de la poesía popular." *Aranzazu* (January 1968): 2-5.

———. *"Txapel" bertsolaria*. Tolosa: Auspoa, 1969.

———. *Xenpelar bertsolaria*. Tolosa: Auspoa, 1969.

———. *Pastor Izuela (1780-1837): Ezkioko ta Segurako itxuak*. Tolosa: Auspoa, 1971.

———. *Txirritaren bertsoak*. 2 vols. Tolosa: Auspoa, 1971.

———. *Zepai bertsolaria*. Tolosa: Auspoa, 1971.

———. *Mendaro Txirristaka bertsolaria*. Tolosa: Auspoa, 1974.

———. *Zapirain anaiak*. Tolosa: Auspoa, 1975.

———. *Ustu ezin zan ganbara*. Tolosa: Auspoa, 1976.

———. *"Bilintx." Indalecio Bizcarrondo. (1831-1876)*. Donostia: Caja de Ahorros Municipal de San Sebastián, 1978.

———. "Bertso paperak." *Jakin* 14-15 (April-September 1980): 115-133.

———. *Txabolategi, Elkoro eta Leunda bertsolariak*. Tolosa: Auspoa, 1980.

———. *Ameriketako bertsoak*. Tolosa: Auspoa, 1984.

———. *Euskal jokoak bertsotan*. Tolosa: Auspoa, 1984.

———. *Kristaubidea bertsotan*. 2 vols. Tolosa: Auspoa, 1984.

Zubimendi, Joseba. "Lenengo bertsolari eguna." *Yakintza* 3 (1935): 141-154.

———. "Bigarren bertsolari eguna." *Yakintza* 4 (1936): 141-158.

Zulaika, Joseba. *Bertsolarien jokoa eta jolasa*. Donostia: La Primitiva Casa Baroja, 1985.

INDEX

tradition by, 14, 70; used as theme by payadores, 129-30
Renaissance period (1935-1968), 99-111
Rhyme: "amaia da hasera, atzekoz aurrera" technique of, 32-33; assonant, 28-29; Basque types of, 27-28; Bilintx's use of, 84-85; guidelines to bertsolaritza, 29-30; Lasarte's use of, 109-10; poto egin error in, 46, 61; Xalbador's use of, 181-83; Xenpelar's use of, 77. See also Verses
Roman-Cantabrian war, 90
Romanticism period, 74-85

Saiburu. See Lujanbio, Juan
Sallaberry, Jean Dominique Julien, 31, 140
San Sebastián, José Antonio de (Padre Donostia), 31, 125
Santos Vega, José, 131
Sarasua, Jon, 51-52
Sardui, Deunoro, 45
Sasoia joan da gero (Uztapide), 103
Schools of bertsolaritza, 206-7
Sein, Emmanuel (Xanpun), 50
Sei puntukoa verse model, 22
Serbia, 133-35
Serbo-Croatian poetry, 3-4, 133-34
Sestina, 133
Showmanship, 39-40
The Singer of Tales (Lord), 4, 133
Sirventès, 18
Slavic Balkan bard, 3-4, 133-34
Sortetxe (family farmhouse), 169
Sortu zaizkidanak (Basarri), 101
Spanish-American War, 91-92
Suffixes, 59
Syllables, 31

Tolosa, José, 170
Topet, Jean, 141
Topet, Pierre (Etxahun): as contest participant, 44, 75; influence of, 137-41; life of, 141-47; themes and style of, 147-53
Treku, Mattin (Mattin), 39, 47-49, 106-8
Troubadour: bertsolaritza vs., 18-19; poetry used by, 17-18
Troveros, 128
Trueba, Antonio, 83
Txabalategi. See Erroizena, José Joakin
Txapel. See Eizmendi, Eusebio
Txapela, 48
Txapelketa: 1935, 46-47; 1936, 47; 1960, 47; 1962, 48; 1965, 48; 1967, 48-49; 1980, 49-50; 1982, 50; 1986, 50-52, 206, 212n. 24

Txapelketak: analysis of specific, 46-52; dialectal/partisanship issues of, 48-49; elements considered in, 18; improvisation used in, 32-33; music and song used in, 31-32; organized by bertsolariak, 51-52; origin/development of the, 45-46; political themes used in, 36-37; role of gai-jartzaile in, 52-53
"Txepetxa" (Otaño), 165-66
Txikia verse model, 22
Txirrita. See Lujanbio, Joxe Manuel
Txotxojeuri. See Enbeita, Juan Antonio

Udarregi. See Alkain, Juan José
"Ume eder bat ikusi nuen" (Iparragirre), 79
Unamuno, Miguel de, 58, 81, 161-62
Urkiaga, Esteban (Lauaxeta), 96, 105
Urretxindor. See Enbeita, Kepa
"Urruxolako gudu-kanta" (War song of Urrexola, 1388-1401), 66
"Urxaphal bat" (Etxahun), 142, 148
Ustu ezin zan ganbara (Zavala), 89
Uztapide. See Olaizola, Manuel

Verb, 60
Verse models: bederatzi puntuko bertsoa, 26-27, 38; desafio, 133; described, 22-23; hamarreko handia, 24-25; hamarreko txikia, 25-26; zortziko handia, 23; zortziko txikia, 24
Verses: bertsolaritza types of, 53-56; created by Amuriza, 201-2; created by Chilean payadores, 130; created by Txirrita, 92-95; created by women, 68-70, 135; created by Xalbador, 180-81; loias, 127; systems for expressing, 211n. 6; txapelketa criteria for, 50. See also Poetry; Rhyme
Virgilio. See Amuriza , Xabier
Vlahovljak, Munin, 134

Women: African Bedouin, 135; Basque, 68-70; increased bertsolaritza activity of, 207

Xalbador. See Aire, Fernando
Xanpun. See Sein, Emmanuel
Xanti (Balendin Enbeita's uncle), 105
Xenpelar (Francisco Petrirena), 26, 53, 73, 75-77
Xirulari (performer), 5

Zabala, 42, 73, 125
Zabaleta, J., 48

THE BASQUE SERIES